POST OFFICE
BOX 377

MISHAWAKA, INDIANA

December 8, 1950

Family H. Bernard Veldman:

Dear Friends:

In the first place we must thank you for the lovely english l
wrote to us in the early part of the year. It was well writt
easily understood and it means so much to know more than one

When you receive this letter you will also receive a letter
that will contain some news which you may or may not be exp
If you have read the papers regarding the conditions of the
now in war in Korea, etc. you are no doubt aware of the fac
of Pete's age are in line for drafting. A few weeks ago P
a notice to be examined for this purpose and since he is w
received a notice of his acceptability to the Army, and l
received his word of being drafted for the Army on Decemb
He will write you more about this; but our purpose of wri
tell you that he is very brave and realizes that he is i
other boys of his age. It is a little hard for him to wr
to you for he fears that you will worry about him. He wa
told him that we would write you a letter also. We want
we are trying to do what we can to make it easy for him
he getsa furlough or permit he will come here. If you
addressit here as you have done and we will send it to
he will hear from you sooner than if you wait until he
address. Please continue to write to him often and wri
always do. Do not worry too much for it is ha
to serve in the army; just pray much that o
will protect him and bring him home sa
ever for t ey would rather keep Pe
ll obey.

ase tell him to be
Holland in M
im not to
the

CARDINAL'S RESIDENCE
452 MADISON AVENUE
NEW YORK 22, N.Y.

February 20, 1952

Dear Friends:

You will be pleased to know that during
my recent trip to Korea, Japan and other places in
the Far East, I had the privilege and pleasure of
meeting your dear one from whom I am happy to bring
affectionate and prayerful greetings with the hope
that before a very long time has elapsed, your loved
one will be able to greet you personally. At the
time we met, he was doing well, was in good spirits,
and very courageous in facing the problems that
confront him and bravely bearing the burdens of a
serviceman's life.

Begging God's blessing on you and all
those dear to you, I am

Prayerfully,

Francis Cardinal Spellman
ARCHBISHOP OF NEW YORK

Mr. and Mrs. H. B. Veldman
"Hees"
Didam, Holland

AIR MAIL

AIR M

U.S. POSTAGE

VIA AIR M

Jeff,

Thank you for all you do
for our Chamber of Commerce.

Enjoy reading this biography

Peter Veldman

Wilma Veldman

Peter Veldman

Dutch Immigrant
American Entrepreneur

Andrea Midgett

Library of Congress Catalog Control Number: 2009902473
ISBN: 978-0-692-00234-6

In loving memory of
Wilhelmina and Bernard Veldman
– Oma and Opa –
who loved, nurtured, and faithfully pointed
twelve children in the right direction

Family of Bernard and Wilhelmina Veldman

Bernard Veldman	Wilhelmina Van Kesteren (Veldman)
October 12, 1898	September 30, 1898

Petrus "Pete" Veldman
April 4, 1926

Wilhelmina "Willemien" Veldman (Coenen)
May 23, 1927

Theodora "Dolly" Veldman (Ensing)
June 1, 1928

Rieka Veldman (Seesing)
May 9, 1929

Allardus "Al" Veldman
June 16, 1930

Bernardus "Ben" Veldman
June 14, 1931

Theodorus "Ted" Veldman
February 24, 1933

Maria "Mary" Veldman (Goris)
January 23, 1935

Johanna "June" Veldman (Wynen)
June 6, 1936

Francisca "Fran" Veldman (Beidinger)
September 10, 1938

Willibrordus "Willy" Veldman
December 30, 1939

Henricus "Henry" Veldman
August 16, 1941

PETER VELDMAN
April 4, 1926

WILMA ZENTS (VELDMAN)
January 22, 1927

TOM VELDMAN
December 19, 1953

DAVE VELDMAN
July 2, 1955

CONNIE VELDMAN (JOINES)
September 24, 1957

SHARON VELDMAN (EDMONDS)
August 3, 1959

AUDREY VELDMAN
October 18, 1961
† January 9, 1996

MARCIA VELDMAN
December 23, 1963

MARK VELDMAN
September 28, 1967

Peter Veldman as a young man

Pete Veldman is all about family: His own wife and children. His birth family. His numerous siblings and their extended families. He is also about the Netherlands, and immigration, and making a successful go of it in America. Pete is about energy and ambition – at 82 years old he still works in the family business, always looking ahead to the next big thing. And he is about memory. Pete is a great storyteller. With characteristic charm and optimism, what he remembers most, what he holds onto, are memories of a life well-lived, a life defined by people, places, determination, hard work, and faith.

This is his story.

THE NETHERLANDS

VORDEN
●

ARNHEM
●

VELDMANS' FARM

RHINE RIVER

●DIDAM

GERMANY

NORTH SEA

THE NETHERLANDS

AMSTERDAM ●

ROTTERDAM ●

BELGIUM   GERMANY

I

"We will move toward the Allies"

IN EARLY APRIL 1945, Pete Veldman had just turned 19 years old and was living with his family near Didam, Holland, on one of the largest farms in the area. By that time, Holland (also called the Netherlands) had endured five years of German occupation as World War II dragged on. Over 200,000 Dutch civilians had died under Nazi rule. As the end of the war neared, tight-lipped stoicism had yielded to intense suffering as thousands starved, especially in the country's densely populated western cities. Tulip bulbs and sugar beets were all that kept countless men, women, and children alive. At least 10,000 individuals died as a direct result of the famine in what became known as the Hongerwinter, the Hunger Winter, the unparalleled, freezing winter months of 1944-45.

The Veldman farm was situated on the extreme eastern edge of Holland, less than a mile from the German border and east of a bend in the Rhine River. The Allied troops had been fighting for weeks between the farm and the river, inching their way ahead. The Germans controlled Didam and most of the countryside east of the Veldmans. German soldiers were scattered around the farm, as they had been sporadically for five long years.

Forever, it seemed, the two stalled military giants had taunted each other in the late afternoons, lobbing artillery shells over the Rhine and into the enemy's territory. Whatever passed over the Rhine passed over the farm. Or landed on the farm. As Pete recalls, the Veldmans did not stop living during those tense moments. It had been going on for too long and there wasn't much danger, he says, "Unless, of course, you took a direct hit." If he or his father or brothers happened to be out on the farm when the shelling started, and if the explosions sounded too close by, they jumped into one of the many trenches the Germans had forced the Dutch to dig on the Veldmans' land. Likewise, Pete's mother and sisters and whoever else was in the house ran outside and hid in an underground bomb shelter if the danger sounded too threatening.

The day the Allied forces began advancing toward the farm in large numbers, Pete's father, Bernard, was told by the Germans that he and his family would have to fall back with the German troops and move toward Didam and beyond as necessary. Bernard did not protest. But when he got home, he gathered his large family together and calmly said, "We are not going to do that. We are not going with the Germans. We will move toward the Allies."

Few people in Holland had cars in those days, unless one lived in a large city or was very wealthy. So Bernard and Wilhelmina, Pete's mother, gathered all 12 of their children, from Pete, the oldest, to the youngest, a brother not much older than a toddler, and made plans to move the family. They would use the wagon and one of the remaining horses. They would ride bicycles. Or they would walk, the older siblings keeping hold of the younger ones.

The odds were in the Veldmans' favor. Pete had told his parents what he had seen a few days before as he traveled the countryside on his bicycle seeking news of the war. He had spent several hours with a unit of Canadian soldiers, reveling in their cigarettes and chocolate, optimism and courage. The Allies were on the move. Their target – the liberation of Holland – was within sight and they were not backing down. Small towns and farming communities were slowly being freed, one by one by one.

There was no guarantee that moving toward the Allies was the right thing to do. Whatever move the Veldmans made, one way or the other, there would be consequences. If they listened to Bernard, disobeyed the German directive and moved toward the Allies, and if the Allies successfully crossed the Rhine and moved through the farm and onward to Didam, the family could probably return home soon. If they followed German orders and moved toward Didam and the worst happened – the Allies were defeated and the Germans held onto Didam – the Veldmans would probably still be allowed to return home. The occupying soldiers were intent on staying alive and maintaining their hold on Holland. They could not be bothered by anything that would keep them from their mission, including the needs of a large family.

On the other hand, if the Veldmans followed orders and moved toward the Germans and if the Allies successfully captured Didam and pursued the enemy, no one could say where or in what circumstances the family might find itself. They could be pushed along with the Nazi army, forced to find their own way farther and farther from home, searching for friends or strangers willing to take them in.

While victory seemed certain this time, the Veldmans knew the Allies had failed before in their protracted conquest of Holland. They had been thwarted repeatedly by the Germans, even forced to surrender strategic gains. The previous September, the Allies had failed to secure Arnhem, the closest real city to the Veldmans' farm. The nine-day battle and its tragic results were well-known through-out the country. The near-victory for the Allies was a crushing disap-pointment to the Dutch, who listened secretly to radio reports of the Allied advance, hoping against hope for an end to their increasingly dire circumstances.

The Veldmans' greatest risk lay in disobeying. No one knew how the Germans would react to an openly defiant family if the Allies failed to liberate Didam. The occupying soldiers were beginning to feel desperate as the noose slowly tightened around them. Because the family did not want the Germans' attention or anger directed at them in any way, the safest choice would be to quietly obey orders.

But the decision facing the Veldmans was no longer just about safety. It was about opportunity.

Those children old enough to understand weighed the seriousness of the situation. The day before, Pete and his oldest sister, Willemien, had narrowly missed being killed as they fled Didam. Traveling to town to attend Mass on Easter Monday had allowed Pete the opportunity to share with friends what he had learned from the Canadians. He and Willemien had left Didam buoyed by their friends' reaction to the hopeful news. Every teenager they had spoken to had been thrilled by Pete's reports. With great anticipation, they sniffed freedom in the air.

The siblings had fallen in with a small group of foot-travelers as they left town via side roads. Suddenly, without any warning, the group had found itself being repeatedly shot at by German soldiers perched high in the second story of a nearby house. Pete and Willemien had finally returned home safely, shaken and giddy with relief. But it had been a very close call – one young woman who had been running with them lay dead in a field beside a line of railroad tracks. Pete's parents said little at the time, but they must have been greatly alarmed at what could have been.

The siblings' close escape and the hard reality of the family's situation were now on everyone's mind. Wilhelmina considered what Bernard's proposal could mean for them all – positive or negative – from her husband to their youngest child. What would happen if Bernard's plan did not work? To him? To her? To the children? What if they successfully reached the Allies? Would there be enough food to eat? Where would they sleep? Could they stay together?

Eventually, everyone old enough to voice an opinion agreed to follow Bernard's lead. They would move as a family. They made plans to head toward the Allies, toward what they hoped would be freedom and liberation.

As it turned out, the Allies swept through the Veldmans' farm without serious resistance that very day; the family never had to move. But the story reveals much about Bernard and Wilhelmina Veldman's resolve. Their decision to stare down fear and move ahead was true to character, for they both were determined, hardworking, protective, and honest. Devout Catholics, their perspective on their troubled country and world was tempered by a firmly held belief that there is more to this world than what can be seen with the eyes alone. Though their faith had been tried, it had not been defeated. And though they never would have courted disaster for themselves or their children, they were weary of the war, weary of the Occupation, and ready for change. Perhaps most importantly, they were willing to take the risk that change always requires.

It was a lesson in living that Pete took to heart.

જી

II

The Netherlands

Childhood

Henricus Petrus Theodorus Veldman was born on April 4, 1926, on a farm in far eastern Holland. Germany was little more than a stone's throw away, a distance that would prove too close and too beguiling for Hitler to ignore as he reached across Europe during World War II. Didam, the closest small town to the Veldman farm, was about two miles to the west. Pete spent his entire boyhood traversing one dirt road or another to Didam, by foot or by bicycle. It was unusual for him to travel to town or neighboring farms by horse and wagon, unless it was raining heavily or a delivery needed to be made. Sometimes a seat in the family's more stylish buggy was available to catch a ride to Sunday Mass, but not often, for the family was large and growing. There was always a new baby to welcome.

No one in Pete's childhood family or circle of friends ever had a car. The owners of the farm, the baron's daughter and her husband, had a car, as did her father the baron. And they were friends of sorts. But they were also members of the aristocracy; the almost 100-acre parcel of land the Veldmans farmed and the house they lived in belonged to the baron. Regardless of a good working relationship, there remained an insurmountable gulf between those who owned the land and those who toiled upon it.

Owning a car was beyond the reach of any Dutch tenant farmer in those days, even one like Pete's father, who worked one of the largest parcels of land around. In fact, Pete's father never sat behind the wheel of an automobile until after he retired and followed his son to America, and then only because Pete helped him get his driver's license. But even as a young boy, Pete dreamed freely of what his parents could hardly imagine. In time, car ownership would be a first step in a life marked by ambition, entrepreneurship, and eventually, great success in businesses involving automobiles. The baron's family never would have guessed.

Pete was the oldest of 12 children. His mother, Wilhelmina, and his father, Bernard, were committed Catholics. Unlike western Holland, which was heavily Protestant, Didam and its neighboring population centers were almost exclusively Catholic. Most businesses were Catholic-owned and Catholic-run. Didam even boasted a Catholic milk factory and Catholic soccer clubs. (Protestants could play for the clubs, Pete says, but had absolutely no say in managing them.) So one can imagine that Pete's birth early on Easter Sunday morning brought indescribable joy to his young parents. First born. A son. Easter day, the holiest of the Catholic liturgical year. As was the custom, he was baptized at church that very morning, while his mother remained home in bed for several days.

Wilhelmina bore all 12 children at home over a span of 16 years. The thatched-roof house they rented, on the land they leased, was very large, even by farm-family standards. Each child found a place in one of two huge upstairs bedrooms or in the spare bedroom close to Bernard and Wilhelmina on the first floor. The entry hall was wide enough to kick around a soccer ball, a favorite winter pastime of the young children. There was also a large kitchen, with a table long enough to seat all the children, their parents, three live-in helpers employed on the farm and in the house, and up to six additional daytime helpers who did not live on the farm but who ate lunch with the family. Female live-in helpers slept upstairs in the girls' bedroom; males lived in a bedroom that was part of the barn. The house included a sitting room that was reserved for guests and family celebrations, and an additional upstairs room where grain was stored.

On the backside of the house, beyond a firewall, was an attached barn. Pete never noticed if the house smelled like the barn. It was just home. But, he says, farmers who went to town carried with them the smell of their work-a-day world, even if their clothes were clean. Entering the Veldman house via the front door or through the barn, a visitor would see numerous pairs of wooden shoes lined up along the wall. All sizes were represented, for everyone wore them – the parents, the help, the children – though Pete remembers his mother changing into something more fashionable when she went to town.

Pete's family taught him a lot about loyalty and ongoing responsibility, for there was always someone else whose needs required attention. Hard work, day in and day out, was essential to keeping such a large family clean, fed, and functioning. And then there was the farm to run, with all kinds of animals to care for, orchards to tend to, and numerous crops to plant, cultivate, and harvest. Wilhelmina and Bernard excelled at it all, Pete says.

"My parents did everything in a big way, except make money!" he recalls with a laugh.

The Dutch are generally known for being responsible and emotionally reserved. They are not as openly passionate and boisterous as the Italians, or as fiercely enamored with themselves and their culture as the French, or as preoccupied with class and status as the British. The Dutch can be all these things, of course. But generally speaking, they are men and women of quiet determination, tolerance, industry, and amazing resourcefulness.

Geographically, the Netherlands, which means "low lands," is a country where almost half of the land lies below sea level. As far back as the Middle Ages, the Dutch began building an incredibly extensive system of dikes and levees to hold back the North Sea and create land out of water. The resulting rich, arable soil has long made the word

"Dutch" synonymous with abundant crops, flowers, and tulip bulbs. And they have kept at it, upgrading the system throughout the centuries, though sometimes not soon enough, as a disastrous high-tide storm in 1953 proved. After the levees were breached in hundreds of places, drowning 1,850 people, many in their sleep, the stunned country declared, "Never again." So far, their advanced technology and fortitude have not failed them.

For young Pete, the diminutive country, roughly twice the size of New Jersey, was anything but small. His parents traveled the 90 or so miles from the farm to Amsterdam only two or three times in their entire lives. A trip to Arnhem, the closest real city about 10 miles away, would be talked about for a week before and a week after it took place. And it would seldom be a trip for children – their world was even smaller.

Pete's days revolved around the farm, his many siblings, school, church, and his parents.

❧

Wilhelmina Veldman was the first one up every morning, even before Pete's father. She stoked the wood-burning stove and began preparing the family's traditional breakfast of skillet-baked pancakes with apples and bacon, called *pannenkoek*. Meanwhile, the live-in helper the family employed to assist her in running the house was upstairs with the children, making sure they were clean and dressed appropriately for school. The children rose at 6 a.m., summer or winter, whether school was in session or not. A vacation day meant they didn't go to school – nothing else in their daily routine changed. Between the house, children, crops, and animals, there was always work for the adults to do. And for Wilhelmina, the workday always began with breakfast.

Born Wilhelmina Van Kesteren, her father died when she was a young girl, leaving her and her older sister to be raised by their grandfather, who was a farmer. Wilhelmina's mother was chronically ill and in a wheelchair for many years; the weight of her care naturally fell to her daughters. (Pete has no memory of any of his grandparents. The last one died within a year of his birth.) Because Wilhelmina was a good student with a real passion for learning, her grandfather kept her in school as long as he could. Her formal schooling ended after she completed the seventh or eighth grade, an advanced education considering the times and the family's financial circumstances. She spent the next several years helping her mother, her grandfather, and her sister.

"Mama had a lot of responsibility at a young age," Pete says.

It prepared her well. Managing her own home (she was 28 years old when Pete was born), Wilhelmina was known to be a good housekeeper and a good cook. She ran the kind of house where everything "stayed well and in good order," according to Pete.

The baron's daughter's husband would occasionally drive out, sometimes with friends, to hunt, visit, or collect lease money from the Veldmans and their neighbors. Wilhelmina used the opportunity to her family's advantage: She dispatched Pete to let the other farmers know ahead of time if rent was to be collected, while she made sure that the house sparkled and that the meals were especially good for such important guests.

"My mom was glad to have them come, and so was my dad," says Pete. "And they were glad to come."

Along with Bernard's good humor, Wilhelmina's hospitality and finesse helped the family cement a good relationship with the landowners. For a few years during the Depression, when cash was painfully scarce, the owners did not collect any rent at all from the Veldmans. As far as Pete knows, they never had to pay it back.

As a parent, Wilhelmina was thoroughly immersed in the lives of her children: what they ate, how they dressed, how they acted, whether they were home from school on time or not. She was a disciplinarian whose rules extended to her own life. Her activities were regulated by the time of the day, the ages and lives of the 12 children, and the seasonal life of the farm. She did not procrastinate when work had to be done. She napped for an hour every day after lunch – the children were taught to respect that. And she never argued with her husband in front of their family.

"She told me that in all their years of marriage, they (Wilhelmina and Bernard) had their disagreements, but they were never angry with each other. I believe that," says Wilma Veldman, Pete's own wife of more than 55 years. "I think it was true of them."

Pete confirms that he never saw his parents openly argue in front of the family; any misunderstandings they had were discussed in private. They were also outwardly reserved toward each other in a way that was typical of their culture and era. In keeping with their reserve, they did not constantly hold and hug their kids. But, Pete quickly adds, no one ever felt unloved. Much later in their lives, Wilhelmina and Bernard followed Pete and eight of his siblings to America. Oma and Opa, as they were then called, were known for walking to Mass every day. Holding hands.

"But Mama was very strict," Pete recalls. "If you were home five or 10 minutes late from school, you were sent to your room for an hour before supper, which really cut down on your time to play. And she kept a long wooden ruler at the kitchen table to use if your elbows were on the table or if you were using bad manners. She would reach across the table and crack your hands with it."

Wilhelmina administered a "good spanking" when needed and "was picky about our language," he continues. "She would not allow us to speak slang. And we were not allowed to be unruly or overly argumentative with each other as kids.

"Both of my parents were very strict on the point that you would do what they told you to do, without a lot of rebuttal. It was expected that we would be obedient. And Mama was very good at that. There was very little that we didn't agree with her about, that we would speak up about. We just didn't do that.

"We challenged her a bit more when we became teenagers. But we still had rules, such as when we needed to be home. She never gave up on that. She would lock up the house at night if you weren't in on time."

Pete remembers his mother as being bright, alert, an extrovert, and a leader in Didam. She was president of the Farmers' Wives Organization, a group that met regularly to discuss issues involving education and health, cooking and sewing.

"Mama was more interested in education than most other farmers' wives," he says.

The Farmers' Wives Organization often hosted speakers normally heard in larger cities. They came because Wilhelmina knew who they were. She worked hard to bring them to Didam. Once they arrived, many of the guests were surprised at Didam's small size, just six to seven thousand people.

"Mama liked to read," Pete says, "though she didn't have much time for it or much to choose from. There wasn't such a selection back then as there is now. We got a few farm journals and the local newspaper, but there wasn't much to them."

Though Wilhelmina could do little about the available selection of reading material for herself and her family, she could be sure her children measured up to her standards of respectability, from the way they conducted themselves at home and in public to the way they dressed. She was indefatigable. Because of her, Pete says, other farmers sometimes thought the Veldmans had more money – and class – than they in fact had.

"We were a little different. We looked like we were a bit more well-off than we actually were," he chuckles. "It wasn't that we dressed fancy, but our clothes never had holes. And they were always clean and mended. I remember Mama standing up late at night, darning our socks. She stood because if she sat down she would fall asleep.

"And when Mama went out, she dressed pretty fancy," he continues. "Much fancier than the rest of the farm girls. She had a nice bit of flair.

"In those days, women wore hats when they went out. Mama

always had a touch that was just a little bit different. Wherever she went, she became known for that.

"When she bought something, she bought quality. And then it would have to last for a long time."

Wilhelmina knew a little about running the farm, but not much. Pete says his parents divided up their responsibilities: She managed the house. Bernard ran the farm. When she needed extra help, to sew for the family for instance, a job at which she did not excel, she hired a seamstress to come in. But she was in constant motion, always working alongside her helpers and overseeing the numerous household projects that were underway, from preserving food to washing laundry in a big room in the barn to cooking for extra farmhands to caring for sick children.

"She was always real busy, no doubt about that," Pete explains. "My dad took it a little easier. He always had a lot of help from his farmhands.

"On the rare occasions Mama wasn't home when we got home from school, the house just seemed empty. She was very good with her helpers, Papa as well. But they were different. Mama was a good conversationalist, but she was perhaps a bit more serious than Papa. He was a good storyteller and a little easier going. Friends would come over to play cards with me and would sometimes wind up playing with him. I wouldn't even be in on it.

"Mama wasn't stern, but it didn't take her long to get across what she felt needed to be done. She deserved a lot of respect. And she got it. Papa, too," he concludes.

"They were a great example. No doubt about it."

❧

Bernard Veldman also worked hard, day in and day out. With so many children to feed and such a large farm to run, he, like his wife, had few idle moments between sunup and sundown.

Both of Pete's parents were industrious, and both were fair and honest in their relationships with their employees and neighbors. They were respected as individuals and as a couple. They could be counted on in times of crisis. Neither of his parents were introverts, Pete says. Both liked to talk and be around people. Bernard, however, was a little more outgoing and carefree than Wilhelmina. Even though he was considered a leader in the community, he was not one to push an issue to the point of conflict. Perhaps growing up in a family of nine children had honed his ability to get along with almost anybody. He liked to have fun and was quick to laugh. He was close to his siblings, especially his brothers, trading labor and tips, livestock and jokes. He loved to play cards.

Perhaps surprisingly, beneath Bernard's imperturbable temperament existed a curious mind and strong will. Though naturally a merry soul, he was not foolish or irresponsible. Nor was he afraid of risk. To the contrary, as his occasionally unorthodox farming practices demonstrated, Bernard liked a challenge. He was an entrepreneur when it came to running the farm, both for the thrill of trying something new and in hopes that some new crop or animal husbandry idea would eventually lead to financial security.

"Papa would get excited and change everything around on the farm, instead of sticking to one thing," explains Pete. "All the attention would be on the new crop. He always thought he would one day make a lot of money with something new."

Holland's cool summers and mild winters are suitable for growing a wide variety of crops. Like his surrounding farmer friends, Bernard grew grain (wheat, oats, rye, and barley), vegetables (sugar beets, chicory, potatoes, and turnips), fruit (apples, pears, and plums), grass, and clover. Livestock included draft horses, milk cows, sheep, chickens, ducks, and pigs. Unlike his neighbors, he was always willing to try an improved way of planting or tilling or pruning, a new way of raising livestock, or a brand-new crop. For example, tobacco, a significant cash crop in the southern United States, requires sustained summer heat. Bernard tried planting several acres of it anyway.

Wilma says that when she first began dating Pete, his father was not known in the surrounding communities as "a real conservative farmer," an esteemed description of most Dutch farmers – and she lived some 20 miles away. In fact, some of Bernard's ideas shocked Wilma's father, who ran his smaller farm very conventionally, and who had more money in the bank to show for it. No doubt, some of Bernard's entrepreneurial efforts shocked his close-by neighbors as well.

Not that the opinions of other farmers mattered much to Bernard. He had friends everywhere he went, no matter what they thought of his farming techniques. Besides, what they thought was true: He liked new ideas and was determined enough to try them. He did not need to be right all the time. He did not need to always lead, at home or in the community.

"Papa had loads of friends, young and old," Pete says. "But he was not the leader. Mama was."

Bernard was comfortable with it that way; it was perhaps more a case of his allowing Wilhelmina to take the lead than her taking it from him. He did not wrestle with caring for 12 growing children and the myriad of details surrounding their lives. He did not worry about feeding a very long table of family and employees three times a day, or worry over the children's education, clothing, and religious training.

On the other hand, Bernard did not flinch from the demands of running the farm, however he chose to run it. He did so with the help of two live-in and as many as six daytime hired hands, without any mechanized equipment. He never had a day of vacation. But though they all worked hard, Bernard was no slave driver.

"During harvest, everyone worked longer and harder days, with extra help from the children and some exchange work between family and neighbors," Pete says. "But Papa also took a nap every day after lunch, although that wasn't so unusual for men. Some of the farmhands even took naps."

Despite the fact that Bernard was so well-liked, and despite the fact that he and his employees looked and dressed the same, it was clear that he was the boss, Pete recalls. Something about his demeanor alerted newcomers to the fact that he was the person in charge.

And Bernard was respected, not just by his employees but by his peers and individuals outside the farming community as well. Farming practices aside, he was known for being an excellent judge of livestock and a good salesman. Other farmers often consulted him before doing their own buying and selling. Even the baron, who served as both "jury and judge" in Arnhem, occasionally stopped by the farm to discuss the merits of a particular case with Bernard. Though it was understood they would never be social equals, the baron appreciated Bernard's opinions and common sense.

"Papa was well-regarded, though not necessarily as a farmer," explains Pete. "It was true that he didn't follow the rules of farming as strictly as some other farmers. But he was very good at trading and he liked to buy and sell. His whole family was like that.

"Some of my uncles (Bernard's brothers) lived close to the Belgian border. For a while, horses were worth a lot more money there than in Holland. My father and his brothers figured out a way to smuggle some across the border to make a better profit. That didn't happen often, just a few times, when prices were unusually high.

"If Papa had been born in America, I don't think he would have been a farmer. But in Holland, in those days, if you were born on a farm, you were pretty much expected to be a farmer. That changed in later generations, as farmland became scarce. Children began to hire out to learn trades, and might become electricians or masonry workers, and so on."

That Bernard leased as many acres as he did was itself an accomplishment and came about because of family connections and reputation. Bernard's farmer father knew a baron, who knew a baron some miles away, and when a farm became available, the owner wanted young Bernard to lease it. It was the way the system worked. It was not unusual for a man in Bernard's position to rent, his entire life, the land he cultivated every day. Even a fairly prosperous farmer might never own the land he worked or the house his family lived in.

"It was basically a good decision," Pete explains. "We could lease the land for less than owning it, less than coming up with the money to pay the bank for it. But if you already had money, that was different."

Historically, Dutch landowners were most often aristocrats. They had inherited the land to begin with, and had little incentive to sell it. They could lease their holdings indefinitely, increasing their gains appreciably whenever they chose to sell what would always be a diminishing commodity in the small, heavily populated country.

No matter how hard Bernard worked, he knew that unless he hit upon some new, great agricultural advance, he would never be able to purchase land himself, not even with a bank loan. He was powerless to stop the escalating price of the ground beneath his feet.

At the end of every day, Bernard remained a tenant farmer. But he was also a maverick, and his great sense of optimism propelled him forward. He walked a taut line between the demands of managing one of the largest farms in eastern Holland and his dreams of financial independence. Perhaps he would have tried a different vocation altogether if he could have been guaranteed a large enough income to support his family. But farming was what he had been born to, and any improvements in his financial circumstances would come from within the world he had inherited as a farmer's son.

Some months after the end of World War II, Holland received its very first shipment of modern tractors. Typically, one of them went to Bernard, for he was always willing to spend money in an attempt to make more money, as long as he remained financially solvent. He also loved the idea of doing generations-old work – plowing and harvesting – in a new way.

But the tractor wasn't Bernard's ticket to success either. Despite all of his attempts, Bernard never made a great deal of money. He never struck it rich, never owned a shovelful of Dutch soil. Though many of his principles were sound, he never got the break he hoped – and worked – for. However, his willingness to try and try again left an indelible mark on his children. For Pete and his siblings stood at Bernard's side when that tractor rolled onto the Veldman farm. They watched their father set out on a new path that he hoped would make all the difference, as they had watched him many times before.

Pete, in fact, had urged his father to purchase the farming marvel. The two had talked it out, discussed the money and how it would impact the hiring of employees, etc. Together, they had decided that Bernard would never know if the purchase was worth the expense until he tried it.

Not long afterward, Pete immigrated to the United States. He took with him his father's determination to go after something until you find what you are looking for. Being an immigrant was not easy for Pete, though he loved the challenge of creating a new life for himself. He had a few false starts as he figured out what would and would not work in his new surroundings. But after a while, his business ventures began to move forward in a way no one back home in Holland would have dreamed possible.

No one, that is, except Bernard. He was cheering on his son from afar. Working the farm, as always.

❧

Pete's childhood was happy and secure. "My life as a boy could not have been better," he says unfailingly. Together, his parents wove work, love, and expectations into a tight fabric that blanketed their ever-growing family.

But though the cloak Bernard and Wilhelmina fashioned

around their children was pulled close, it was not impregnable. Tragedy could strike any one of them at any moment, the cloth could be rent despite their best efforts. Even as young children, Pete and his siblings understood that life and health were not guaranteed. They occasionally saw grief and calamity upend the lives of those around them: schoolmates, relatives, neighbors. Fortunately, no child or adult was ever lost to illness at the Veldmans', though the family was quarantined a few times, including once for diphtheria. No one was ever killed or maimed in a farm accident. But they all knew terrible things could happen. One friend of Pete's, a young girl, was electrocuted when she mopped her family's kitchen floor and then, unthinkingly, threw the wet mop over an electrical wire to dry. A few other friends died of childhood diseases.

Young or old, life was uncertain at best – Pete's parents acknowledged that. But they did not let fear or uncertainty immobilize them. They did what they could, and prayed that God would do the rest.

For adults and children alike, routine was the thread that tied one day to another. Though different seasons called for different kinds of work, few events altered the predictability of everyday life. New babies might join the family. The hired help might change. There were occasional holidays and festivals. But cows needed milking, chickens needed feeding, fields and grain and orchards needed tending, floors needed scrubbing, and clothes needed washing regardless of the calendar.

Sundays were the weekly exception to the rule. On Sundays the family did only those chores that were essential. They all went to morning Mass in Didam, and from there met other farmers and their families at a local café for coffee. Pete and his siblings might check out something to read from a small, one-room library where the librarian often held new books for the family. When they reached adolescence, the children were allowed to return to town on Sunday evenings for Vespers and church youth group, and maybe, afterward, a game of pool and one beer (never more) consumed under the watchful eyes of the bar owner.

"It seems like everyone was in on raising us," Pete comments. "The teachers, the baker, the owner of the bar, the Church."

Weekdays followed their own routine. Everyone woke early in the morning and ate breakfast together before the children were sent off to daily Mass, which was followed by school. From the time they were in kindergarten, Pete says, he and his siblings walked the two miles to town and back in their thick wooden shoes, kicking "something that approximated a soccer ball." The Veldman farm was the farthest out; neighbor children joined them along the way. Adults did not accompany the youngsters. Bernard and Wilhelmina did not fear for their children's safety, and there was too much work for them to do to leave the farm.

The walk to town took about 45 minutes, with time for play figured in. School was out at 4 p.m. The children walked back home kicking the same soccer ball, did their chores (in the house for the girls, on the farm for the boys), had supper a little past 5 p.m., and then played until bedtime, which was 6 p.m. in the winter, 7 p.m. in the summer. There was never any homework for grade-schoolers.

The children took their lunch with them and ate at school, while their town friends went home to eat with their families. Back at the farm, the noon meal was the hot meal of the day. It was prepared by Wilhelmina for all the adults living and working on the place. The day-help brought their own meals, though they were free to sit with the Veldmans and live-in workers if they chose. Also included were any children who were not yet school-age or who were home from school.

All of the children were present for the evening meal, which typically consisted of light sandwiches and lunch leftovers. Pete and his siblings sat at one end of the long kitchen table. His parents, the one live-in house helper, and the two live-in farmhands sat at the other end. The children were not allowed to speak unless they were spoken to; to disobey was to risk a sharp crack across the hands with Wilhelmina's ruler. There was a spoken prayer before and after every meal of the day. After the prayer that followed the evening meal, the children were excused to play until bedtime.

"Religion was not discussed much in our house. It was just part of life. There were always prayers before and after every meal and prayers before bed," says Pete. "We were always looking forward to that prayer after the meal, which meant we were free to leave the table.

"We always played a lot. It was simple, but it was fun. We were inside the barn and out. The animals were a fun part of our daily lives. There were newborn colts, lots of calves, little pigs, and thousands of chickens. It was a lively place to be a part of."

The family and live-in help gathered together once more in the evening before going to bed, to pray again and say the rosary together. Only the youngest children were excluded. Sometimes the adults ate again, a porridge-like dish, before retiring. As the children grew older, they could gradually stay up later and enter into the adults' evening conversation. It was a rite of passage they looked forward to.

"You brought along your own stories to add to the mix," Pete recalls.

If talking to the adults did not appeal to the older children, they could bike and spend time with friends. Bicycles, a common, easy, and inexpensive means of transportation, grew in importance as one aged. Adults and children alike biked as much as they walked, if not more. They biked more than they used horse-drawn carriages and wagons.

Though many farmers did not have bikes for the smallest of their children, somehow the Veldmans did.

"I guess I learned to ride right after I learned to walk," Pete says.

"I remember my little sister riding a new, little bike into a wall. It was from Japan, and in those days things from Japan were not well-made. The accident was almost the end of the bike," he chuckles.

Though the daily routine was essential to keeping the Veldmans' large family and their livelihood moving forward, it was not inflexible. It was not routine just for the sake of routine. It could be interrupted when necessary, when friends, family, or neighbors needed help. People mattered.

From very early in his childhood, Pete observed his parents' generosity and care toward others. When Wilhelmina's sister was widowed at a young age, she and her only child, a son named Harry, moved in with the Veldmans for several years.

"It was a great time for me," says Pete. "Harry was about four years older than me, so it was like we were brothers. We played on the way to school, on the way home from school, and at home. We also had our disagreements, but not many."

By the time Pete's aunt remarried, she had become a second mother to him, and Harry was considered one of the Veldman siblings. With the remarriage came relocation to another farm, however, and the two moved away. But Pete and Harry remained fast friends. Whenever his parents allowed him, Pete would walk the hour and a quarter it took to reach his cousin's new home, or he would ride his bike. After visiting for a few days, he would walk or ride home.

When Pete was around 11 or 12 years old, he went to visit Harry during the spring floods experienced annually along the country's large rivers. Pete had heard about but had never seen land covered by water as far as the eye could see. It was an experience he was looking forward to. The two boys were out in a flat-bottomed boat, poling along on a cool day, when Pete leaned too far over to look into the water and fell in. He could not swim. The weight of Pete's wet clothes and shoes made it difficult for Harry to pull him out of the water and back into the boat. It took Harry a few minutes to fish out his younger cousin with a pole, a few minutes that seemed like forever to both of them.

Pete identifies the near-drowning as one of the two scariest moments in his life, second only to the time he was shot at by German soldiers as he fled Didam with his sister. Even serving in the Korean War after he had immigrated to the United States was not as frightening as hopelessly trying to keep his head above water with only Harry to come to his aid.

Though he could not have known it when he was growing up, the model of caring Pete saw exhibited by his parents and relatives – the cloak they pulled in around their children and each other – was one he would later draw from as he helped almost every one of his siblings, and finally, his parents, settle in America. One by one he helped them learn the language, find a job, go back to school, or gain financial independence until they were on their feet and able to care for themselves. He generously lent himself to their needs until their heads were above the swirling waters of a new culture.

What Pete probably knew, even as a young boy spending time with his siblings and cousin, was that hard work would be crucial to whatever measure of professional success he eventually achieved in life. For if routine was the thread that stitched daily life together, work was the needle that conveyed the thread. And his parents never let him forget it.

❧

M y parents were adamant that you had to work, you had to work," Pete says of his childhood.

"They maybe wore nice clothes (when they went to town) and had good food to eat, but they never had any money."

Though the family was poor by today's standards, poor must be placed in context. To be rich in Holland in those days meant one owned land, a house and furnishings, and had money. Few people were rich by those standards, including the Veldmans. Their daily needs were met, but they owned very little. And they were perpetually strapped for cash.

"We just didn't have cash," Pete explains. "And even if they had had money, my parents would not have shown it. We (children) felt poor in the sense that our parents saved money and impressed upon us the importance of saving. That, and the fact that everyone was always working.

"Every May, the town had two days of celebrations. Mama would give us maybe 25 cents to spend any way we liked. But she highly recommended that we save some of it, put it back in the bank. She would check with us, to see how we had spent what she had given us, and what we had saved."

Though Pete was too young to understand it at the time, the worldwide Great Depression devastated the Dutch economy in the 1930s. Banks and companies went bankrupt. International shipping and trade, upon which the national economy was dependent, ground to a near halt. High unemployment, severe wage cuts, and widespread poverty contributed to social unrest and political instability, and played a role in the eventual rise of the NSB, or Dutch National Socialistic Party. Such bleak economic conditions set the stage for a small percentage of citizens to believe, at least initially, that Holland would more quickly regain its economic strength if it sided with Germany in World War II.

Though farmers could at least feed their families during the Depression, the guilder (Dutch currency) was extremely difficult to come by. When the baron's family excused Bernard and Wilhelmina from paying their annual house and land lease, they saved them not only financially – they saved them socially. To stoop to a handout was unthinkable: Anyone receiving any kind of government assistance was severely stigmatized. Much to their shame, individuals exempted from the country's bicycle tax were required to wear on their clothing or carry on their bikes a sign that identified their needy status. In the cities, those who received aid were required to wait in line two times a day at relief agencies, while government inspectors made regular "house calls" to scrutinize need. Unending lines of Dutch men and women dressed in red, government-subsidized clothing became a symbol of the country's lingering difficulty. By the time the country began to pull out of its dire economic straits, World War II was upon them.

Pete remembers his Uncle Piet, one of his father's brothers, "coming down" to borrow money from Bernard so he could make payroll for his farm employees, when there was still money to be borrowed. But as time passed, Bernard's farm, too, brought in less and less cash, until what savings he had were also depleted.

However tight the money supply, daily life for the Veldmans continued much as always. The routine was just that much harder. The family had little or no cash, but there was security in the known. The farm was kept up and running, clothes were mended and mended again, and children walked to school, did their chores, and obeyed Wilhelmina, ever mindful of her ruler.

One of Pete's earliest childhood memories is walking along with a farmhand on their way to feed the chickens. Pete was very young. When a rooster landed on his head, the farmhand immediately stepped over, grabbed the bird, and killed it instantly, right in front of Pete. The memory is vivid, he says, not because the bird was killed, but because he was in a potentially harmful situation that was dealt with without a moment's hesitation. The rooster's sharp spurs could have badly cut Pete's face or damaged his eyes, but he never even had a chance to think about being afraid.

Home was a safe place for Pete and his siblings. No matter what was going on in the world outside the farm, Pete was secure inside his world, and it didn't have a lot to do with money. For those few years between childhood and adolescence, he knew what to expect.

"I remember Mama cutting one banana into several slices for all of us," he says. "And everyone was happy with a sliver.

"Looking back, the Depression must have been a very worrisome time for my parents, but it didn't trickle down to us kids."

For a young boy who didn't know better, a banana slice was just fine. Poor was relative, and to have a banana at all must mean the family was rich enough.

☙

Pete loved school, at least when he was young. He remembers hearing missionaries talk about far-off places like Africa and Asia, and seeing pictures of poor, impoverished children from around the world. It convinced him at a very tender age that he wanted to be a missionary when he grew up, not so much to do missions work, but to travel to those parts of the globe so beyond the reach of almost any man, woman, boy, or girl living at that particular time and place in history. The idea of learning, adventure, and challenge in a new setting captivated him. As Pete grew older, he realized that missions per se held little appeal for him. However, his interest in "going someplace new, someplace far away" remained intact throughout his childhood and adolescence. Dreams of countries far removed from Holland helped sustain him during the long, grim years of World War II.

"My idea of becoming a missionary went by the wayside," he explains, "but not my idea of seeing the world."

Academics were another matter. By the time Pete was ready to move up to high school, which began in the seventh grade, he wanted to quit altogether. But first he had to convince his parents. Most importantly, he had to convince Wilhelmina.

"My parents had a good attitude toward education," he says. "They didn't push it too much. But they definitely wanted me to go to high school."

The discussions between Pete and his parents went back and forth. Bernard and Wilhelmina thought a higher education would benefit their eldest son, and they told him so, repeatedly. They wished for him the educational opportunity they had never had. Besides, they said, the world was changing. Farmland was becoming scarce as Holland's population continued to grow. Bernard and Wilhelmina worried about what kind of work their sons, in particular, would one day find as adult men with families of their own. They could not all stay on the family farm and work with Bernard. It wasn't big enough to support them all. But nothing his parents could say changed Pete's mind.

Finally, Pete and his mother reached an agreement: He would

attend the first year of high school. He could quit if – and only if – he made all A's for the entire year. He would follow Bernard's footsteps by going straight from the classroom to the farm, working alongside his father. One can imagine Wilhelmina shrewdly thinking that if Pete rose to the occasion and made the grades, he would be persuaded to stay in school as long as there was an opportunity to do so.

Pete upheld his end of the bargain by making the grades. But proving to himself and to his parents that he could do high-school work with such aplomb did not change his mind about quitting, for his decision had never been about ability. Young as he was, Pete was simply ready to get on with his life, and he did not consider furthering his education to be part of the equation. Reluctantly, Bernard and Wilhelmina honored their promise: They allowed their obviously bright, determined son to drop out of school after he finished the seventh grade. Pete was 13 years old, and no longer a student.

"School was easy for me," he admits. "But I didn't like high school. I didn't feel I should be there. I thought I knew everything. But I had to have real good grades for my mom to let me get out."

❧

In contrast, Pete enjoyed grade school from the very beginning. He liked everything about it – getting there on his own two feet; his teachers (even the less-qualified ones, whom he and the other boys harassed); the academics, at which he excelled; his friends; and school parades where all the children dressed up as church saints or poor kids from around the world and followed Veldman workhorses in a procession through the streets of Didam, cheered on by townsfolk every step of the way.

Pete even tolerated the daily morning fights outside the schoolhouse, though he never understood why he and the other boys fought. Or why he, of average size and build, never walked away.

There was, he says, a town boy/farm boy divide among the students, but the fights were never between the two groups. The farm boys were stronger and would have won if the spars had been about who was from where. (Pete says he and his friends always won physical competitions such as races if they were pitted against the town boys.) But the fights were between individual boys, not groups of boys. Were the fights about accepting challenge and facing down fear? About who was stronger, quicker, or tougher? Pete didn't know then, and years later, he still doesn't know. Perhaps why the boys fought doesn't really matter, for usually, within 30 minutes of their ritual squaring off, the combatants resumed their friendships.

"It was a challenge," Pete says. "I guess that's why I participated. But if I met someone within half an hour of the fight, in the hall or outside of school, it would be over. We would act like nothing had happened."

Perhaps Pete fought to convince himself of his courage, perhaps to prove himself to others, perhaps because he was a good athlete. (He was competitive and strong, and an exceptionally fast runner. He once placed eleventh in a race of several hundred young men, by "pacing myself while the others didn't.") Or perhaps he fought because he could not stand to lose, could not walk away without at least trying.

Whatever the reason or combination of reasons, as soon as Pete got to the schoolyard, he deposited his few belongings and took his stand. He might not win – he accepted that. But then again, he might. He would not know until he joined the fray and gave it his best shot. There were no entrenched bullies in the group, he says. The way he looked at it, he had as good a chance of victory as anyone else.

For Pete, the possibility of winning made fighting worth the risk. Win or lose, the next morning promised another match-up, another chance at victory.

☙

Pete remembers with great fondness his kindergarten teacher, a nun who had a way of keeping 30 or more five-year-olds in order. He also remembers his fifth-grade teacher, a gregarious man who always opened the class with a joke or witty remark and who was invariably followed through town by students during their lunch hour. He was a congenial Pied Piper.

"It was just so obvious that this man loved students," Pete says. He and his fellow classmates could not help but love him back.

"He just taught differently from any other teacher I ever had," Pete adds. "He was such a neat guy. He made the whole class laugh and then we went to work. When he would go home for lunch, he always had 10 to 15 students surrounding him. He was the leader of the bunch."

Pete was not above misbehavior or taking advantage of a bad situation, especially if by being mischievous he captured the attention of his classmates. In particular, he remembers a teacher whom he often tormented by shining a mirror toward the front of the room while the teacher stood with his back to the class, writing on the blackboard.

"I would flash a mirror on the board to make the light dance," he says with an embarrassed laugh, "and I would keep at it."

Invariably, the teacher turned around in great agitation and demanded to know where the light came from. Invariably, Pete and his classmates said nothing. Time after time the teacher jumped around, and time after time the students remained silent. Pete is convinced that if the teacher had paid no attention to the light, had just gone on teaching, he would have given up and put the mirror away. But the teacher's response was too much of a temptation for Pete to ignore. The teacher could not stop reacting. And Pete did not stop instigating.

"He just could not keep order at all," Pete says. "And he was a terrible teacher.

"But I still feel bad about how I treated him," he adds after a brief pause.

If Pete's parents had found out about his antics, he would have had no ground to stand on, no matter how bad the teacher was or how poorly he controlled the classroom. Blaming the teacher for one's misbehavior or poor academic performance did not work for the Veldman children.

"To my parents, the teachers were always right," Pete says. "We never had a teacher that Mama or Papa disagreed with in our presence. There was no use in coming home and saying that the teachers had done something wrong, or got the situation wrong."

☙

As much as Pete loved grade school, he also loved breaks from it. He remembers lining up along a sidewalk in Didam, surrounded by classmates and adults, to catch a glimpse of Queen Wilhelmina, who ruled the Netherlands through two World Wars over a span of 50 years. He had no idea at the time that the great lady he jostled to see would one day govern her country from exile during the long years of World War II, communicating weekly with her subjects via radio, resolute in her belief that Holland would one day again be free. Pete only knew she was the Queen, descended from the House of Orange-Nassau, beloved by most of her subjects. She was royalty. For a young boy whose family supported the monarchy, the excitement of seeing her pass through the streets of his small town was a big enough thrill to last a long time. He waved a small orange flag and cheered as loudly as he could.

"For Holland, a queen was nice. It had a lot to do with our old history. Seeing her was the highlight of the year," he says.

"But," he adds, "you don't need a queen in America."

The event also allowed Pete and his friends time away from school, a huge treat for all of them. None of the adults with whom Pete associated ever had a vacation. He never knew anyone who traveled away from their farm for an extended period of time to sightsee or for rest and relaxation. Nevertheless, the Veldmans and their friends and neighbors knew how to take a break and have a good time. They just didn't travel very far to do it.

"All the pleasures were celebrated within a distance of 15 to 20 kilometers (9 to 12 miles)," Pete says.

"The pleasures" included baptisms; First Communions; a Fall celebration in Didam; St. Nicholas Day; Christmas Day (a strictly religious holiday); Easter, a two-day observance that often fell on or very near Pete's birthday; a two-day May celebration in Didam when "rides would come to town, booths would be set up, and a lot of Jewish people would make a lot of money off us, although we never had much money"; family birthdays; the Queen's birthday; etc.

St. Nicholas Day was celebrated on December 6. The night before, Dutch children traditionally left out their wooden shoes to be filled with candies and treats. At the Veldman farm, St. Nicholas Day was a big event, eagerly anticipated by the children and willingly staged by their parents and a few family employees.

"St. Nicholas would come around on a horse, dressed as a bishop, with a staff and miter," Pete remembers. "He came with his sidekick, Black Peter, who carried a very large sack. If you had been bad, Black Peter would put you in the sack and carry you off.

"In the end, Black Peter didn't really take anybody away with him, but he always pretended he was going to. It was an exciting evening for us," he continues. "We would each get one present from St. Nicholas, not like all the presents American children get today.

"Black Peter would always dress up in special clothes that were usually hidden away. But one year, my brother Al was becoming suspicious of the whole Black Peter myth. He found the clothes, so then he knew about Black Peter."

One of the most prominent celebrations in Pete's memory is an early summer party hosted yearly on the Veldman farm. It was a day the whole family looked forward to. There were four large farms in the Didam area; each family hosted a party of its own. The party at the Veldmans', called Schuttersfeest, always began in town with early morning Mass. From there, most of the family's neighbors would return to the farm for a full day of games, a "good deal" of drinking and partying, and later in the evening – after everyone had returned home long enough to milk cows and take care of chores – music and dancing back in town.

"One group would begin the day by shooting clay pigeons for points," Pete says. "The winner would become King, and he would then choose a Queen for the day. Another group would compete riding horses, grabbing a ring suspended by a pole. Once again, a winner would be declared King, and he would also choose a Queen. Another group would put on a flag show."

And so the day went, from one event to another, with cards and games and food and drink. Pete had his first taste of beer at Schuttersfeest. Though he was young, there was no legal age limit for alcohol consumption in Holland at the time. He thought the beer tasted awful.

"It burned my tongue for hours," he says.

Pete's family recognized and embraced the role they played in their farming community on these celebratory occasions. Their lives, joys, and sorrows – and those of their friends and neighbors – were validated as they came together for a few hours or a whole day. The men and women in attendance all worked hard, no matter the size of their farms. They all struggled when crops failed or tragedy struck. They worshipped together on Sundays and special holy days. Their children walked to school together and became friends, fought each other, competed against each other on ice skates in the winter and in other contests of strength and endurance in the summer, rode bikes together, traded labor during harvest, and sometimes grew up and married each other.

Entire families got together to laugh and drink and play games and put aside their worries for a short while at the Veldmans' farm on these special days. But before Pete was out of his teens, the farm would be used to gather friends and neighbors and strangers for another purpose: to house those who were displaced by the fighting that was taking place all around them between the Allies and the Germans. By the time World War II ended, 40-50 people would be living with the Veldmans. Some slept in the house. Many more slept in the barn. One family slept in what was essentially the basement cellar. Every man, woman, and child living with the Veldmans was waiting for a change in their situation that would allow them to go home. Like their hosts, they hoped it would be liberation. Meanwhile, they all coped as best they could.

Pete was happy as a young child. But there was always something deep within him that yearned for adventure and challenge, something that wanted the un-ordinary and the un-secure in the most ordinary and secure of lives. His parents had their own dreams – for financial security, for the education of their children, for a place in society. But they had too many mouths to feed to allow their idealism to take the upper hand. They were forward-looking people, able to hold onto their aspirations with one hand. They were also realists, and their other hand gripped tightly the reality that they must work diligently to provide for their family.

One hand would not have been enough. It took both hands to build a life for Pete and his siblings that was responsible and challenging, that met their needs and gave them wings.

And then came World War II, which threatened to tear apart their entire world.

ↄ

World War II

I *had biked about 10 kilometers (6 miles) to visit my aunt and uncle and my cousin Harry. I liked going there and I was young enough that my dad would sometimes just let me leave work on the farm and go visit for a few days. I enjoyed Harry, and his mom was like a mother to me. If her husband, my Uncle Theo, needed a little additional help on his farm, I would go over.*

Really early in the morning, right before dawn, there were suddenly hundreds and hundreds of planes flying overhead. They were coming from Germany. You could not have slept through it. We immediately knew what was happening: The news was in the air. We knew we were being invaded. German troops started coming across the border. They could just pretty much cross over – there was nothing to stop them.

It happened by surprise. We did not think it would happen. Planes probably passed over for six or seven hours.

My aunt and uncle lived in a kind of isolated area, a little out-of-the-way, where you wouldn't expect to see many Germans coming through. But a few came by on motorcycles that were mounted with a machine gun on an attached side-cart where another soldier sat. I thought the motorcycles were neat.

There was no fighting around us, but my aunt and uncle told me

I shouldn't go home until we knew it was safe. We had no telephones and we didn't know what was happening anywhere else, so it was best to stay right where I was. I stayed with them for two or three days, then ventured home to my family's farm on my bike. I knew the smaller side roads and didn't have to be on the highway much.

When I got some distance from our farm, I could see lots of horses and wagons and at least 100 German soldiers standing around. There were German soldiers everywhere. I didn't know what to think, so I went to a neighbor's house.

"Oh, don't worry about it. Go on home," they said.

I don't remember hearing that my parents had been worried about me or had been looking for me, but I'm sure they were relieved to have me home. There was a whole lot of talk about what had happened: A supply unit for the German army had moved onto our farm.

My parents said fighters had gone through first, then the supply unit came. We knew we couldn't fight the Germans. No, no, no, no. When the supply group said they were moving in for a while, my parents probably asked, "Can we stay, too?"

At first, we knew nothing about what was happening in the rest of the country. My dad had only been to Amsterdam, which was 90 miles away, a few times in his life, and that was for a church event where he went to pray all night. I think we already had a radio, because it would have been hard to get one after the invasion, and I know for sure that we had one after they were banned. But I don't remember anyone listening to the radio in the early days of the Occupation or when the German supply unit was on the farm. We did not hear the Queen's first broadcast from London. We heard sometime later that she was safe.

We had so little news back then. It wasn't like it is now. Almost any news we got from the Didam newspaper was about farming or our town. But we were used to not getting the news on time. The local newspaper didn't write much about what had happened right after the invasion because the Germans threatened to shut it down, which they did after a few weeks anyway.

The Germans did not want any news coming in. After the troops went through Didam, they left behind enough soldiers to control the town. They shut down or controlled all communications and directed how the Dutch police department should be run. No one could leave the country, of course. All the borders were heavily guarded.

Basically, there was not much the Dutch could do about the invasion. The German army was huge; it was also very well-trained. Dutch soldiers fought the Germans for five days, which helped a little, but it was insignificant in the big picture. There was not much Holland could do to stop the Germans. There was not much Austria could do. Not much people from Hungary could do or people from Czechoslovakia, or Belgium, or Poland.

The German supply unit staying at our house was good to us. They did not scare us. That was not what they were out to do. They were just there to supply the troops ahead of them. Some of them obviously did not want to be there – they were not much older than me – but they had no choice.

I got right in the middle of them. We were always trying to see what they had. We stole whatever we could from them, whenever we could, just because it was loose – and because they had invaded us. They spoke German and we spoke Dutch. The German language didn't sound that different, but we couldn't understand much at first, though by the end of the war I could understand a lot more. They didn't have that much to communicate, anyway. We knew what they wanted. We understood quite well.

The Germans didn't take over much of the house that first time, maybe a few rooms for the officers. Most of them slept in the barn or outside under wagons or trucks or such. They cooked for themselves. My mother did not have to cook for them, and we never ate at the same table. They took the barn to hide a very large bus they didn't want out in the open where it could be seen by planes flying overhead.

They separated themselves from us quite well. They stayed to themselves. Out on the farm, away from the officers, the soldiers might try to talk to us. Sometimes we could understand a few words. For them, it was important that we weren't fighting them.

My parents weren't afraid for my teenage sisters. The Germans were, at that point, a disciplined army. I think they were as well-disciplined then as the Americans were later on.

The Germans were also well-supplied. But it was strange. In the end, the supply unit was only at our house for about 10 days. When they came, we didn't know if they were going to be there for 10 days or 10 weeks. But in about 10 days, they got the order to move on, and they left.

This was the first time we had Germans living on the farm during the Occupation. But it wasn't the last. They moved in with us two other times before the war was over. About 10 to 20 of them would move into a part of our house, and would come and go from there. We tried to go on about our lives as normally as possible. The officers-in-charge always told my mother she did not have to worry about the soldiers bothering my sisters. They were "good soldiers," my mother always said, as long as they were with their units. Their discipline and organization began to fall apart later on.

I was 14 years old when the invasion took place.

❧

Though World War I, also called the Great War, affected the Netherlands socially and economically, the country escaped conflict on its home soil by declaring itself neutral. When World War II erupted in 1939, Holland once again claimed neutrality. It was well-known that the country was as unprepared for war psychologically as it was militarily: It had not engaged in battle for over 100 years; as a result of the Paris Peace Conference that ended World War I, many politicians were confident that the country would be defended by the League of Nations, if necessary; the defense budget had been neglected, partly because of the country's late recovery from the Great Depression; and the army was skeletal, with most of its weapons dating back to the late

1800s. Also, before the invasion, an undetermined number of Dutch citizens were pacifists, belonged to the National Socialist Movement (NSB), or sympathized with Germany. (After Holland's surrender, Germany outlawed all political parties in the country except the NSB, at which point the NSB openly collaborated with the occupiers.)

After France and Great Britain declared war on Germany in 1939, the Netherlands slowly awakened to the reality of what was happening on its doorstep. The Dutch government began to mobilize its forces should the unthinkable happen and war come to its people. However, the small, abysmally equipped army found it was too late to modernize. Though it tried to buy firearms and other equipment from several countries, it failed. At best, the Dutch army had a few old tanks and an equally small number of modern aircraft in its arsenal when Germany stormed the country.

By early spring 1940, ominous war clouds were gathering across those few Eastern and Western European countries that were not already actively engaged in the fight. Yet in the months preceding the invasion, many Dutch clung to their hope that Holland's neutrality would be honored by Hitler and his giant war machine, even as that machine marched into neighboring countries. The self-proclaimed Führer promised as much. But Holland, with its international ports, heavily populated cities, and shared borders with Belgium and Germany, was not to be spared.

On May 10, 1940, German troops invaded the country. Suddenly, German soldiers were everywhere. The invaders had a new word for their strategy – blitzkrieg – or lightning war, based on speed, surprise, and a large military. The soldiers came in tanks and in trucks, on foot, on motorcycles, and in horse-drawn wagons, spilling over the German/Netherlands border, including the border within a mile of the Veldmans' farm. Simultaneously, an endless procession of planes split the quiet skies of early dawn. Some of the planes dropped bombs to destroy rail lines, roads, and communication centers, and to create a sense of panic among the Dutch; others dropped paratroopers who hit the ground equipped and ready to fight.

No matter how the German soldiers entered, the majority was headed west, toward Holland's densely populated cities and ports, and toward its government seat, The Hague. Holland's civilians – young and old, in cities and in the country – stood horrified as they witnessed what was happening all around them. The unthinkable had happened.

Pete, visiting his aunt, uncle, and beloved cousin, Harry, had turned 14 the month before the invasion began. Though he and his family had no way of knowing it, Dutch agents operating from inside Berlin had sent repeated warnings to their government of what was to come. But the numerous, seemingly empty warnings were largely ignored by the authorities, including the last one on May 9: Tomorrow morning at dawn. Hold fast!

By daybreak May 10, it was too late. The Dutch army could do little to thwart the large, efficient, well-supplied militia that rushed into the country. However, despite Holland's apparent military weakness, the Germans were surprised by the five-day conflict that followed. Holland may have been tardy in preparing for war and had only a small number of soldiers when compared to the invading army, but her sons fought with courage. Plans to flood a vast area of the country's outlying farms, and thereby slow the enemy, failed. The soldiers of Orange fought anyway. One of them, Piet Bodde, a former farm employee of the Veldmans, had been drafted into the Dutch army as the military scrambled to pull itself together shortly before the invasion. He died on the second day of fighting in another part of the country.

Another young man from Didam who died some distance from home was a son of one of the local butchers, a well-liked and well-established family with whom the Veldmans did business.

"He was a Jew, a real quiet type of guy," Pete says with difficulty. "A good soccer player. He said, when he was drafted into the army, 'The Germans will never get me alive.' And they didn't."

The Germans did, however, presumably get the young man's

parents, for they were never heard of or seen again after the war ended. They almost certainly died in a concentration camp, knowing that their son had, at least, been spared the slow horror of their fate. Had they survived, Pete says, they would have returned to Didam or contacted someone there after Liberation.

German paratroopers landing in The Hague expected to capture Queen Wilhelmina, her family, and key advisers in a day or two, thus immobilizing Holland's government. But the Queen escaped to a British ship shortly after the invasion began.

Sixty years old, intelligent, forceful, and unafraid, Wilhelmina was a "soldier's queen" who had unsuccessfully tussled with her government for a small, well-trained, and well-equipped army in the aftermath of World War I. Unsure of what would happen as World War II gathered momentum, Wilhelmina had made plans to flee to Zeeland (southern Holland) if Hitler disregarded her country's internationally declared neutrality and invaded. From Zeeland she planned to coordinate resistance efforts until help arrived for her beleaguered country. (Before the invasion, most Dutch did not think it would take long for the Allies to liberate the country if Hitler seized it.)

Shortly after the determined monarch was safely aboard the British cruiser, the captain informed her that he could not, in fact, was not allowed to contact shore, as Zeeland was under heavy fire from the German air force, or Luftwaffe. He also said it was too late to backtrack to the capital city, which would be heavily bombed if she returned.

Faced with the graveness of what was happening to her country, Wilhelmina reluctantly sailed for London. From there she established a government-in-exile, calling Hitler the "archenemy of mankind." From the outset, Wilhelmina insisted that Holland was right to have not cut a deal with Hitler before the invasion, and she was resolute that no deal would be forthcoming, as was later suggested by German officials and her own prime minister. Under her rule, the Dutch government would never legitimize Hitler's breach of international law, would never sanction the invasion and subsequent oppression of its people. In a test of power and wills, her prime minister was eventually removed from office.

Churchill would later reportedly say that Queen Wilhelmina was the only "real man" among all the leaders-in-exile living in London during the war. Following her first radio communication after her re-location, in which she assured her subjects of her safety and convinced them of her resolve to stand firm on their behalf, her weekly broadcasts over the BBC's Radio Oranje (orange) were eagerly anticipated by her countrymen, who listened illegally and in secret. She unfailingly offered her people hope, and rallied staunch resistance against the Germans for five long, worsening years of occupation. She never gave up hope for a free Holland. More importantly, she never let her country-men give up hope.

Pete does not remember hearing any recriminations after the Queen's escape. "Our family supported the Queen," he says, "though maybe we didn't feel as close to her as some people did. Before the in-vasion, we celebrated all the festivals and holidays associated with her and her daughter, Princess Juliana.

"There was no need for the Queen to stay in Holland and be overtaken by the Germans," he continues. "She would either be killed or made a puppet ruler. She did not leave for a lack of courage. It's not courage to stick around if you are for certain going to be killed.

"I never heard anyone say anything against her going to Lon-don. She needed to be there, to keep the government going. We couldn't leave. We didn't have the opportunity she had. But it was important that she left."

Though many of the Veldmans' countrymen disobeyed Ger-man law by celebrating the Queen's birthday during her years of exile, the Veldmans did not raise a toast in her name or sing in her honor. (In at least one case, the Germans fined an entire Dutch town for commemorating the sovereign's birthday.) The Veldmans also never displayed a picture of the Queen in their house, before or after the war. With so many Germans passing through the farm, either to live for a short while or to check on the harvest or oversee the counting and distribution of livestock, it would have been an antagonizing gesture for the family to suddenly hang a portrait of Queen Wilhelmina on their wall.

Flagrantly antagonizing the Germans was not something the Veldmans wanted to do. They had too much to lose. Many Catholics in eastern Holland feared that Hitler would hunt them down after he eradicated the Jews, Pete says. Perhaps he would have gone after all Christians. Pete's neighbors felt he would most certainly go after Roman Catholics.

"We would have been next," he says with conviction.

On May 14, 1940, a day or two after Pete returned home from his aunt and uncle's, Germany demanded that the Netherlands surrender, vowing to bomb Rotterdam and its extensive port heavily if surrender was not immediate. By then, the invasion had been going on for five days. Thousands had died in the fighting. Holland surrendered against a force it could never have defeated on its own. What the Dutch did not know as the surrender was being negotiated was that German bombers were already headed for Rotterdam. (The ultimatum was unsigned when it was issued and a Dutch commander returned it for a signature, thus delaying the process.) The threatened German attack could not be or was not called off, and Rotterdam was bombed anyway.

By the time the conflict finally ended, more than 7,000 Dutch soldiers had been killed or were missing and at least 900 civilians had died. Germany moved quickly to establish its own rule of law in what just days before had been a proudly independent country. Occupying soldiers patrolled city and town streets alike, the North Sea shoreline was closely watched, and all international borders were placed under heavy guard. For the next five years, Holland's citizens would face a deepening, constricting darkness that ultimately threatened to sabotage civilization, hope, and decency.

The lives of the Veldmans and millions of their countrymen would never be the same.

છ

More than 60 years have passed since Pete lived through his stories of growing up in occupied Holland, stories he recalls vividly and with the timing and good ear of a true storyteller. Though he recalls many incidents with good humor and a twinkle, he sometimes stops in the telling because of tears. After all these years, after repeating his stories to family and friends countless times, he still occasionally loses his composure as he relives the pain he and his family and his country-men endured.

"I'll get back to you on that," is a common refrain. Or, "I don't know why, after all this time, I still can't talk about it."

For Pete and his family and their fellow farmers and nearby town folks – indeed, for most of Holland – the years 1940 to 1945 were consumed with thoughts of liberation. Who would govern Holland when the war finally ended was not the most pressing question. The passions and energies of millions were centered on a far more important question: Who would liberate Holland?

Pete and his countrymen were determined to endure occupation as long as they had to, though the costs would grow with each passing year. They went about their lives as best they could, all the while hearing whispers of what was happening in other parts of the country. The Occupation would eventually all-but-strangle the Netherlands and its free society. Pete spent his teenage years watching – and learning – as the invaders gradually tightened their grip. He learned to dodge, feign innocence, and whenever he could, defy the authorities. He learned to remain attentive, ever alert to what was happening around him. He learned not to let fear itself defeat him. And he learned to wait.

Pete grew from boyhood to young adulthood during the span of World War II. His memories of that time mark his journey in understanding – from boyish excitement at seeing soldiers on motorcycles to a young man's growing realization that living without freedom is no way to live. From acceptance of what was beyond his power to control to a steadfast determination to one day change the course of his life if he could.

As Pete matured, he anticipated liberation each step of the way.

છ૭

There were two good things that came out of the war. The first was a lake that was created on our farm when the Germans started building the autobahn. Our farm actually produced the sand needed to build the road and a railroad overpass. The road construction was contracted to a Dutch company; no Dutch were forced to work on it. Employees who had traveled the world over came to do the work. Their presence created a lot of excitement for our small community.

This happened very early in the Occupation. The road divided our farm in half, right through the middle. The sand that was needed to build it was hauled away in a special little railroad with a small locomotive. While the locomotive was traveling from one place to the next, pulling 12 lorries (trucks) full of sand, I pulled 12 empty lorries into position to be filled again, using a well-trained horse. We worked slow, but sure. I was hired by the contractor – I'm sure for some small amount of money, though I don't remember what – to do the work. It was tricky because it made the horses nervous. That's what I liked about it.

The German who was in control of Holland at the beginning of the Occupation had a real interest in a toll road being built in the country. He wanted to extend the road into Germany. But the person who eventually took over command from him did not have the same interest. He decided that the project was not that important and that there would not be enough concrete to finish it because of the other needs of the war. So the road was left unfinished. It was just a dirt road until sometime after the war when Holland started rebuilding the country.

The road construction crew used a machine that sucked out dirt, separating out the sand. The hole that was left created a five-acre lake on our farm that gradually filled with water. During and after the war, our family and friends used the lake. Once the Germans quit working on the autobahn, there was no more soldier activity around there at all. The lake had water flowing in one end and out the other. The sand made a beautiful beach. I learned to swim in our lake, and we skated there in the winter with friends. We were not watched by the Germans. It became our very private swimming hole in the summer and skating rink in the winter. It couldn't have been better.

The second good thing was that toward the end of the war I met the woman I would one day marry.

∽

*E*verybody had to carry an ID at all times. If you lost it, you would be questioned by the Germans and the Dutch police as to how you lost it. Anytime you were stopped by the soldiers or the police, you might have to show your ID. Because we lived out in the country, I wasn't constantly stopped. We didn't travel that far, and everyone knew each other. I knew which police would wave me on and which would give me trouble. Some Dutch were real sympathizers with Germany and some weren't. The ones who would wave me on, say if I was driving the wagon, wouldn't really look for me. Even when the Dutch police thought they had to stop us – for their own safety, because they were being watched by the Germans – they would kind of look the other way. Later on, they would stop by our farm, looking for something in return – a payback – like milk or grain. We had those things because we lived on a farm. But they needed them, too.

There was danger all around during the Occupation. But when

you're in the midst of it, you don't feel it that much. I didn't. I was young and thought, at first anyways, that it was pretty exciting. Now I think of my parents and all their children and know they must have been very concerned from the beginning.

For me, it was a lot of excitement. When you live on a farm, life goes along pretty quietly. And then, all of a sudden, here come the Germans invading the country, and some come to live on the farm, then they move away. It's exciting stuff.

Some German sympathizers lived in Didam. Some of them were well-known. Maybe some of them hid it and were more sympathetic than they showed. But the real sympathizers – we knew who they were. None of them were friends of ours. Before the war, being a German sympathizer was nothing that serious. Politics was a pretty open thing. That changed after the invasion.

When I was 14, I used to ride my bike from the farm to Didam to attend a gymnastics class. I would pass by the house of a well-known sympathizer who had a big sign in his yard showing his support for the Germans. One day four or five of us stole the sign out of his yard, took it behind the school, and tore it up. The next week when we went to gymnastics the guy came in, looking us over in class. He had figured out who had taken his sign. But he didn't say or do anything.

Most people living in Didam weren't sympathizers. The mayor gave us most of our directions, which came from the Germans. For instance, the mayor shut down the newspaper when they told him to. That's probably how he stayed alive through the Occupation. It's not that we had Germans or sympathizers all over. But some Dutch were real sympathizers, including some of the police. One policeman in particular was probably a sympathizer, but then again, maybe not. Maybe he just had to keep his job. Maybe we were better off having him over us than a real sympathizer. Sometimes you never knew.

If you weren't doing anything illegal, you could go just about anywhere you wanted to, at least at first. Where I lived, out in the country, I didn't pay too much attention to the nighttime curfews the Germans imposed on us. I was only going from one farmhouse to another, and there weren't police in between. But if you lived in Didam, you had to pay more attention to those kinds of things. No matter where you lived, all the houses had to have their windows covered at night, so if the Allies flew over they would not see lights and mistake a few houses for a town or city. Covering windows protected both the Germans and the Dutch from Allied bombs. We could not even have a light on our bicycles at night.

At the beginning of the Occupation, my cousin and I would ride our bikes about 100 kilometers (60 miles) in one day, to visit relatives. We would stay for a few days, exchange news and information about the Germans and the war, and then ride back in a day. We did this a few times. It was quite a challenge. That's why we did it.

If I had been told to swear loyalty to the Germans when I was 14, I would have probably done it and then gone on living as I wanted to. I was young and looking for a challenge.

ങ

*T*he Germans set up indoctrination camps for young boys pretty soon after they invaded. I think it was partly to keep young boys off the streets, to keep them from aggravating the soldiers. It was also to train the minds of young boys. If you train the mind early enough, it stays with you for a long, long time. The Germans did this a lot more successfully in Austria than they did in Holland. They started with younger boys in Austria.

I never had to go to an indoctrination camp, though I was just the right age. I did have to take a fitness test. Later on, we received word that they had found something wrong with me. But there was nothing wrong with me. We knew someone at The Hague had helped keep me out, someone who had contacted my parents and said they would try to help keep me home if they could. My brothers were too young to be tested.

So I never had to go to an indoctrination camp, although once I went to visit a friend of mine who had to go. I wasn't afraid to go there to *visit him. I went with a couple of other boys. We went by train, which was a very big deal for us, and then we came back. The boys I knew who were sent to indoctrination camps weren't sent to train as soldiers. They were too young for that. They may have been sent to dig ditches and trenches for the Germans. Later on, we all had to do that. Boys and men were sent all over the country to dig for the Germans.*

The Germans didn't have to go looking for boys our age. We were everywhere. A future brother-in-law of mine was forced to stay in one of the camps for a long time. I think it was a little hard for him when he first came out, to change his thinking. He was a year older than I was. But the Germans didn't take everyone who was a year older. Maybe they took some of the older ones to keep them from joining the Resistance.

❦

The beginning of the Occupation was a time of unnatural quiet for the Veldmans and other isolated Dutch farmers. While their lives had suddenly and catastrophically been turned upside down, they knew little about what was happening in the rest of the country. Most small-town newspapers were shut down following the invasion; all communications were closely monitored by the Germans. Radios were either quickly confiscated by the authorities or hidden by their owners, who dared not tell anyone what they heard over the airwaves for fear of sympathizers.

Though many German sympathizers brazenly supported Germany, others were covert – and willing to report any countrymen they suspected of any kind of illegal activity. Some Resistance workers even posed as sympathizers to get inside information from the Germans. No one knew for sure who could be believed.

It was an uneasy time. The Dutch, known for their tolerance and acceptance of all kinds of political and religious beliefs, were thrust into the uncomfortable position of not being able to trust people they had lived beside and worked with for years. Open-mindedness was replaced by suspicion and fear.

Before the invasion, travel between different parts of the country had been minimal, especially among farmers; there was even less travel after. Little news could get in by word-of-mouth, and very little could get out. The Germans wanted it that way. The Veldmans and their neighbors were particularly inaccessible, for one could travel no farther east without being in Germany itself. Pete says that he and his parents knew almost nothing of what was happening outside their small community for quite a while. That their house was full of soldiers made it that much harder for them to find out what was going on elsewhere. They did not hear Queen Wilhelmina the first time she spoke from across the North Sea via BBC radio. It would be several days before they knew the full story of the invasion – how many lives had been lost, the bombing of the western cities, the installation of a German civilian governor, the gradual elimination of all non-Nazi organizations.

Nonetheless, life soon returned to some sense of normalcy in eastern Holland. Children once again walked to school. Farmers returned to their fields. The difference was that everything now happened under the watchful eyes of the occupying troops. Although the German supply unit living at the Veldmans' house moved on, other troops remained in Didam for the duration of the war.

"There was no shooting of any kind in Didam during the invasion," Pete says. "And afterward, there were enough German troops around to keep everything under control. Some strange things happened once in a while, but it had to happen pretty close by or you never found out. Like when the Germans started hauling away Jews. It happened real quick-like because they didn't want everyone to know what was happening.

"When you don't even have a small newspaper to inform you about what is happening in your own country, well . . ." he pauses, never finishing the sentence.

"No one really thought about trying to leave Holland. If you drew a little circle on the map, we were in communication with everybody within a two- to three-mile radius. Everybody within that circle was pretty much OK, except that we were under German occupation, which was a bad deal.

"The Occupation was just a miserable situation because the Germans were always there. There was a lot of mistrust. You had people you really knew, people you could communicate with. But you were always watching out for sympathizers.

"If you were really against the Germans, you didn't tell everybody. Let's put it that way."

The creation of the lake on the Veldmans' farm, a by-product of the attempted construction of the autobahn, was one of "two good things" that resulted from the Occupation, according to Pete. Hitler began building the autobahn, or motorway, in Germany well before the beginning of World War II. By the time war needs halted construction in that country, over 2,000 miles of road were finished, though few Germans could afford to buy automobiles. Even fewer Dutch would have used the autobahn in the early 1940s had the Holland motorway been completed soon after it was begun. However, the modern road would have been a boon to the German army for quickly transporting soldiers and supplies from Germany to Holland's port cities and beyond.

How and when and if the road was ever used by the Dutch mattered little to Pete and his family and their friends: Few of them would ever use the road for its intended purpose, for very few of them would ever own any kind of motorized vehicle. As far as they were concerned, the lake was a reward for enduring a situation they hated but were powerless to change. What the Germans started but could not complete offered the Veldmans and their neighbors a year-round venue for entertainment during the war years and for as long as the family lived on the farm.

The Germans did not force the Dutch to work for them very

much in the early months following the invasion – not even on the autobahn – partly because Hitler wanted to win them over. He considered the blond looks of the Dutch to be superior and thought Holland could contribute toward creating the ideal Aryan society if it were eventually annexed to Germany.

Even to a boy Pete's age, the thought was laughable.

There were many scary moments for everyone, but still, it was pretty exciting for a young teenager. We didn't work so much after the Occupation started. The farm was neglected – there was just a very negative attitude toward life.

We would steal from the Germans whenever the opportunity came along. It was our little part of fighting the war. You did not openly oppose the Germans – that was always the wrong thing to do. You couldn't gain anything, and you put yourself in a lot of danger for no good reason. You knew you couldn't win. You just kept your mouth shut.

We knew other people who were also opposed to the Germans being in Holland, people we associated with. Some of them could do more things to get back at the Germans than I could as a young teenager. For me, being so young, it was pretty challenging and exciting to do any of the things I was not usually supposed to do. Like stealing. Can you imagine? I would never have been allowed to steal from anyone other than the Germans. But all I heard from my parents was, "If you steal, don't get caught." Or, "Be careful that you don't get caught!" That made it even more challenging to do.

Almost everything we stole was useless, small stuff. We did it to aggravate the Germans. But once one of my uncles and I stole a cow, and that was pretty serious. Or it could have been. Most products from the farm had to be turned in to local, approved authorities. Everything was regulated after the invasion. All of our livestock – cows, horses, pigs, not

58

"Landgoed Hees," the farm where Pete grew up in far eastern Holland. The main barn was an extension of the house. The autobahn is visible in the background.

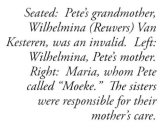

Bernard Veldman's family in front of their home in Duiven. Bernard stands in the back row, third from the right. Bernard's parents, Petrus and Theodora, are seated.

Seated: Pete's grandmother, Wilhelmina (Reuvers) Van Kesteren, was an invalid. Left: Wilhelmina, Pete's mother. Right: Maria, whom Pete called "Moeke." The sisters were responsible for their mother's care.

Bernard and Wilhelmina on their wedding day, June 18, 1925. Pete remembers his mother wearing her wedding dress on many special occasions.

From left: Willemien, cousin Harry, Dolly, Pete.

Wilhelmina and Bernard stand behind their children. From left: Pete, Willemien, Dolly, Rieka, Al, Ben, Ted, Mary, June, Fran, Willy, baby Henry.

Wilhelmina and Bernard dressed up for a special event. Wilhelmina was known for her flair, though her resources were limited.

Wilhelmina's wartime identification card.

Wilma Zents, 18 years old, in apron and wooden shoes (1945). Wilma met Pete at a clandestine dance before Holland was liberated.

*Mr. and Mrs. Seesing,
Pete's sponsors in
Leopold, Missouri.*

Pete stands on board the Leerdam, *second
from right, in Rotterdam. It took 14 days for
the freighter to cross the Atlantic Ocean.*

TRAVELERS AID SOCIETY of *New York*

Date *5/6/49*

To the Conductor
Name *Peter Sleldmon*

Is going to *H. Seesing Leopold, Mo*
NAME   ADDRESS

Travelers Aid Society has~~ has not~~ been notified at *St. Louis*

Remarks: *Speaks Dutch - little
English*

N T A A—Conductor's Letter - No. 4 - 10M - 12-47

*The ticket given to Pete by members of
the Travelers Aid Society after he found
the train station in New York City. The
ticket helped Pete make his way across
the country. Note the "remarks." Inset:
Pete as a young man, sometime before he
immigrated.*

*The convent of the Poor Sisters of
St. Francis of Perpetual Adoration in
Mishawaka, Indiana.*

Pete in basic training in Breckenridge, Kentucky. Despite the freezing temperatures, he was never issued a coat.

Pete stands at the 38th Parallel, which divides North and South Korea.

From left: Herman Kruis, John Kruis.

Pete "at home" in Korea as a United States soldier.

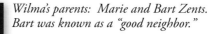
Wilma's parents: Marie and Bart Zents. Bart was known as a "good neighbor."

Wilma's family. Standing, from left: Riek, Theo, Ans, Jos, Ada, Wilma, Jan. Seated, from left: Mary, Bart (father), Marie (mother), Bertus.

Pete and Wilma on their two-day honeymoon in Frankfurt, Germany.

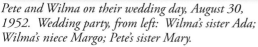

Pete and Wilma on their wedding day, August 30, 1952. Wedding party, from left: Wilma's sister Ada; Wilma's niece Margo; Pete's sister Mary.

chickens — had to be counted regularly and registered. It was controlled partly so people with ration cards could get meat and other food to eat.

Farmers could only sell to those Dutch who had been approved by the Dutch government, and the Dutch government had to work with the Germans. Before the Occupation, we would have sold to the butcher house owned by the Jews, or to others, who would then resell the meat to whoever they wanted to sell it to. Now we could only sell to the Dutch slaughterhouse, which was controlled somewhat by sympathizers. They, in turn, could only sell to specific food centers. Without an approved ration card, no one could get food, unless you lived on a farm like we did.

Frequently, someone in authority would come to the farm to count our livestock and make sure the numbers were right. Any difference in their numbers and ours could be a real problem. If we had any extra animals, we kept them in hiding. My dad had a good relationship with one of the local authorities, who would often let us know ahead of time if there was an inspection in the making.

Once, my uncle and I worked together to steal a cow from the Germans. They had a whole herd of them fenced together. Whenever it was late at night, the soldiers who were on duty would come together to talk, and when they did, we stole the cow. We lay in hiding, waiting for a long time, and then when we got the cow out we walked away with it, trying to keep it quiet as we went. I don't remember, but I'm pretty sure we butchered it.

Another time we butchered a cow of ours that had drowned. We weren't even supposed to do that. It was against the law for us to butcher. But the cow had drowned and we wanted the meat. There was a man working with us that day who owned a truck. He was helping us move our cows back to the farm after they crossed a river. My mom never liked those guys — there were two of them — who owned the truck because they were rough and foul-mouthed. When I was younger and they came to help on the farm, before the war, she always made us go inside the house because she didn't want us to hear their language.

The guy with the truck said he would haul away the dead cow for us. But after he had loaded it into the back, he had to stop unexpectedly and wait to cross a bridge. There were guards watching the bridge. So he got out of the truck and leaned against it, to hide the blood that was dripping out from underneath. (We had slit the cow's throat in order to preserve the meat.) What he was doing, hauling away that butchered cow, was certainly against the law, and he was nervously trying to cover it up. He didn't get caught. We probably paid him back by giving him some of the meat.

Another time, some friends and I stole a whole bunch of tires from the Germans. We worked all night to steal those tires, though we didn't even have a vehicle to drive. No one on our farm had a vehicle to drive and none of my friends' families had anything to drive. We just wanted to take the tires. I had seen them in a pile by the soldiers' camp during the day. The Germans were camped out, living out of tents, and the tires were off to the side.

My friends and I took the tires little by little during the night. The next day, we found out there wasn't one good tire in the bunch! They were just old, worn tires, no good at all. We had rolled them out, one by one, probably eight or 10 of them. But they weren't worth hauling home. The Germans probably watched us take them.

ᕗ

*O*nce I had to spend the night in jail because I was caught hauling some of our own grain to the baker. I was actually stealing our own grain! We had to turn in the grain whenever it was harvested. The authorities knew when it was harvest time. They probably even knew who was harvesting on particular days. We were watched by the Germans, or by a Dutch man they placed in charge, to be sure the grain that we brought in from the fields was sent where it was supposed to go. I don't remember needing ration cards, because we lived on a farm. But people living in towns and cities needed them, and were allowed only so much of certain kinds of foods, including so much bread per family. Farmers had to send *their grain to be milled so people would have enough bread to eat. Where we sent the grain was regulated.*

When we needed extra grain, maybe to trade for something like shoes or more bread because we were such a large family, we would steal from ourselves, take a little off the top. That is what I was doing the day I was caught. We got along pretty good with the guy, a Dutch fellow, who was supposed to be watching for the Germans as the grain was bagged and loaded onto wagons. Underneath one of the wagons, where the spare wheel should have been, I hid several bags of grain. We didn't talk about it, but I'm sure he saw me and knew what I was doing.

The Dutch police stopped me once I was on the road, driving the wagon into town. I was on my way to the baker, to trade the grain for extra bread when we needed it. The police found the grain, of course, and wanted to know where I got it and where I was going. I wouldn't be surprised if they knew we were threshing that day and were on the lookout for us. I told them that the grain was leftover from the fields, that I had gathered and bagged it up. Naturally, they didn't believe that, and they threw me in jail for the night.

My family didn't have a way to communicate with me, though I guess they heard where I was pretty quick. The jail was creepy, but after hours of interrogation, the authorities let me go the next day. When I was let out, the first thing everyone I met asked me was, "Did you talk? Did you tell?" But I hadn't told the police who helped us out, who we secretly traded with, or anything like that. I was a hero for the day.

I was 14 or 15 years old when this happened.

The Dutch police took the grain. They probably kept it for themselves.

છ

The Germans did away with newspapers, radios, sometimes even our bicycles, very early on. They wanted to keep everyone close to home. We hid our radio after they became illegal. I don't think our neighbors had a radio, but maybe they did. If they had one, we never knew. But they never knew we had one, either. You had to be very careful about things like that.

We hid the radio up in the hayloft, surrounded by bales of hay. We made a secret room up there; the walls were made out of hay. We disguised it well. If you wanted to listen to the radio, you had to step up on the fourth cow in the barn, lift a bale of hay, and climb through an opening in the ceiling.

My dad was up in the hayloft at night quite often, listening to news of the war. My mother was never up there. I was there almost every night.

Looking back now, I think how serious the war was for my mom and dad. They had a whole household of children and all of these things going on around them. Soldiers were sometimes living on the farm. People were watching our harvests and counting our livestock. It wasn't that serious for me at first, but life was totally different during those years of the Occupation. The amount of danger that was all around you affected you at all times. You never forgot you were occupied.

My mother was always very alert. She was a very sharp woman, calculating. One time, later on in the war, some Germans and a Dutch man came to our door around midnight. Everything would have been blacked out if any lights had been on, but they weren't. No one used electricity that late at night. It was too expensive – if you could get it. We had electric lights, but we didn't always use them. We often used kerosene or other types of fuel lamps.

Anyway, the house was dark when the Germans came to the door. Everyone in the house but my mother was sleeping. The Germans had probably been alerted by a sympathizer, who was with them, that we might have a radio we were hiding. They knew that midnight was when we would be listening to it if we had one. That's when they could catch us. They also probably came to steal some food. The German soldiers were pretty much on their own by then. There were no supplies left for them, which meant they had to find their own food. But they still had guns.

My dad and I were listening to the radio up in the hayloft, along with a man who was living in the hayloft in hiding. The way we had fixed it up made for a real neat room up there. My mom had to quickly think of some way to alert us. Before she went to answer the door – she knew it would be trouble because it was so late at night – she threw the main electric switch a couple of times. The only thing running was the radio, and we knew something was wrong when it went on and off. We immediately turned it off and just lay there in the hayloft.

We stayed there for a long time. We heard the Germans and the sympathizer walking around down underneath us in the barn. They probably stayed in the barn for about an hour or more, listening and walking around. Then they finally took some food and left.

It's amazing how still you can be when your life may depend on it.

∞

*Y*ou could only trust your family and a few very close friends during the war. We trusted our aunts and uncles and just a few others. You always had to be careful about what you said and what you did and where you did it.

I was too young to be in the Dutch Resistance and my father was too old. They would not have wanted me to be in the midst of all that, and my father had no business being in it with a family the size of ours. It was very, very dangerous work. Anyone even suspected of being in the Resistance could be executed on the spot, without a trial. You didn't have to be much involved. If they even thought you were involved, that was good enough: It was instant execution.

After the war was over, I became friends with a young teacher in the agriculture school who had been in the Resistance. But I didn't know him during the Occupation. I met him when I took some classes after the war.

I also had an uncle, Uncle Jan, who was part of an underground group that tried to help any Allied pilot who was shot down get to safety, usually to France and from there to Switzerland. From Switzerland, a pilot could get back to wherever he needed to be. The group had a real good system worked out. Everyone involved would take the pilot only a certain distance, only in the part of the country he knew well. There would be someone waiting for the pilot at the next point. A certain word would be spoken and the pilot would be handed over. Men like my uncle operated only in their own areas, where they knew the roads and language and people, where they could get around without arousing suspicion.

I didn't know my uncle was involved in this until after the war was over. He would have never told me during the war. I didn't know – and I shouldn't have known. But my father probably knew what his brother was doing. This uncle was never married and did not have a family of his own. He was the best sort of person to do this kind of work. It was extremely secretive. It had to be that way.

ꙮ

As the war went on, we were forced to work for the Germans in lots of different ways. This happened all over the country. Some Dutch were sent to work in factories in Germany, some had to work in Dutch factories that were controlled by the Germans.

I had to work with a group that was building a big ditch to stop invading tanks, a tank-defense line. This happened many times. We were told to bring a shovel with us whenever we went to work. I always made a point not to work, as much as I could get away with it. And I always brought the smallest spade I could find. I told the soldiers it was all I had.

Once, a German soldier came and stood over me and watched me. Finally, he said, "I've been watching you. And I haven't seen you move one shovelful of dirt yet." So I shoveled a little dirt for him. But when he moved away and was no longer looking, I shoveled it right back. I put the dirt back in the trench.

The trenches were being built to stop tanks from coming in whenever the Allies arrived. Lots of Dutch civilians were rounded up to dig trenches and fortifications. We had to dig foxholes everywhere, including some of the foxholes that were all over our farm. Thousands and thousands of foxholes used by German soldiers were dug by the Dutch. When it got to the end of the war, and the Allies and Germans were shooting artillery shells over our farm, my dad and brothers and I would jump down into one of the foxholes if the shells seemed too close.

Who knows, maybe we had dug the foxholes we were crouched in.

❦

Once the Netherlands surrendered, the Germans began employing a number of different tactics that psychologically, physically, and practically limited the public and private lives of the Dutch. One of the simplest, most unrelenting means of domination exercised by the occupiers was their demand that the Dutch carry identification cards at all times; this was especially true for residents of the big cities. Being stopped – for little or no reason by soldiers and the police – and coerced into showing an identification card was an intimidating form of harassment at a time and place in history when most people did not even carry a driver's license because they did not drive. As time passed, identification cards also became an effective way for the Germans to identify those Jews who might have otherwise escaped detection.

No matter who you were, if you were stopped, you had to produce identification for the authorities to let you pass. Or you had to use some other means to convince them that your business was legitimate. Anyone who did not comply risked relentless questioning, beating, being thrown in jail – or worse. Because he lived in such a small community, and maybe because he was young, Pete does not remember that he always carried an ID. He does remember being stopped and questioned regularly by German or

Dutch authorities, even when he was recognized.

Pete's answers were not satisfactory the night he was tossed into jail. He would not tell where the grain had come from (his family's farm) or where he was taking it (to the baker). Though he was clearly a minor, the police did not just take the grain and send him home. They locked him up. For a few fleeting moments following his release the next morning, Pete felt like a hero. He relished the admiration he received from his family and friends for bravely keeping his mouth shut.

To this day, Pete recalls the baker – for whom he sometimes delivered bread during the early years of the Occupation – with fondness. He got the job, he says, because he knew where all the farmers lived. Not surprisingly, he loved the challenge of balancing a very large basket full of fresh bread on the front of his bicycle and riding carefully from one farmhouse to the next to deliver each family's regulated number of loaves. That he had to work hard to control the unwieldy bike and its cargo as he avoided deep ruts in the road made the job fun.

In time, the manufacture of fake IDs became a primary job for many Resistance workers who toiled to keep themselves and others alive. For instance, a Resistance worker who had been identified under one name had a chance of continuing his or her work – and staying alive – if a convincing fake ID could be made using a different name. Such false documentation also helped a small number of Jews live undetected in Dutch society. It helped move others Jews into hiding and even out of the country, an undertaking that was very risky in the early years and nearly impossible toward the end of the war.

With "proper identification," Allies who had been shot down or otherwise detained in Holland had a chance of being moved from point to point by the Dutch underground until they were put on a train or boat and transported out of Holland. Pete's uncle, who helped move Allied pilots from one part of the country to another, had more to worry about than securing a farmer's disguise for a soldier-on-the-run. If a pilot was stopped and did not have convincing papers, and if he could not pull off the daring stunt of impersonating a Dutch farmer, both he and the man putting his life on the line to get him to safety could pay a terrible penalty.

Another seemingly benign method the Germans used to intimidate and control was to impose curfew hours throughout the country. If nothing else, curfew regulations were a constant reminder that the Dutch were no longer in charge of their own lives in even the simplest of ways. Where you went, and when, was no long a personal decision. While curfew hours were sometimes relaxed in the early years of the Occupation, they were more tightly controlled as time went by, especially in larger cities.

At first, many of the restrictions put in place by the Germans seemed "exciting" and "challenging" to Pete. It was exhilarating to irritate the occupying soldiers, to stand up to them in small ways. But the stakes increased as the years passed. Toward the end of the war, the German army itself was growing desperate. Nazi soldiers guessed the end was coming, but they could not leave their posts. They were running low on supplies and often stole to feed themselves. They ransacked houses for anything of value in "no man's land" – areas the Dutch were forced to flee as the Allies slowly fought their way into the country – and sent the goods back to Germany for "safekeeping."

Teenagers often complain that time moves slowly: It can't hurry up enough for them to get on with their own lives. For Pete and thousands of other Dutch youth growing up during the Occupation, time was dominated by an overriding situation over which they had absolutely no control. Motivation ceased to be personal and became instead an external keeping of rules or following of orders. There was little to reach for when the goal was someone else's. There was no moving forward.

The restrictions placed upon Holland worsened with every passing season, until, for Pete, time came to a near standstill. By the end of the war, his circumstances were no longer exciting. He was no longer a young boy thrilled by the challenge of annoying an occupying soldier or undertaking a long bike ride. He knew more, he had seen more, and he understood more.

A year, a month, a week, a day, an hour – time is crucial for anyone straining to get on with his or her life. Conquering time, moving forward, and gaining independence would become the older Pete's greatest goal.

 भ

There were different people who hid on our farm during the five years of occupation. One man, the farm owner's brother, was a professional who had gone to college. He was a very nice person, about the same age as my parents. For a short time, maybe a few months, he lived in the hayloft where we hid the radio.

He was a city person, but my mother tried to disguise him so he could walk around during the day without the Germans or sympathizers recognizing him. She got him farm clothes and wooden shoes to wear. He had never worn wooden shoes before – they were worn by poorer people and farmers – but she told him that on a farm he had to look like a farmer.

The day after my mom got him the clothes, he came walking out wearing wooden shoes and reading a book. My mother snatched the book out of his hand and said, "Give me that! Have you ever seen a farmer walking around reading a book?"

I don't know why he was hiding. Maybe he was a judge or something like that. He was probably not being looked for by the soldiers, but by German sympathizers. I don't know where he went after he left the farm, but he eventually made it through the war and became a free man.

My dad had pretty good contacts on the outside. Sometimes he would get a message, a tip that went something like: You'd better watch out. They – German soldiers, sympathizers in the police force, etc. – are coming to your house. Then the people hiding on our farm would go to the woods, or if possible, find somewhere else on the farm to hide. They would not usually go to their hiding rooms.

We had one person in hiding for over a year. A former farm em-

ployee of ours had been told that he had to work for the Germans. He didn't show up when and where they told him to, but came instead to our farm to hide. He lived in the chicken coop for a year or more. He worked on the farm most of the time, but not if the Germans came around or were living in the house, and not if we thought there were sympathizers around. Then he went to the woods until it was safe. The chicken coop was a pretty good-sized place since we had lots of chickens. Maybe he cleaned out a little area of it for himself. I don't know. You do what you have to do to stay alive.

The children in our family who were maybe 8 years old and older knew we had people living and hiding on the farm. Not the younger children. It was too risky for them to know what was going on because they might tell people outside the family. The Germans may not have made a big issue out of our hiding evaders if they had been caught. But you could never be sure what would happen – it depended on the day and who was in charge at the time.

If we had been caught hiding Jews, that would have been different.

❦

We didn't know much about the treatment of the Jews for a long time. But just beyond the edge of our land, we would sometimes see trains go by. I would hear a train coming and would ride my bike over to watch it, or go by wagon if I was out in the fields.

After a while, I realized the trains were full of Jewish people being sent into Germany. I could tell because the train cars had open sides and the cars were full of people, but no one was sitting down. And there were soldiers with them, guarding the people so they wouldn't try to jump off.

I figured out what it was after I saw it a few times.

Sometimes people were able to escape the trains, but not often. Usually they were shot by the guards after they jumped. The father of one of my future brothers-in-law jumped off a train and escaped as it was on its way to Dachau, a concentration camp in Germany. I don't know why he *was picked up by the Germans — if he was a political prisoner or if they were going to force him to work in Dachau. The important thing is, he jumped the train and made it. He stayed in Germany for the rest of the war, working on small farms, moving from place to place to keep from being arrested again. He finally made it back to Holland after the war was over. Sadly, he died soon afterward from eating canned food that had gone bad.*

He made it through the whole war, and then he died.

ↄ⅃

*A*t first there was enough food for everyone, but toward the end of the war many people were starving. Thousands died of hunger in the big cities. Farmers were the only ones around who had food. We always had enough to eat; it just wasn't very good. But my mother had a way of making the most out of it.

We had a family friend, a young woman, who worked at a food distribution center. I got ration cards from her for a Jewish family, a man and wife, who went into hiding near where we lived. By this point, Jewish people all had to wear the Star of David on their clothes to identify themselves as Jewish. Gradually, we learned that all the Jews were being captured and sent to death camps. They could be picked up by the Germans anywhere they went.

My dad knew this Jewish man and his wife because he had done business with the man. The farmers were well-acquainted with the Jewish groups before the war, for they bought from us and sold to others. Some of them were very good at what they did.

The Jewish man and woman came to my dad needing help. They were little known in our community and would not have been readily recognized by the locals when they came to us. But it was too dangerous to hide them at our house. There were always too many people around, including German soldiers, and if the couple was discovered, we could all die with them, depending on who was in charge and the circumstances. It was just very dangerous.

My dad helped the man and woman find a place to hide out in the country, with a Dutch couple living in a small farmhouse. It was not a place where you would expect anyone to hide, but they did, and it worked. It was not much of a farm, and there was not enough food for them there. The Dutch couple did not have enough food to share, but their house was near a town, and they could get food at a distribution center there if they had ration cards. The Dutch couple still had to pay for the food, of course, because that's how ration cards worked, but they could at least buy more food if they had the cards. They would take the cards in and get food and take it back to the house for the Jewish man and woman.

The neighbor girl I knew got me the ration cards each week for the Jewish man and his wife. She worked at the office that distributed the cards. I have no idea how she got extra cards for people who needed them.

I took the Jewish couple their ration cards so they could get food. I delivered the cards to them each week at a predetermined time. It would have been dangerous if I had been caught, but at that time it was more of a local thing to be decided. It was not like hiding a Jew in your house. The consequences would have had a lot to do with which Nazi or Dutch policeman was in charge when I was caught.

One day I got to the farmhouse about 30 minutes late. I rode my bicycle, like always. When I went up to the house there was no one there. I knocked on the door and looked around and waited for several minutes. I did not go in the house. I thought it was really strange that no one was home. It was late in the season and the grain was high, all around the house. There wasn't anyone in sight – just fields of grain.

I finally picked up my bicycle and got ready to leave. And suddenly the Jewish man and woman came out of the field of grain, where they had been hiding. They thought that because I was a half-hour late, something had happened, something had gone wrong. All the other times I had been on time. They were so worried that somebody had caught on to what I was doing, that maybe I was being followed.

They were so afraid that they had been sweating out there in the field. I remember them standing there, their clothes drenched with sweat.

I took them ration cards every week for several months, until they felt it had become too dangerous for them where they were staying. I made sure I was never again late. They had been so afraid. I will never forget how afraid they were, standing there wet from sweating.

One evening they came back to our house. We could not keep them there, although I think they stayed for one night before my dad took them to the train station. They had decided to go to one of the big cities. I don't know why, but they thought they had a better chance of blending in somewhere else where there were more people. Exactly where they were going, I don't know. They did not tell us. It was better for them and better for us if we did not know their plans.

When it was time to go, my dad took them to ride on the locomotive. There was a special spot on the train where the conductor hid them. I guess my father had somehow let the conductor know beforehand that they were coming.

They must have made it to wherever they were going, but they did not survive the extermination. They were not so young when they left, and they looked Jewish. We knew they didn't survive because we never heard from them again after the war was over.

We didn't want to communicate with them right after they left, and they would not have wanted to communicate with us. It was too dangerous. But we never heard from them again. And we would have, if they had survived. They would have let us know that they had made it out alive.

Most of the Jews did not survive the war. There was just no place to hide in Holland because the country was so small. A few of the Jews had contacts in other places who helped them get out of the country right at the beginning of the Occupation, but most did not.

All of our extended family hid individuals during the war, but not Jews, as far as I know. There were only three or four Jewish families living in Didam at the time of the invasion. There were more in other *nearby towns, and of course there were lots of Jews in the cities. It was just too dangerous to hide them. If you were caught, you would also be sent to a death camp. We had too many children for my parents to risk that. They would have killed all of us.*

What I did, getting the man and his wife ration cards, wasn't that dangerous. I knew the man and his wife. We traded with him. I couldn't see how the authorities could catch me. It was just a few, little green cards that fit in my pocket, and I was on my bicycle.

But I didn't want to get caught.

℘

Food rationing, severe hunger in the cities, the horrific search for and subsequent deaths of most of the Jewish population, the establishment of concentration camps within the country, forced manual and factory labor by the Germans, the abandonment of homes, low fuel supplies, the tightly regulated distribution of farm products, conscription into the German army, the illegality of newspapers and radio broadcasts, the constant threat of sympathizers, relentless propaganda – all contributed to the gradual strangulation of Dutch society.

Very slowly, as he grew older, Pete's eyes were opened to what was happening around him. His only reliable source of information about conditions in his own country was what he heard in secret on the radio up in the hayloft. But first, that news had to be smuggled out of Holland and into London. Then it was written into a BBC broadcast. Accurate information was a long time coming, if it ever arrived.

For instance, Pete never knew – had no way of knowing – that Germany eventually established three concentration camps for Jews within Holland. Ironically, one of the camps, Westerbork, was built by the Dutch before the invasion took place to house Jewish refugees fleeing Germany. It was meant to be a place of life and protection. But in an unspeakably cruel twist of fate, the Germans utilized Westerbork as a transit camp. Throughout the long years of occupation, thousands of men, women, and children wearing the Star of David were rounded up and sent to Westerbork and from there to Auschwitz, where the vast majority died in the gas chambers. Most Jews never knew why they were being sent to Westerbork; they only knew that no one ever returned home from there.

Only 30,000 of Holland's 140,000 Jews survived the war. In all of Europe, Holland was second only to Poland in the percentage of its Jewish population that died in the death camps. Well-maintained Dutch civil records aided German soldiers charged with ferreting out the country's Jews, no matter where they lived. One by one by one, the soldiers kept at their task.

From the very beginning of the Occupation, it was almost impossible for Jews to get out of the country. Even if they succeeded, their only option was to enter a bordering country that was also under Nazi control. Holland offered no mountains and had no great stretches of forest in which to hide, and the sea was heavily patrolled by German small craft and U-boats. When Bernard Veldman put the older Jewish couple on the train bound for the city of their choosing, he could only have guessed at their complete desperation.

Pete always gets emotional when he talks about the couple coming out of the grain field – the image of their abject, sweat-drenched fear is burned in his memory. He could not have understood then that their fear was not that he had let them down. He was a young teenager. They feared for their very lives, and rightly so. As Pete grew older, as the rumors increased, as trains full of human captives continued to roll past the Veldmans' farm, the Jewish couple's fear became for Pete a grim reminder of what was at stake for his country, perhaps for much of the world, should Germany win the war.

Pete was maturing in a world where anyone could be thrown into jail for refusing to answer a question or play the role of an informer. Where wearing a six-pointed star on one's clothes marked one for death. Where any "lawbreaker" could be sent to a concentration camp, not in another country, but in his or her own country. The list goes on. "The Occupation was a terrible time for the country," he says.

It was a terrible time to be young.

∾

*T*oward the end of the war, country farmers and people living in small cities and towns were forced to evacuate because of fighting between the Allies and the Germans. The Allies were right on the other side of the Rhine River. Whenever the Dutch had to leave their homes like this, the Germans would go through them, taking whatever they could use.

On more than one occasion the soldiers made me go with them, along with a group of 10 or 15 drivers, horses, and wagons. The soldiers took belongings out of Dutch houses – or made us carry them out – and loaded up the wagons. Then they made us drive the wagons into Germany where they were emptied.

They took most anything you can think of. I once had a wagon full of canning jars. Along the way, as we drove toward Germany, we passed Dutch people on the side of the road who knew there was stuff in the wagons. They would run up to us and try to get whatever they could off the wagons as we passed. There was always a German soldier with a gun at the head and foot of the line, but people could get a few items off the wagons in the middle without being seen.

This time, the Germans caught a Dutch man trying to steal something off one of the wagons in a long line. For some reason, they made him sit down beside me, on the wagon I was driving, all the way into Germany. But the Germans released him once we got there. I'm sure he was home before I was.

While he was with me, before we got into Germany, he watched me stop the wagon and hide a few items for my family that I took from out of the pile of stuff. There were foxholes all over the place, and before we crossed the border I spotted a particular one and put a small bunch of tools in it that I had taken off the wagon.

"That was a good idea," he said to me once I was back beside him on the wagon seat. He meant it was a good idea to not take the tools into Germany and risk getting caught when I didn't turn them in. If I didn't have them on my wagon, maybe they wouldn't be remembered. And there would be no chance of getting caught with them hidden on my wagon after everything else had been taken off it if I hid them in the ground before I rode into Germany.

The Dutch guy left Germany before I did. He caught a ride home on another wagon that left before mine. When I got back to the foxhole, to retrieve the tools I had placed there, they were gone!

I think he, the Dutch man, took them.

❧

There were shortages of everything as time passed because there was no manufacturing going on. But farmers could trade for almost any-thing. People really needed food and would trade almost anything they had for it. I even traded food for bicycle tires, which were very hard to get. No one needed money.

We did not send food to the big cities from where we lived. But people from the cities would walk miles and miles to get food. If they had known us before the war, they would come even as far away as we lived from the big cities. They would get enough food to live for a while and then take what they could back with them to their families.

There were also fuel shortages. Some people cut wood out of their own houses to build fires to stay warm. That's all they had. There was no other fuel around. There were no woods near the big cities, so there was not even firewood.

We were not totally dependent on electricity at our farm. We still had kerosene lanterns, which we used quite a bit. Only one or two rooms in our house were heated by a wood-burning cook stove or a coal-burning stove. The other rooms in the house were not heated at all. We had plenty of wood because we were in the country, but we could not always get coal. Sometimes, during dogfights between German and Allied aircraft, planes would be forced to drop their extra fuel. The fuel was in a type of rubberized container, and if you happened to get to it first, it was good to have. But you had to be quick, because other civilians and even the German army were after the same thing. Everyone was always watching for anything that could be used.

When an army is in retreat, they are an unhappy bunch. They don't have supplies. When the Germans first came in, they had plenty of supplies. Everyone got fed well. There was no shortage of anything. But when they had to start falling back, as the Allies got closer, they began to break up. All of a sudden they were on their own finding food, on their own hauling out whatever they wanted to haul out. They began to lose their organization. Soon we had a whole lot of unhappy men on our hands. Then things began to happen that should never happen. As times got worse, the Germans stole more and more from the Dutch. This went on for months. Sometimes they were stealing just to live.

Because there were occasionally German soldiers living on our farm, we were somewhat protected from them stealing from us. Whenever Germans were officially living at our house, the farm was actually protected from other soldiers stealing our livestock or anything else. But no Germans lived on the farm after the Normandy invasion, and when there were no German soldiers officially staying on the farm, they stole our cows for meat and our horses for transportation. They stole whatever they could get.

Basically, we knew not to challenge the Germans. There wasn't so much to be afraid of, as long as you didn't confront them.

But once I did challenge a German soldier. He came in with some others to steal one of the few horses we had left. I decided that I wasn't going to give him the horse. We exchanged words, and finally the soldier shot into the ground right at my feet. He more or less told me that I could either give him the horse freely, or he would shoot me and then take the horse anyway.

I gave him the horse.

I was older then, and challenging the soldier wasn't a smart thing to do. They were going to get the horse no matter what I did or said. I could have been killed over a horse.

A very terrible thing happened in the last few months of the war. A German general lived in Didam, though I'm not sure how well-known that was. One night in March 1945, our freedom fighters ambushed the vehicle he was riding in. They had no idea who was in the car – they just needed the vehicle. When they found out who was inside, they started fighting. All of the Germans were killed except for the big boss. He was seriously wounded but not killed.

The next day, German authorities randomly rounded up 263 innocent Dutch people, mainly men who had nothing to do with the war, and killed them in retaliation. Over 100 of them were transported to where the ambush took place and were shot down at that spot, then their bodies were buried in a mass grave.

This all happened about 20 miles from our home, but the big man lived in our town.

~

The last several months of the war got harder and harder for everyone. Houses were blacked out to keep them from being a target. Rainy, dark nights were always welcome. The Allies would fly over the farms and cities and towns at night, and if they saw anything that looked suspicious, they would bomb it. Later on, the Allies started flying over during the day, when the Germans no longer had as many planes to fight back with. If the Allies saw a train passing, they wouldn't really question who was on it, they would just shoot it up if for some reason it looked suspicious to them. It all depended on what the pilot thought was a target. A train might be carrying German supplies. The Allies would shoot at German military transports. Even a group of horse-drawn wagons driven by farmers would be looked at. Maybe it was a small unit of Germans moving in disguise, or hiding in the wagon, or moving their supplies.

Once, my sister Dolly was traveling on a train that was hit by the Allies. Whenever this happened, the train would stop, of course, and everyone would get out as fast as they could, move away from the train, and lay flat in the grass, because the plane would probably pass back over and might shoot again. Dolly was not hurt, but she was very, very scared.

We did not feel this kind of activity was an injustice. I knew of several farmers who were killed by the Allies this way. The farmers were just traveling to one place or another on their wagons and were shot from the air. For some reason they looked suspicious. But we did not resent it. To have the Allies engaged in the fight against Germany was our only hope for freedom.

There still wasn't much news — we always knew very little of what was going on. We were all just waiting to be free. And the Allies up in the air? At this point, they were all friends. Even if they shot up trains with Dutch people in them, we didn't bother much about that or blame them. We just wanted the war to end, and the only way it was going to end was to stop the Germans. They had to be defeated.

Toward the very end of the Occupation, the Allies started flying into Germany, bombing their cities. We would see them passing over because our farm was in their flight pattern. We knew what they were going to do.

The Germans on the ground had these huge searchlights. At night, if they got an Allied plane targeted with one of their lights, they would shoot it down. One Allied plane was shot down a few farms over from us. We all heard it go down. It went nose-down, deep into the dirt. Only a little bit was left sticking up out of the dirt. It was obvious there were no survivors.

At other times there were Allied survivors. When a plane went down, everyone in maybe a two-mile radius would know about it. Sometimes we would be watching the planes fight it out up there in the air before one of them went down. If a farmer was going to help an Allied survivor, which most of us would have done, he had to get there first, because the Germans would also be looking for any survivors, to take as prisoners. It was a race to see who got there first. The Germans would get any of their own survivors if their planes were shot down.

Sometimes the Allies parachuted out after their planes were hit, but that meant it took longer for them to get to the ground, and they might be spotted by the Germans on their way down. If they made it safely to the ground, they would hide wherever they could until they found someone to help them. They had to be pretty clever to get away from the Germans. If they could hide in a ditch or behind a small stand of trees, even for a day or two, they would usually be OK. If they could just stay alive while the Germans were looking for them, they had a good chance of making it.

Once an Allied soldier found a Dutch person, or a Dutch person found him, he would need to get a set of farmer clothes like the Dutch wore. Maybe the Allies should have worn farmer clothes while they were flying, under their uniforms! The soldier might need other help as well, especially if he had been wounded during the dogfight or hurt in the crash.

Just about any Dutch person the Allies eventually located would help them. And if the Dutch didn't want to help, maybe because they were afraid, they would tell the soldiers where to go for help. People like us had big farms. It was pretty easy to hide Allies on farms because there were lots of barns and buildings scattered around the property.

My family never actually discussed what we would do if an Allied plane was shot down near us. We never talked about if we would help or not. We just knew we would. It would have been automatic. But it never happened on our farm.

❧

*T*he Invasion of Normandy, which began on June 6, 1944, was a long time coming. But when it finally began, I think that same night we knew it from listening to the radio in the hayloft. It was extremely exciting to know that something was happening on the Allied front. We even told neighbors what we knew about D-Day taking place.

Then the Allies got delayed.

We were somewhat depressed over how long it took between the Invasion of Normandy and our final liberation.

All the next winter, as the Allies got closer to Holland, Dutch farmers and their families who had been pushed off their farms by the fighting came to live with us. By the beginning of 1945, there were 40 to 50 extra people living with us on the farm. It was a big house, but people were living and sleeping everywhere. Naturally, all of the rooms in the house were taken. Many people slept in the barn, some in a basement room that was used as a cellar for keeping vegetables. There was even a Catholic priest in the group who organized school for all the children. (Schools had been shut down as the situation worsened.)

My cousin Harry's family was part of the group that came to us for several months. Many of the other families in the group knew Uncle Theo. My uncle knew a lot of farmers in his area, and when they had to evacuate, he sent them to us. We didn't know most of them at first. We were the last farm around they could go to. If we wouldn't take them in, they would have to go much farther away from their homes.

We fed everyone one meal a day, in the barn. It was quite a sight – and quite an undertaking for my mother to oversee. We ate at long tables set up with wood and sawhorses.

Some people brought cows, hay, and food with them. Some brought nothing. Harry and I would go back and forth to the farms the people had left to get whatever food was available to help feed everyone living at our house. The Germans were pretty busy and were not watching livestock that had been left behind too closely. So Harry and I would get food and bring back livestock. Uncle Theo had the most food and most livestock of anyone staying with us.

I remember one day when I was driving the wagon to one of the farms to get food, and the Allies and the Germans started shooting at each other over the Rhine. It was late in the day, around 4:30 or 5 p.m., about the time they often did this. The road I was driving on had suddenly taken me much too close to the river. There was shooting everywhere. I was really very afraid.

❦

*I*n late 1944, the only other good thing besides the lake that came from the war happened: I met Wilma Zents, who would later become my wife. I was 18 years old when we met. She was a year younger. We met by chance at a clandestine dance that was held in a farmer's barn, in a town some distance from our farm. These dances took place from time to time, but we always had to be careful. I remember that all the windows of the barn were blacked out.

I only got to go to the party because a friend of mine got me an invitation. It was an invitation-only party, and I wasn't invited. I knew the family who was hosting the party because I had dated their daughter a little bit. But it was not a group I knew well.

Meeting Wilma was, for me, as they say, "Love at first sight."

We saw each other a few times after that, but not much. It was a very long bike ride between her house and mine, almost 20 miles.

Some time later, I was part of a group of farmers and wagons, about 10 in all, who helped move the Baron out of his castle. He was the man who had first arranged the lease on our farm. His new destination was the town where Wilma and her family lived.

When we got there, we found out that the castle the Baron was supposed to move into had been taken over by the Germans. We couldn't empty our wagonloads right away, but had to spend the night in the homes of nearby farmers. As luck would have it, the house where I was directed to go was Wilma's house!

I had a good part of the Baron's wine cellar on my wagon. A small part of it could not have been better spent. It was his wine we served that evening, digging in as part of our celebration. We had a great evening, and from that time on we stayed in touch and became more serious in our relationship.

∾

*M*y *father never had a gun. I had one briefly. I took it away from a German soldier I found sleeping by himself in our barn one morning. He had his rifle beside him as he slept, and I leaned over and took it from him. He woke up and yelled when he saw me standing there with his rifle. Then he started to talk.*

He was just as scared of me as I was of him.

This was really at the tail end of the war. I don't know if any of the Allies were over the river yet, but they were certainly close.

The soldier asked me if I would just let him go home, to Germany. It was the one time during the war I seriously debated what I should do. It was the first time I had a gun in my hand and a German soldier in front of me.

I wasn't in a hurry. I had time to think because I was the boss in the situation. I was the one in control. I didn't have to just react quickly out of fear for my own life.

I seriously thought about shooting him.

I could by then pretty much understand what he was saying to me in German.

"I can't leave without the gun," he told me.

"Should I let you leave?" I asked.

This soldier, he was really down and out. He was totally lost, didn't have any idea where his unit was. He just wanted to try to make it back to Germany, and he was so close.

After we talked for a few minutes, I gave him back his gun.

I'm glad I didn't do what I might have done. I just couldn't shoot him. And I'm glad of it. That would have bothered me a lot more than remembering that I let him go.

He was young, probably a little older than I was, but not much. He had been sleeping in the hay. There was hay in his hair and all over his clothes. I'm sure he was a little hungry.

He was done with the war. If the Germans had found him, they would have probably sent him back to the front with another unit. If they suspected he was trying to go AWOL, he could have been shot. There was no way to know. He just wanted to go home, to get out.

In the army, it's always bad if you lose your weapon. You can get in a whole lot of trouble for losing your weapon. There were many soldiers trying to get home to Germany by this time. Anything could have happened to him if he had been caught without his gun.

Regardless of what I decided to do, the soldier was not going to take the gun from me by force. That wouldn't have happened. I was in control of the situation. That much was clear.

I had never even shot a gun, didn't know how to use one. I would have probably used it against the soldier in a different way.

I'm glad it turned out the way it did.

ॐ

*L*ife started to change once the Allies began invading the country, drawing closer to us. There was change all around. We were so close to Germany, and the Allies began pounding the Germans back, pounding them back.

The front line became very clear. It was where we lived. All of the farms between the Rhine River and our house were now evacuated. This is when my father was told by the Germans that we, too, would have to fall back with the German troops. We were now in no man's land. We, and the group of people living in our house, were the only Dutch people around who had not already left.

A day or two before my father was told we must evacuate, I rode my bike to a small, neighboring town near the Rhine that had just been liberated. It was Easter Day, April 1, 1945. When the Canadian Army rolled into town, there was no end to the excitement for the few Dutch who had gathered there to welcome the Allies. I walked through the line to greet the soldiers and spent the afternoon visiting with them. I went home with my pockets full of chocolate and cigarettes and my head full of stories about the Canadians and the coming liberation. I was sure it would happen to us, too, this time.

The next morning, my oldest sister, Willemien, and I walked to Didam to attend Easter Monday church, since we had not gone the day before. We crossed the front line, and found ourselves back in German territory. After church, we went to visit some friends so I could fill them in on what was happening. I wanted to tell them about meeting the Canadians. I guess I wanted to brag a little about what I had seen and heard.

It was when Willemien and I started to walk home that we learned something about an active front line. Because the Allies were now somewhere behind our farm and the Germans were in Didam, it was not so easy to get through. We weren't too worried, though. We decided to take a less-traveled side road that would still get us home. We were traveling with a group of six to 10 people. We didn't know the others. We were all just trying to find a way out of Didam.

Suddenly, as we crossed an open field on the outskirts of town, we were fired at. There was a house on the edge of the field – the mayor's house – and when we looked we could see that it was full of German soldiers. They were up high, standing in the windows on the second floor of the house, where they could shoot down on us. When we saw the Germans up there, we realized how dangerous it was for us, and we all started running.

There was a railroad line running down the middle of the field. The tracks were built up on a high embankment. Before we could reach the tracks, the Germans were firing at us. I yelled to my sister that we had to cross the tracks and get over to the other side, where we could crouch down away from the shots. But there was no safe place to cross.

The only way to get to the other side was to go up and over, in full view of the soldiers. I started crossing, still yelling for Willemien to follow. She was right there with me. We crossed over together. The others who were running with us didn't cross the tracks. They just kept running along the side, in front of the soldiers.

Right before Willemien and I went over, a young woman who was running in between us was shot. We knew she had been hit before we crossed over. There was nothing we could do but keep running.

The shot killed her, but we didn't know that at first. We only knew that she fell between us.

Once we got to the other side of the tracks, we laid there for a long time. We tried not to move. You can imagine how much we were shaking. We had our noses in the ground, pressed down as close as we could get. Finally, when everything had quieted down, we crept along the backside of the tracks until we felt safe enough to make a run across the field. And then we ran for all we were worth.

You know, you hate to get killed the day before freedom comes. To go through all of a war, and then, on the day before freedom, to get killed – when you get to the end of a war, you just want to live.

I think Willemien and I ran a little faster than the others. I don't know. Everything was going well, and then, just before we got to the tracks, the Germans started to shoot. It all happened so suddenly, and we had to think of some way to get out of there. We could see the shots hitting the dirt all around us.

Willemien had blood on her clothes when we got home. Other than the time I almost drowned as a boy, it was the scariest day of my life. Even being sent to Korea as a soldier myself when I was older was not as scary as trying to get away from the German bullets.

The next day, April 3, was when my father was told to move. But we didn't do it. The Allies came through the farm before we had a chance to go to them. We heard the noises in the next town over as the soldiers began liberating it. No one was still living there. We heard tanks and shots and all these strange noises coming from there. By the time the Allies got to us, at 3 or 4 o'clock in the afternoon, we, and all the people who were still *living with us on the farm, were in our yard waiting for them. (I think some people had left our house because the fighting was getting so close.) We gave the soldiers a great welcome.*

The first group of Allies swept through the farm and eventually did a lot of fighting in Didam and beyond. The second group came with supplies and such. We did a lot of visiting with them. Both groups were Canadians, and we sure were cheering them on.

I think it was good for them to see how happy we – the Dutch – were to be liberated.

When Didam was liberated, it was not considered temporary. We all knew it was the beginning of the end. There was no real German army left in our area. What was left was disorganized and in retreat.

We knew this freedom was the real thing.

೧

*E*very town in Holland had its own freedom parties and celebrations after it was liberated, and after the war was finally over. The festivities went on for months. There were parades and floats and dances in the evenings. This was a most joyous time – like nothing ever before. We went from town to town to join in the fun. Our hometown, Didam, had a parade as well. Our family did a lot of work on a float honoring Piet Bodde, our employee, who had died in the invasion. It turned out beautiful.

The celebrations were perfect for a young man in need of lots of fun days. I took in a good share of the evening celebrations. I attended them with either Wilma Zents, who was now my girlfriend, or Willemien, my sister, and the rest of my family.

Many of the Dutch farmers I knew were unhappy with the agreement that came out of the Yalta Conference that was made by the Allies, who were understandably sick of the war. The American President, Franklin Roosevelt, was very ill and died before the war was officially over. The farmers came back from a meeting in town where they heard the decisions that came out of the Conference. They were shaking their heads and talking politics. They disagreed with the division of Germany, and with the eastern block that went to Russia. They felt that it was a setback and a future setup for another conflict. But, regardless, Holland was no longer an occupied country.

For us, the war was over.

❧

E ach of Holland's numerous small towns, as well as its big cities, endured its own unique form of German occupation for five years. The several months between the Allied Invasion of Normandy (D-Day, June 6, 1944) and Holland's liberation were long, hard, and excruciatingly slow for those who waited.

Most of the country's eastern towns were liberated by the Allies over a several-day period in early spring 1945. However, the Allies stopped short of entering the crowded western cities, for fear of massive civilian casualties. Though the Germans eventually allowed shipments of food to enter to help feed thousands of starving Dutch citizens, the cities were not freed until about a month after Pete and his family and their friends began attending victory celebrations in Didam and the surrounding area.

Until the singular moment of liberation of each town, farm, and city square, all of Holland was waiting – desperately, fervently waiting – for the Allies to come to them. Despite the casualties, despite the fact that the entire country was not yet free, as the Allies secured the outlying regions of the country, the Dutch began celebrating their achievement: They had withstood German occupation for five years, and now they were free. And the next town over, and the one after that, was free as well. They celebrated for days, weeks, months, until the whole country was caught up in a huge commemoration of what it had endured, what it had been freed from, and what it could finally look forward to.

Pete turned 19 years old on April 4, 1945 – the day after the

Veldman farm was liberated. No one thought of it at the time; he has no memory of his birthday ever being mentioned that year.

The many individuals and families who had lived for months in the Veldmans' house and barn left as soon as they could for their own homes. They did not wait until the country was officially free – there was no holding them back. But about 10 years later, several members of the group commissioned a stone thanking Bernard and Wilhelmina for their sacrificial role in keeping so many people housed and fed during the last, long months of the war. The stone was engraved with the names of all the evacuees, and installed in the hallway near the front door of the Veldmans' farmhouse, a blessing, of sorts, to anyone who entered.

Wilma Zents, who would later become Pete's wife, remembers going to liberation parties and dances with Pete – and sometimes with his family and siblings – regularly after the war ended, though it remained a very long bike ride from his farm to hers.

"I was 17 when we met at the secret party," Wilma says. "I remember that I had never seen Pete before, and I thought he was very good-looking. He was dressed nicely and his hair was wavy. But I was nervous that maybe he didn't like me the first night we met, until he asked to take me home, to a friend's house since my family lived 35 miles away from where the party was taking place, a very long way by bike."

Now that the war was over, Pete and his siblings and Wilma wanted, more than anything else, to live. They wanted to meet and dance and celebrate with friends and acquaintances. They wanted to laugh, look good, and dress as fashionably as possible. They wanted to hear airplanes flying overhead without flinching, uncover the windows, and turn on the lights.

They wanted to find adventure in living and in pursuing their own dreams, not in dodging death.

෪

III

America

Immigration

World War II was over, the long years of occupation ended. Queen Wilhelmina returned from exile and began touring the country, motivating her subjects to undertake what would inevitably be a long post-war recovery. Occasionally, the venerable lady traveled by bicycle. The Queen's years in London had spurred new ideas for her about how Dutch government and society should be run, beginning with a Cabinet she hoped would be comprised of individuals who had been active in the Resistance. However, within a few short years of her homecoming, politics in Holland returned to business as usual, and in 1948, after more than 50 years of rule, the disappointed monarch abdicated the throne in favor of her daughter, Princess Juliana.

Meanwhile, in the months following Holland's official liberation on May 5, 1945, the countless jubilant parties gradually ended. Ecstasy gave way to the hard work of reality. Schools and businesses gradually reopened, the rebuilding of cities and industries began, families worked at reuniting, and farmers returned to the land. Everywhere one looked, there was work to be done. Material goods and cash were in short supply. Food remained scarce, despite the relief efforts of other countries.

Like thousands of his countrymen, Pete could be found back

on the farm, working diligently alongside his father for the first time in years.

"I finally became serious about the farm," he says. "There was lots of work to be done. The farm showed a lot of neglect from the wear and tear of the war, and a large number of our cows, horses, hogs, and other livestock had been taken away."

Pete had been too young for much earnest work before the war, and too demoralized during the Occupation to invest personally in the farm's success or failure. For five years, the farm had not really mattered as long as the Veldmans had enough to eat. The family did enough to get by and whatever work the Germans demanded of them, such as digging some of the thousands of foxholes that scarred the land everywhere one looked. They let go of the rest.

"The farm was not taken care of during the war," Pete explains. "We mostly sat around and talked about the war. I think even my father lost interest."

Now, 19-year-old Pete was working hard physically every day. He was also thinking hard about new ways to do the work, manage employees, and increase productivity. Most importantly, he was mulling over what the future might hold for a young man who was both determined and ambitious. The war, or more specifically, Pete's contacts with the young soldiers of the Allied forces, had opened up a world of possibilities for him.

"The Allies always had a little cash in their pockets, and they were willing to spend it on cigarettes and chocolate, which they passed out to us during liberation. To have money to spend was new to me, and very exciting," he recalls.

For the first time in his life, Pete seriously began to envision life outside the Netherlands. All the while, he toiled beside his father, and for two years he took classes at a special agriculture school. Though he did not know it then, the certification he received for completing the program would be an invaluable admissions ticket when the opportunity to immigrate to the United States presented itself.

Looking back, Pete says, "Going to the agricultural school was one of my better ideas. It was a very practical sort of education about how to run a farm and manage land. It was important for helping Dutch farmers get back on their feet after the war.

"Meanwhile, I talked my father into hiring new people to work on the farm. I told him we needed new people – and not just a few – because anyone we kept on would train the new people we hired. We had people on the farm who had been there for 10 or 12 years. But you just couldn't get them to work after the war like you could before, and they certainly weren't going to work harder because of me. I was only 19 years old.

"It took a lot of convincing, but in the end we did it," he continues. "We had a changing of the old guard on the first day of May, the traditional day for employees to leave a place of employment because they were asked to or because they wanted to. My father kept just one farmhand. Everyone else we hired was new. It was not my idea to keep even one. But it worked.

"We got one of the first of five tractors to come into Holland after the war. It came from America. We had a lot to learn about this new piece of equipment. We had to learn the simplest of lessons, like you couldn't mix any water with the gasoline! But we learned fast."

❧

As he worked to assimilate new methodologies with an ancient livelihood, Pete began hearing of farmers who were leaving for other countries where they hoped it was still possible to tend the land and become financially secure. He was offered free passage to Brazil in exchange for caring for several horses and other livestock that a Dutch group who had started a commune there were having shipped across the seas. He knew of a few farmers who had emigrated the short distance to France; more who had settled in Canada, where the Dutch were given preferred immigrant status; and a very few who had made it into the United States, which was simply called "America" because it was easier to say. Getting into America was the hardest of all, for most immigrants were required to have a sponsor who would guarantee housing and employment.

"Even though my dad had a nice farm, he wasn't really very good at farming. It was well-known that we had a fun place, but that we weren't very good at farming itself. And there were fewer and fewer farming opportunities in Holland. It was clear I was never going to be the kind of farmer I wanted to be if I stayed. I was never going to make it in the Netherlands as a farmer, and I began to think seriously about immigrating," Pete says.

"I had enough information to know France did not look good to me, and my mother talked me out of going to Brazil because she thought I was too young and it was too far away and I would be too much on my own, which turned out to be good luck for me.

"I did not know that much about America," he continues. "What I knew was from a few movies. That is probably why it looked so good to me. The movies showed acres and acres of wheat fields being combined with 10 to 12 machines in a row, large dairy farms in California, cotton fields in the South, and grain and beef farming in the Midwest. It was a young farmer's dream.

"I still wanted to be a farmer, and I thought I could be a farmer in America. It was not really a well-thought-out plan. It was just a dream. But there was something about America!

"It just seemed, from where I was, that there was so much more opportunity in America. Also, my experience with the Allies had been good. The American soldiers always had money. And they spent it. It looked to me like all Americans were rich.

"I had basically always worked for my dad, and when you work for your dad, you don't get paid. So I never had any cash."

Some time after Wilhelmina talked her oldest son out of going to Brazil, a friend of Pete's, Benny Seesing, who later married one of Pete's sisters, stopped by the farm to tell Pete he had just received an invitation to immigrate to the United States from distant relatives living in Missouri. Benny told Pete that while he personally had no intention of pursuing the opportunity, he would be glad to facilitate contact between Pete and the Seesings if Pete were interested.

Pete did not think twice, but jumped at the rare, fleeting chance. Ten months of slow-moving correspondence later – and after completing loads of U.S. government paperwork – Pete made reservations to cross the Atlantic Ocean on an inexpensive freighter, the *Leerdam*. He bid a tearful farewell in Rotterdam in April 1949 to his parents, siblings, and Wilma Zents, who was by now his fiancée.

Pete hoped, even then, that if his situation in America worked out, a few of his brothers might join him in the distant future, but no one could say for sure when the family would see each other again. The trip to see Pete off was an exciting experience for everyone, until the ship began to pull away from the dock and the family started to cry.

Watching their oldest brother grow smaller and smaller in the distance, the younger siblings thought Pete was gone forever. Their grieving and fear was alleviated only by the thrill of traveling all the way to Rotterdam and back in a flatbed truck (sitting on potato crates in the back), and being treated to ice cream on the way home. The older siblings knew there were no guarantees: They really might never see Pete again. His sister Fran remembers waving good-bye to Pete at the dock – and crying for the rest of the day.

"This was big. We didn't really think we would see him again. After he left, it was a kind of letdown. I don't even remember going home," she says.

For Wilma, left standing with the Veldman family, Pete's leaving created deep emotional conflict.

"I wasn't too excited with the thought of going to America at the time," she says. "But the problem was, I was in love with Pete.

"I'm not as adventurous as Pete was – and still is – and I was very concerned about the future in a different country," she continues.

"You only traveled to America by boat at that time, and I was not at all sure that if I went to America with Pete I would ever come back to see my family.

"But I wanted to do it, and I tried to be positive about it. It would have helped if my parents had been cooperative, but they were not. They liked Pete, but they did not like his plans. They did not see the need for him to leave Holland. They didn't see that at all. And that did not help me. If they had been more for it – or even not so against it – it would have been a lot easier for me.

"Pete and I decided before he left that we would wait for each other. We thought he would be back to get me in a year or two. After he left, my parents did not really talk to me about Pete very much. It was as if they were hoping he would come back to Holland to stay. Meanwhile, it was better if he were just not discussed."

Pete, on the other hand, was ever the optimist, even as he left Wilma. He was convinced it would all work out – with her, with navigating the uncharted waters of life as an immigrant, with finding profitable work. And unlike Wilma, he had his parents' support to buoy him along.

Bernard had, for a long time, harbored his own personal dream of immigrating to North America; his entrepreneurial heart applauded Pete's spirit and courage. That one of Bernard's brothers had lived in Canada for a while only sparked his interest in what his son was undertaking, even though the brother had eventually returned to Holland because he found Canada to be too cold. In some ways, Pete was fulfilling his father's dream as well as his own.

"When I talked about leaving, my father could understand it real well. He thought it was a good idea, which meant a lot to me." Pete says. "In fact, one of the very last things he said to me before I boarded the ship was: Let me know if you see anything over there for me and our family.

"Mama was a little more apprehensive, but she could see it coming. And she knew and was very concerned about the fact that there would be no future for all of us if we stayed on the farm. She understood that real well."

Wilhelmina was also relieved that Pete was not going to Brazil or even Indonesia. She knew of some young Dutch men who had returned from those parts of the world with different values than what they had grown up with. It had become clear to her that Pete was going to go somewhere. Living with a family of Dutch heritage in Missouri seemed about as much as a mother could hope for. Meanwhile, she had heard about the terribly cold North American winters, and before Pete left she had scurried about, securing for him as many winter clothes as she could find. Helping him pack took her mind off his leaving.

Pete was 23 years old when he resolutely left everyone he knew and loved. Though he was on a ship full of immigrants, mainly Dutch, he uncharacteristically made no lasting friends on the ocean crossing. Everyone was too intent on getting to America, too wrapped up in their own fears and dreams to interact much with each other.

"It was my first step into the unknown," he says. "Suddenly, I was all alone, for the first time in my life." After a pause, he adds, "It was hard to leave, but it's true that some part of me had always wanted to leave."

Pete had no regrets, no second thoughts as the *Leerdam* left the dock. In many ways, he knew he had been preparing to leave his homeland his whole life. He left with everything he needed – a strong back, youth, faith, ambition, loyalty, and deeply instilled moral values. Everything, that is, except much money. He sailed from Rotterdam with a couple of suitcases and $80 in his pocket, the most he was allowed to take out of his war-torn country. His suitcases contained the winter clothes his mother had found for him; wooden shoes, which he did not wear until several years later when he and Wilma tried running their own farm; and his one heirloom, a watch that had belonged to his grandfather, which was lost at some point in his travels. (He returned the money to his parents as soon as he made a few American dollars, knowing how much they needed the cash. He also returned most of the winter clothes, shipping them back home where they could be doled out to family members. "I wanted to start from zero," is how he puts it.)

Pete was deeply aware that this first step wasn't just *his* first step. He was determined to return and marry Wilma, and bring her back with him. And after he had made it in America, he would do whatever he could to help any family members interested in following in his footsteps.

It was, however, up to him to lead the way.

∾

Crossing the Atlantic on a freighter filled with about 100 immigrants and the ship's crew was not much fun for Pete or anyone else on board. Many passengers were seasick for the entire 14 days it took the ship to pass from shore to shore. When stormy weather was encountered for a few days, those who were already sick got worse, while others who had thus far escaped such misery found themselves also in poor condition.

The air on deck was too cold for passengers to remain topside for long. There were no recreation areas on the vessel, no places to mingle; the only place passengers could pass the time was in their cramped, shared rooms. There was little or nothing to read. Playing cards was a possibility, if you could find someone well enough and willing to join in.

"We were mostly just waiting to get to the other end, to New York," Pete says. "We did stop in Antwerp, Belgium, soon after we left Rotterdam, where I ate my first banana since 1940. It was a real treat for me, and I didn't have to share it with my brothers and sisters! Also, the food on the ship was pretty good. And it was my good fortune not to get seasick.

"Finally, early in the morning 14 days after we left, there she was – the Statue of Liberty. She looked like an invitation to come to America. It was a beautiful sight, couldn't have been nicer. To begin with, we'd been all those days on the water. And all of a sudden there was land, and then there was the statue. There were shouts from all the passengers – we were all standing on the deck – when she came into sight.

"It was a good time of the year, springtime, and everything just looked so pretty. And there was all the activity of the harbor, which I had never seen before. New York looked great. It was truly 'America, the beautiful.'"

❧

Pete entered the United States on April 6, 1949. He did not pass through Ellis Island but disembarked in Hoboken, New Jersey. One of the biggest challenges he would face – learning to speak and read English – slapped him squarely in the face the minute he got off the ship. He was immediately aware of his inability to communicate, but he didn't flinch, and it would not have occurred to him to back down. The Dutch schoolboy thrilling to a scuffle in the schoolyard had found a big enough fight to keep him on his toes for a long time.

"My papers were all ready and I was accepted into the country easily enough," he recalls. "But I had not prepared myself for the challenges in communicating. And though I didn't go all the way to America to just get nowhere, I should have learned to speak English before I went!

"I had to spell my name to one of the immigration officials, and that was quite a big deal because I had never spelled a word before. In the Dutch language, we don't spell words. Instead, we write it as we listen to it. My complete name is Henricus Petrus Theodorus Veldman. I kept being asked if Veldman was with a 't' or a 'd.' When

I wrote down my name for the official, he thought we should shorten it to Henry. He just shook his head when I tried to tell him it was Piet. Finally, he understood that I went by my second name and not my first.

"From that point on, I was Peter Veldman."

～

Newly named, which he did not object to, Pete was fascinated by all the sights, sounds, food, people, and size of the buildings as he made his way to the train station in New York City. He was unprepared for how absolutely new and different everything was to him. He was in awe. One thing, however, puzzled him: He could not understand how people seemed to know he was new to the country just by looking at him, without hearing him utter a word, but he was sure they knew he was not one of them.

Somehow, Pete found the train station, and a good Samaritan took him inside to a Travelers Aid Society booth. Half an hour of attempted conversation passed before the person working inside the booth made a desperate phone call to someone outside the station who spoke Dutch. The unknown speaker translated for Pete and the aid worker until Pete understood how to go about getting a train from New York to St. Louis, Missouri.

"I was instructed to find another Travelers Aid station when I got to St. Louis, which I made sure to do!" he remembers with a laugh. "Meanwhile, my train trip across the country could not have been better. I had never slept on a train, had never had dinner on a train or seen an American menu, and I couldn't read English. A stranger took me along and bought me my first meal. I saw large, beautiful farms outside the windows, a dream after coming from a 100-acre farm, which was the largest in my hometown but small in comparison.

"Once I got to St. Louis, I was directed to travel by bus to

Cape Girardeau, Missouri," he continues. "When I got there, the bus driver called my sponsor's daughter-in-law, who soon appeared with her young son to pick me up. It was just unbelievable how friendly everyone was to me. I felt absolutely at ease with her, though I couldn't understand what she was saying! Our speaking conversation didn't go too well.

"Her husband, John Seesing, managed the commercial side of the Cape Girardeau airport. The following Sunday afternoon he took me up in a little two-seater airplane. It was my first time in the air and was a great way to see the area. John could understand a very little bit of what I said.

"Later in the day on the afternoon of my arrival, John and his wife took me to his parents' home in a tiny little town, Leopold, in the Ozark Mountains, where my sponsor and his wife lived. Though English was their primary language, Mr. Seesing spoke Dutch and his wife spoke German, so we had an easier time communicating. They were the nicest people you could ever meet. He told me the first order of the day was to change out of the clothes I was wearing and into some American pants. And then everyone was happy.

"I had on what would have passed for my Sunday best in Holland, which was knickerbockers," Pete says with a laugh. "No one in America wore pants like that – they were short and came to my knees. Now I knew why everyone could tell with just a look that I wasn't American!"

❧

Leopold, Missouri, where the elder Seesings lived, surprised Pete. With a population of about 1000, he could not believe how small the town was – one school, one church, a couple of modest stores, a diminutive post office, and the Seesings' tavern, above which they lived. It was not at all like the American towns Pete had heard about or seen in the movies. The surrounding farms were not sizable and were connected only by gravel roads. There was no blacktop. Almost everyone around was Catholic.

"The Ozarks were not that different from being in a small town in Holland," Pete explains. "A lot of immigrants had settled there. My sponsor hardly ever left Leopold. His parents had immigrated from Holland, and he was looking for news of the war. What had happened in certain parts of Holland interested him."

Like most of their neighbors, the Seesings lived modestly, but what they had they freely shared with Pete the short time he lived and slept in their upstairs apartment, which he describes as "three rooms under a tin roof." The small space was not much to speak of, but because of the Seesings' generosity, it was an adequate starting place for Pete.

Though it was threshing time when Pete arrived in Leopold, he quickly learned that most of the farms around were too small to hire extra labor. He found a little work here and there, for 10 to 15 cents an hour, but it was not enough to keep him busy. Traveling from neighbor to neighbor with a small group of farmers who helped each other out during the harvest, he remembers being impressed with the good lunches the wives prepared for all the workers. At most, he worked only about five hours a day, from after the sun had burned the moisture off the grain in the morning until quitting time, around 3 p.m., which allowed the farmers plenty of time for taking care of their chores and livestock. Since Mr. Seesing owned neither land nor livestock, Pete spent the rest of his day piecing together conversations with his hosts about America, Holland, and World War II; eating; and trying to stay cool.

"It was hotter than blazes in the Seesings' apartment," Pete says. "There was no air-conditioning, of course, just a fan in the window. I was used to working, but I wasn't used to that kind of heat and humidity.

"On my first Saturday morning there, I traveled with Mr. Seesing to Marble Hill, where we stopped at the license bureau. He told them I needed a driver's license. From there the conversation went to World War II and Europe, and an hour later I walked out with a driver's license."

At this point in his life, Pete had never driven a car. He certainly did not have the language, driving, or reading skills needed to pass a driving test. But thanks to Mr. Seesing, who perhaps did not fully understand how much simply riding in a car thrilled Pete, the newly arrived immigrant was issued a license without being tested.

After a few weeks, a nearby son-in-law of the Seesings was hospitalized, and Pete moved over to his and the Seesings' daughter's farm to help with the work. He was shocked to find their farm almost as poorly equipped – and no more modern – than his family's farm back in Holland. Once again, this was not like the movies. That the couple used mules instead of workhorses was new to Pete, and he liked learning how to work with and care for the sturdy animals.

☙❧

Five weeks later, Pete moved about 30 miles away from Leopold to Sikeston, Missouri, a larger town with bigger farms and a greater need for seasonal workers. There he lived with Elmer Pobst, a cousin of the Seesings who farmed the largest place Pete had ever worked on. The cousin had four sons who befriended Pete and who all eventually became farmers themselves. Here Pete began learning how to use modern farm machinery. And here he hoed the weeds out of cotton for several backbreaking days, unwittingly picking up some language that would have shocked his mother.

"The farms were larger in Sikeston and there was a variety of crops. The most labor-intensive was cotton. I worked in rows cleaning out weeds.

"I came back with language that I heard the other workers using," Pete laughs. "I didn't know better! I didn't know what those words meant. When I visited Mr. Seesing back in Leopold, which I sometimes did on the weekends, he would say to me, 'Pete, you can't use those words. You can't talk like that!'

"My coworkers in the cotton fields were very poor African Americans. They lived in such small houses, but they seemed happy, talking from early morning until late at night."

It was a real boon for Pete that the Pobsts' youngest son took an interest in the family's foreign field hand and began to teach him a few English words. (No one on the large spread spoke Dutch.) Pete was as eager to learn as the little boy was to show off his command of his native tongue.

"We would take long walks on Sunday mornings," Pete remembers, "and he would point out things to me and teach me the English word for it. He would have me repeat the word over and over until I got it right. He was such a cute little boy. And there was no one around who could speak Dutch, so I learned fast. I had to!"

❧

Early summer moved into mid-season, and although Pete was thriving on the adventure of his nomadic lifestyle, his experience so far had not matched his dreams. He had taken a huge personal risk in leaving Holland. And he could have stayed there, with his parents and siblings and the woman he loved. He did not have to leave. He perhaps would not have found the kind of opportunity he was looking for, but he would not have been living a hand-to-mouth existence as an itinerant farm laborer who did not know his host country's language.

From the very beginning, Pete planned to do a lot more than eek out a living. He had traveled to America with the aspirations and ambition of an immigrant – not the fears and desperation of a refugee. He had not crossed the ocean searching for peace, running for his life, or seeking political asylum. From the moment he stood on American soil, Pete had a goal in mind, and though he wasn't sure how he was going to reach it, he was determined to go after it: He was looking for success. At the very least, he would keep on trying, even if he might occasionally get the wind knocked out of him. He was not down for the count, not about to head home.

"So far, it was not really what I had expected," he recalls. "But I always thought it would get better. I had only ever gotten spending money from my dad, so I wasn't used to making money. I could live with that. I was never a spender because I didn't have much to spend. Now I had to make my own money. But even though I got started with very little, I never felt I was short. I never felt too poor. I always thought there was a better day coming.

"Not knowing the language kept me from getting better work. I'd get to the farms, and the farms were all different from what I had known. And I couldn't understand the people. Everything was new to me. The houses were different. The cities. The farmers. The food. I'd catch a ride to work on a farm somewhere and then walk back."

He thinks for a moment, then stresses, "Still, just to ride in a car was exciting for me. And it was America!"

From Missouri, Pete found work in Illinois, then Tennessee, then Michigan. Sunburned and tired as he rode in the back of a truck headed for southern Illinois to pick peaches, he knew he was not living the kind of life he had been brought up to live or to expect for himself. But he had faith it would not always be this way. His life would change for the better once he learned the language and gained his balance. He was sure of it. Meanwhile, he added a new word to his expanding vocabulary:

mi-grant *a worker who moves from place to place to follow seasonal work*

"Many of the migrants I worked with were prepared to be that poor for the rest of their lives. I never felt like that," Pete says. "Some needed the money much more than I did. That was their life. I didn't see it that way. I knew someday Wilma would be here, I'd have a car, we'd have a different kind of life together."

☙

I picked peaches during the day and loaded them on trucks at night," Pete says. "I'd sleep in the back of a truck, or sometimes in the back seat of a nice Buick, until the peaches needed to be loaded, then work loading a semi for a few hours before I went back to sleep. Four hundred bushels later and a few dollars in my pocket, I would be done for the night.

"Anna, Illinois, was a small town of about 6000 people during most of the year, but it swelled to many thousands more during the harvest with all the migrants and their families," he continues. "The problem was that no one could find a place to stay. It took me two days to find a place where I could sleep and take a shower. I slept in a horse stable the first two nights I was there, then someone connected me with a nice room in a house for about a week. The amazing thing was the whole thing – all the crowds and work – came to an end overnight in a town like that."

Once a crop was picked, the migrants left for the next harvest in the next location just about as quickly as they had appeared, Pete included. But once, the owner of one of the trucks Pete had been loading at night asked Pete to travel with him to Memphis, Tennessee, to supply several fruit stands he operated in the area. Pete said yes. He thought it was a great opportunity to see another part of the country; he especially remembers the lights of Memphis at night. "A real stroke of luck" landed him overnight in the truck owner's house. Pete was surprised that a man who was officially his boss would extend such hospitality. It was a different kind of lesson in American, egalitarian living. He was also impressed with the house.

When the fruit-stand owner informed him it was time to head north again – to pick more peaches, this time in Benton Harbor, Michigan – and showed Pete on a map where Benton Harbor was and the route they would take to get there from Memphis, Pete was astounded. The distance was unbelievable to him, akin to traveling from Amsterdam to Rome. No one in the Netherlands would have considered such a trip.

From one part of the country to another, Pete wrote weekly letters home, one to Wilma and one to his family. He told them about his work, his travels, and the people he met. But though they heard from him regularly, it was difficult for their return mail to catch up with him; he was working too hard and in too many locations to let the dust settle. Wherever Pete went, he worked as much as he could, doing whatever he could. Slowly, he began to save a very little bit of what he was making.

"I had real drive because there were no handouts. No one was providing me any money at all," he explains. "When I came to America is when I started to work really, really hard. Even when I worked for another person, I felt I should give him an honest day's work. And when I (later) worked for myself, I had to work even harder. Soon as you're on your own, your income depends on how hard you work. Or how smart you are. Since I wasn't too smart, I had to work hard.

"Even when I was working as a migrant, I started to save a little of what I was making. Even though I made just a little, I managed to save a little. Since having cash was new to me, I didn't feel a need to spend a lot. And I wanted to get Wilma here."

Pete was also watching and learning lessons about American employers and employees. Though he verbally understood very little, he could tell what attitudes and actions were effective, and which weren't, on both sides of the work force.

"I think all of us, my brothers and sisters and I, thought that at some point we would employ people," he continues. "We were used to employing people, not that we thought it was wrong to work for someone else. At this point, I was still stuck on farming as my future career. It stuck with me for quite a while. And I used to think about it, that one day when I had a place of my own and people worked for me, I wanted it to be a place with a heart.

"I had wanted to go someplace. More than anything, I had wanted to go to America. Next, I wanted to be successful. I could see people around me who were successful, and I wanted that. I wanted to be successful as an American farmer. After only a few months here, I would not have gone back to Holland. Absolutely not."

❧

As he moved from one orchard, one crop, one farm to another, Pete was occasionally offered full-time work. Once, he got tired of waiting for his pay after he and a crew of migrants had finished working at a particularly beautiful Illinois farm. His companions were resigned to spending the rest of the day biding their time as necessary – they needed the money as soon as they could get it, and they would use the free hour or two to catch their breath – but Pete decided he had waited long enough. He wanted to get on down the road, move ahead to the next spot and be ready to begin all over again as quickly as possible.

Pete politely approached the farm owner, a woman, and asked her to forward his pay to the Seesings in Missouri, since he did not know exactly where he would be working next or for how long. He had enough cash in his pocket to live on for a short time, and the Seesings would deposit the check in the bank for him. (He had set up an account in Leopold before he left Missouri, and mailed money to the Seesings to deposit for him whenever he had a few dollars to spare.)

The woman eyed Pete critically and asked, "How do you know I'll forward the check?"

"I don't," he answered. "But if you don't send it, you must need the money more than I do."

Pete's chutzpah and work ethic so impressed the woman that she offered him a full-time job on the spot. He explained that he wasn't interested in settling permanently just yet. But she sure did have a pretty farm, he told her. He would keep her offer in mind.

Though the Seesings reported that they received Pete's pay-check without delay, he never took up the farm owner on her offer.

დ

Work in Benton Harbor, Michigan, was much the same for Pete as anywhere else – picking the harvest by day, loading it by night. He realized by studying a map that the small farming community located on the shores of Lake Michigan was not very far from South Bend, Indiana. Pete decided to travel to South Bend one Sunday, his day off, to try to connect with a Dutch family who had immigrated there from his hometown. He would not have called the couple "friends" before he went to visit them. They were acquaintances. But they were from Didam, and for a young man who was longing for contact from home, it was worth every effort he could muster to find them.

After arriving in South Bend, which is located in far northern Indiana, Pete methodically began calling every Dutch name listed in the phone book. Three calls later he found himself talking to someone who knew the couple he was trying to locate but could not find a phone number for, Bernard and Johanna Peters. He called the Peterses and they rushed to pick him up at the Greyhound bus station.

"Mr. Peters thought what I was doing – traveling around picking fruit – was terrible," Pete says. "And he told me so. But I really didn't think it was all that bad. I moved along from one job to another pretty well. All along the way, people would say, 'Why don't you stay here?' But I thought it was good to move along. I was learning a lot along the way, working for the other person. I thought I was doing just fine."

Before Pete knew it, the Peterses were driving him around South Bend and the neighboring town, Mishawaka, pointing out potential places of employment. Finally, they introduced him to the Poor Sisters of St. Francis of Perpetual Adoration, located south of downtown Mishawaka on Dragoon Trail. The Catholic convent housed several retired sisters and many postulants as well, some American, some not. Pete immediately liked the convent, which included a small farm where the sisters grew food and raised dairy cows. He also enjoyed talking with the sisters; several spoke German, which he remembered well from the Occupation.

The sisters did everything they could to convince Pete to stay there and work for them. They explained to him that with winter coming on, his current life as a migrant would become much more difficult. They showed him a small apartment where he could live, with a "real bed and a shower, which was very inviting." They said his meals would be cooked for him by the sisters and served to him in the dining room. But Pete repeated what had become his standard refrain: He wasn't ready to take up permanent residence. He would not commit.

"But the sisters and I came to an agreement," he says, "that I would call if things did not turn out as well for me as I hoped."

One thing Pete really wanted to try was not hoeing, but picking cotton. With cooler weather on its way and the creamy white bolls almost ready for picking, he hitchhiked back to Missouri as soon as he finished picking peaches in Benton Harbor. He was back where he had started from several weeks before, back at the cotton fields near Sikeston, where work was plentiful and wages for picking cotton were rumored to be exceptionally good.

It was not what he had anticipated.

"I didn't want to miss out on picking cotton," Pete says. "I had heard everyone talk about how much money you could make. But it was the worst job I ever had. I carried an eight-foot sack on my neck, picking until my fingers were bloody, which they were within a few hours. It was bad.

"Two sacks were enough for me. I found myself thinking: This, I don't have to do. Before long, the Poor Sisters of St. Francis came to mind – a nice apartment, with some outside work and some inside work, and a little time to spoil myself. When I called Sister Stephanie, who was like the general manager of the convent, her only question was, 'When will you be here, Peter?'

"I hitchhiked and arrived in South Bend the next day."

୧୬

Pete did a variety of jobs both inside and outside the convent that first fall and winter. Toward spring, he spent a lot of time trimming fruit trees in the sisters' neglected orchard. In particular, the apple trees badly needed pruning. By the time he finished cutting, there was no hope of a fall fruit harvest. Pete had carefully explained to Sister Stephanie what needed to be done, and he had warned her not to look for any apples that fall. He remembers that she simply did not want to hear it. He also remembers that the lack of fruit that year caused quite a stir.

"My work at St. Francis had a nice variety," he says. "My first responsibilities were the fruit orchard and a vegetable garden. Unfortunately, my prediction of no apples came true, much to the sisters' disappointment. But we did have a great vegetable garden, which helped make up for the lack of apples. During this time, I also looked after the convent's sheep, became a dairyman in emergencies, and learned how to drive the van."

From Pete's perspective, the convent was a great place to work. The sisters offered "the best of food, something I had come to appreciate, and they were real good to work for. They even put together some packages for me to send home to my family," he says. However, when he received his first check, written from the Poor Sisters of St. Francis, Pete good-naturedly balked.

"When Sister Stephanie handed me the check, I crossed out the 'poor' part. We could communicate in German, and I explained to her that the sisters were not poor, and that they had to be honest. We had a good laugh. But today, they are just called the Sisters of St. Francis, not the Poor Sisters of St. Francis."

As he acclimated to his first winter in the Midwest, Pete met a few Dutch families who had also recently settled in the South Bend/Mishawaka area. There were not many, not enough to organize their own parish or populate a particular part of town, as was true for some of the other local immigrant groups. Nonetheless, Pete enjoyed the contact with people who spoke his own language and shared his cultural background. On Saturday nights he regularly attended dances held at the YWCA; there he also made friends with the offspring of first- and second-generation Polish, Hungarian, and Italian immigrants. Their evenings were full of (attempted) conversation, table tennis, and dancing. Pete loved all of it. His poor language skills did not make much of a difference when it came to getting along with other young adults his age.

South Bend was a big city for Pete, and he filled letters to his family and Wilma with news of what he saw and heard, including the "rolling staircase" he rode several times in a row at a Sears & Roebuck store. He described how the escalator went up and down, up and down, and how it never stopped moving. For the first time since he had left the Netherlands, he now regularly received letters back, expressing relief and gratitude at his job and living situation, and full of questions about his new life in America.

One Saturday, an older gentleman who was overseeing the construction of a new building at the convent asked Pete if he would like to go with him to a University of Notre Dame football game. Pete happily accepted the invitation. But early in the first quarter, he realized that a "perfectly good ticket on the 40-yard line had been wasted" on him. He did not understand a thing that was happening down on the field, nor could he understand what his host was patiently trying to explain to him about the game in English. It was too much for someone who had played, understood, and loved soccer all his life.

He wrote home a letter that said: In this game called football, they talk for a while, then come out and push each other around some, then go back to talking again.

❦

By the time Pete had been working at the convent for a year, "America was starting to look better by the day." He still had a long way to go with the language, but he was increasingly confident he would remain in the United States. He was proving to himself every day that he could do it. He was starting to think about what his next move should be, where he could find a higher-paying job, when he would have enough money saved to return to Holland for Wilma. Pete was making plans. Perhaps, he says, his life was going along too smoothly for something not to shake it up a bit. What happened next shook him to the core.

"One evening Sister Stephanie came to me as I was eating dinner," he begins. "She had a letter addressed to me in her hand. She had already opened and read it, since I could not read English and could only understand a little of what I heard. She knew I couldn't read it. She also knew what was in it, from the return address.

"She read to me in German, translating as she read: Your friends and neighbors have selected you to serve in the U.S. Army."

Pete did not know what to think. It took him a few minutes to understand what Sister Stephanie was telling him. He had never considered enlisting in any army, much less the U.S. Army. Did this happen to everyone? Was it a joke?

"I really had second thoughts about what I was hearing," he continues. "I couldn't understand it. I had absolutely no desire to go into the Army. That was the last thing I had ever wanted to do. But

Sister Stephanie helped me understand that I had no choice. I was being drafted. The only problem was, I had never thought about the draft, never even knew there was such a thing."

Pete's mind went in a thousand different directions. Everything in his new life would change – again – if he were to enlist as he was being "invited" to do. The letter stipulated that he would owe two years of service to the U.S. Army, which meant it would be at least another two years before he could return to Holland. He would break his promise to Wilma. Would she wait an additional two years for him? He could hardly understand English – how could he possibly survive basic training? Where would the Army send him? What if he never saw Wilma or his family again? Did it matter to anyone that he was only an immigrant? He was just getting on his feet.

True to character, Pete shrewdly assessed the situation and his opponent. After discerning that the only way to move forward was to comply with the summons from Uncle Sam and his "friends and neighbors," Pete decided he would not try to get out of it. He would take it on the chin.

"I was not a U.S. citizen," he explains, "and maybe if I had not really wanted to go, I would not have had to go. I could at least have tried to get out of it. But would that mean I'd have to leave America? There were a lot of good things going on, and I knew this – America – was the place I wanted to be."

When Pete worried out loud about how he would break the news to his parents, Sister Stephanie offered to do it for him. She wrote Bernard and Wilhelmina and explained what was about to take place in their son's life. Back in Holland, the postman in Didam guessed something was amiss when he received the sister's letter; he made a special trip by bicycle out to the Veldmans' farm to hand deliver what looked like bad news rather than wait for the next day's post.

It's hard to imagine how Pete's parents, siblings, and Wilma felt when they received word that Pete was being drafted. Certainly, they hoped and prayed for the best. They probably wondered why he did not just come home for good. Was living in America worth risking his life? Regardless, the implications were clear: Pete would not be returning to Holland in the near future, not to visit and not to live. He had made up his mind. No matter their questions, fears, and misgivings, he would soon be farther from them, not closer. For after three months of basic training in Kentucky, Pete learned that he was being shipped out – not to Europe as he had optimistically hoped – but halfway around the world.

Pete was headed for Korea.

Korea

At the end of World War II, the strategic Korean peninsula was divided at the 38th parallel into the People's Democratic Republic of Korea in the North and the Republic of Korea in the South. The ensuing conflict between the North and South escalated into a civil war that served as a battleground stage for the major players of the Cold War: the United States, which supported noncommunist South Korea, and the Soviet Union, which supported communist North Korea.

The United Nations reacted with alarm when North Korea invaded the South in June 1950. Never officially calling it a "war" and thus bypassing the need for congressional approval, President Harry Truman of the United States condemned the North's aggression and within two days of the invasion authorized U.S. military intervention on behalf of South Korea. Under the command of Gen. Douglas MacArthur, U.S. soldiers from all branches of the military joined troops from 15 other nations in a protracted, fierce attempt to push North Korea back across the 38th parallel.

By the time a truce was declared in July 1953, almost 37,000 American soldiers had been killed in what has been called the "Forgotten War." A great proportion of those deaths occurred early in the conflict, but for all three years the fights were historically brutal and intense, the soldiers far away from home.

ся

Pete had been working for the Poor Sisters of St. Francis for a little over a year when he was drafted into the U.S. Army. The Korean War had broken out less than six months before, as he was busy planting and tending the sisters' vegetable garden off Dragoon Trail. Pete did not know much about the conflict when Sister Stephanie approached him at the dining room table, opened letter in hand. The little he knew had been gained in halting conversation with others. His language skills were slowly improving, but he could not yet read English and he had minimal contact with newspapers.

Pete knew the war was taking place. He knew where Korea was. Knew thousands had died in the first months of fighting. He did not know that though the American people largely supported their country's involvement in Korea, they held it against Truman for not going before Congress at the very beginning of the conflict. Such political nuances were beyond his basic conversational skills.

Because Pete was an alien when the war started, it had never occurred to him that he could be drafted by the United States. But as he contemplated the letter translated into German for him by Sister Stephanie, he decided he would not contest America's call to duty. Even if he was not yet an American citizen, he was intent on becoming one.

Pete had always considered himself to be a lucky man, and as he talked with Sister Stephanie he grew confident that the U.S. Army would send him to Europe. In fact, because of his ability to speak the language and his familiarity with the region, he was sure he would land on his feet in Germany. It made perfect sense. The way he saw it, he would get in his obligatory military service, which might speed up the

U.S. naturalization process, while living across the border from Wilma and his family. Of course, he admitted to himself, if he had been really lucky he would have avoided the draft altogether. (At some point he learned he would not have been considered for the draft had he immigrated six months later.)

Pete explained to Sister Stephanie how he thought everything would work out for the best. When he returned from the European Theater, he would bring Wilma with him. The sisters would see.

"We have to find us some more boys from Holland," the habit-cloaked women told Pete as he gamely prepared to leave the convent. They fretted over him a little before sending him off with promises of prayers and letters.

Notwithstanding the sisters' supplications, the next two years didn't quite work out according to Pete's plan.

❦

On December 11, 1950, Pete reported for duty at Camp Breckenridge, Kentucky, where he would spend the next 16 weeks in basic training. The post, located near the western edge of the state, had been used as a prisoner-of-war camp during World War II. By 1950 it was the training ground for the Army's active 101st Airborne Division, better known as the Screaming Eagles. Camp Breckenridge was in a poor area. The facilities were spartan and the winter weather was frigid.

Pete hated the cold and patiently endured everything else. It could have been worse, he knew, from his time spent bouncing from place to place as a migrant. He had plenty to eat, and he was being paid for every uncomfortable, grueling day spent in training. He did not take food, shelter, and a regular paycheck for granted, no matter how basic they were.

"Basic training would have been a lot better if it had been located further south," Pete remembers. "Kentucky was extremely cold. I spent a couple of days camping two to a tent in temperatures that were well below zero, with no overcoat. We never got our winter coats until after basic was over, which was sometime in April. Even standing in line for breakfast in the mornings would get us off to a bad day."

Despite the bone-numbing cold, Pete earned a medal for sharpshooting during his time in Kentucky. He had come a long way from the teenager who once stood over a German soldier in his family's barn, unsure of how even to hold a gun. Fortunately, he never had to use his newly acquired shooting skills in combat, which was more than fine by him.

"I never enjoyed any weapons," he explains. "Anyway, I was sure the Army would be needing me in Europe, seeing as I could speak German. In the meantime, I immediately began learning a lot about the Army. It didn't take long to figure out there were many ways to do things, and then there was the Army way. But from the very beginning, the Army was one of the best things that could have happened to me, for that is where I really learned to speak and understand English."

Pete made friends with young men from all over Indiana and a few other Midwestern states during training. Additionally, John Kruis, a good friend of his from the YWCA weekend dances in South Bend, showed up about a month after Pete's arrival. Kruis was equally sure he would get a European assignment. Once they completed training, the two friends would be bound for the Old World. They were convinced of it.

Pete was one of the oldest recruits in the camp. Many of the other young men had never been away from home for an extended period of time, had never slept in an uncomfortable bed, had never been without some of the basic amenities of life. They had never experienced living in an occupied country or witnessed the impact war has on vast numbers of people, whole continents even. This, of course, was not true for Pete.

"I had gone through most of these experiences before, like being homesick and not having a nice bed to sleep in," he says. "To my surprise, everyone complained about the food, and we were being fed three meals a day! I gained 20 pounds during basic training. Add that to getting to sleep on time every night – and getting a good night's sleep at that – and it didn't seem so bad to me. For me, this was the best time I had had since I arrived in the country to learn English and learn about the American way of life, all the places everyone was from, etc. I soaked it up like a sponge. I was meeting a variety of people, from the best to the worst, and making many new American friends.

"Even when I was in Korea, we had a lot of time to sit around and talk," Pete continues. "The Army is where I perfected my English, although I had to undo a lot of it when I came home! And I learned a lot about the other guys and their lives. When you're away from home like that, you only remember the good things. That's what the guys wanted to talk about in basic training and after we got our assignments: home. You wouldn't recognize guys you know when they're away from home like that – all of a sudden home becomes very important to them and they talk about it a lot.

"I really enjoyed the Army. At first I thought I should be doing something else. I thought I wasn't getting anywhere. But then I realized I could learn more in the Army than anywhere else. I could spend a lot of time on the language and I could travel, although it's not always the best way to travel. Life has a lot to do with the expectations you have. At that point in my life, just going places was enough for me."

Pete honed his skills in many ways during his two years in the U.S. Army. In particular, the numerous opportunities he had had since he was a teenager to just listen and observe – sometimes in a hostile environment – began to serve him well. Even before he was drafted, Pete knew he could handle a variety of difficult situations. He had been doing just that since the German army marched into Holland – and into his front yard – when he was 14 years old. And then there was his experience of living as a non-English-speaking immigrant in the United States. Unlike most recruits, Pete had begun the process of learning how to live in a different culture without family or close friends to prop him up well before he showed up at Camp Brecken-ridge or was sent overseas.

In large part because he was never engaged in active combat, Pete's time in the Army afforded him the opportunity to become increasingly insightful, sure of himself, and steady on his feet. As he became competent in English, he gained a new confidence in himself as a foreigner among foreigners. His penchant for taking chances grew alongside his confidence, though it's fair to say he never took foolish chances. (His risk-taking has always been driven more by opportunity than by defiance, more by a desire to think for himself than by recklessness.)

The man Pete grew into while he was a soldier is still there to-day, many years removed. The dynamics of his personality are much the same as when he was in the Army. Pete is obviously not a reticent individual. But neither is he glib. When presented with a reasonable opportunity, he takes it without much hesitation. In some ways, he acts out of a honed, fair sense of survival. But his instinct is not rooted in fear. It's rooted in a genuine desire to live life to the fullest, a desire that has been with him since before he immigrated. So, you want both to see the world and make a life for yourself? From Pete's perspective, then and now, the Army was as good a place to begin as any. The Army was what was put on his plate. He took what he got, grew into a man, and moved on.

During basic training, many of Pete's fellow recruits went home on the weekends. Pete did not have a home to go to; he also didn't own a car. Though he and John Kruis occasionally caught a ride to a nearby Kentucky town for the day, northern Indiana was too far away for easy weekend travel. Instead, Pete used the time off for rest and relaxation, letter writing, playing cards, and conversation. Waiting his turn every Friday to pass weekend inspection, he began to notice a pattern other trainees seemed oblivious to in their eagerness to leave the premises.

"I recall the weekends, when lots of the soldiers would leave," he says. "You could not leave camp until you passed final inspection, which began at 10 o'clock Friday morning. Your bunk had to be perfectly made, your living area spotless, and, much more difficult, your gun had to be perfectly cleaned. It would take two or three trips for some of my buddies to pass, especially the gun inspection, which could really be aggravating.

"But what I noticed is this: The sergeants started getting ready to go home themselves around 3 p.m. Friday afternoon. Since I had nowhere to go, I would just wait until it was close to that time before I went for inspection. The sergeants didn't give me much trouble then because they were ready to leave.

"I never had to come back before I passed inspection. Not once. Three o'clock Friday afternoon was the best timing."

ᴄ⋅ꓱ

Before basic training ended in April, Pete learned he was not going to Europe after all. He was not crossing the Atlantic Ocean, headed for Germany. He was crossing the Pacific, headed for Korea after additional training in Japan. The Army did not share Pete's thinking about what made "perfect sense" – and made no apologies for it. Not long afterward, John Kruis also received his orders. He was as surprised as Pete was to learn that he, too, was being sent to Korea. Unfortunately for both of them, the two friends would not be traveling together.

Although he was concerned, Pete doesn't remember feeling terribly anxious about being sent to Korea. He knew the potential for danger was high, depending on his job assignment, but it was what it was. He would just have to wait and see. After spending a few free days back at the convent in Mishawaka, he left by train for Seattle with the rest of his unit.

"Many parents, brothers, and sisters were at our farewell," he says. "After lots of tears and many good-byes, we were on our way."

There was no one to see Pete off as he headed into the unknown.

He stepped back and watched the scene unfold around him: the hugs and kisses, slaps on the back and handshakes, the wet eyes and open tears. He took it all in, and thought about his family and Wilma. He had not seen them for almost two years, had not heard their voices or touched them. Finally, he took a seat, and when the train began moving, he let it take him to a different place both physically and emotionally.

"The northern route the train followed was beautiful," Pete recalls. "Spring had arrived, and it couldn't have been better. For me, it was another good look at America. Traveling like this was one of the things I had most wanted to do. A few days later we arrived at the port in Seattle, where we would ship out. There we had our usual delay, the Army's 'rush and wait.'

"I found myself in a transfer company where nobody knew what was going on," he continues. "I took advantage of the delay and went AWOL (absent without leave) for five days to Vancouver and Victoria, Canada, to visit an old friend of my father's. My Army friends were wondering where I had been when I finally returned to Pier 9 in Seattle. Fortunately for me, the transfer company was still very confused and I avoided confrontation with the officer in charge by going to play pool. Three days later I was on a ship to Japan."

Pete's previous ocean-crossing experience came into good play this time around. He expected a lot of men would be seasick, but he did not think he would be among them. He was right on both accounts. Before the ship left port, Pete convinced some of his mystified buddies to take the top bunks. They could not understand why anyone would choose to sleep that high up, especially since they would likely encounter rough seas in the days ahead. The bunks were stacked in vertical rows of six and did not have guardrails. It was a long way down. But they understood Pete's thinking later, as they spent their time playing cards, reading, or sleeping – suspended above the tortured souls below who struggled miserably with the "unpleasant results" of prolonged seasickness. The constant nausea and vomiting was unbearable for some of Pete's shipmates; it was as bad as anything they had ever experienced, and it lasted for days.

It was Pete's turn to be mystified when a few troops went AWOL during a brief stop at a naval base in Alaska. The air was cold and the island was desolate. He could not understand why anyone would desert the Army in such a place. A half-day there was more than enough for him.

༄

Fifteen days after leaving Seattle, the ship docked in Yokohama, Japan's second-largest city. Looking down as the ship was tied up at the dock, Pete marveled at how "small the Japanese looked and at how fast they seemed to move about on their short legs." He was thrilled, completely fascinated by his new surroundings. After disembarking, the troops traveled to Osaka in a crowded, uncomfortable train built for people of slight stature. Finally, they reached their Japanese destination – the small, lovely island of Eta Jima, site of the Japanese Naval Academy and home to Japan's officers and admirals before and during World War II.

"Here, we received the royal treatment, with white linens at breakfast and candlesticks at dinner," Pete says gleefully. "We truly had the best sleeping quarters and the best food, prepared by soldiers who were training to become cooks! Unfortunately, I found out I was here to be trained as a pole lineman. This was a real problem for me since I have always been afraid of heights over three feet.

"The day after we arrived, the first day of training, we traveled to a field with about 50 poles stuck in the ground. Just poles. Looking at those poles, I knew the Army had made a mistake as far as I was concerned: I couldn't be a pole lineman. I found the sergeant and told him about my problem, and he told me he understood. He said the Army would not want to waste their time or mine. Then he told me I would be climbing 40-foot poles within three days or he would arrange to have me flown to Korea! Taking a second look, I didn't think those poles looked so high after all, and within days I could climb to the top. But it was always very scary for me, to climb straight up a pole like that."

Pete says he "lived like a king" during the several weeks of lineman training on Eta Jima. And he loved every minute of it, as long as he was not high up on a pole. He went to school five days a week and had weekends off. The American dollar was valuable and on weekends he and his friends walked into town where delicious, inexpensive meals were served by dark-haired Japanese ladies.

"The ladies would smile and say, 'One dolla, please.'" Pete says, his blue eyes twinkling. "Even soldiers could afford that."

The weather was so beautiful the men turned in their winter coats, which had been issued before they left Seattle. It was early summer and the coats were useless, or so the soldiers thought.

"We never had overcoats all the following cold winter in Korea," Pete says, shaking his head. "We didn't have them when we needed them in basic training, and we didn't have them when we needed them in Korea."

The life Pete considered luxurious by immigrant standards came to a screeching halt when lineman training ended. His circumstances deteriorated from the moment he left Eta Jima until he arrived at his new station in South Korea – a tented camp located on the 38th parallel. From the time Pete and the other troops left Japan – traveling by ship, open boats, canvas-covered trucks, and grimy, open freight cars that passed through tunnels reeking of smoke – to the first glimpse of his new home, a tent that slept 20 men, Pete gradually came down to reality. He was a drafted U.S. Army soldier living in a country that was at war.

Pete was not, however, on the front line. He was headquartered with the 51st Signal Corps, a communications company. For that he was thankful.

❧

C amping was never my favorite thing to do," Pete says, "and living in a tented camp with the Army did not change my mind. We were in no-man's land, with a few Koreans around who served as our support. There were about 15 tents in our company. All together, we formed a communications unit. There was not much work to do the first few weeks we were there. We basically spent our time cleaning up old wiring. Later on, some of the men ran wires to forward units, so they could communicate from the field back to the base camps or to another forward unit."

Japan had been fun for Pete from the moment he arrived. South Korea was the exact opposite, at least at the beginning. There is nothing appealing about war, no matter who is involved or where it is played out. Pete had been here before, and he recognized what he saw.

"The Koreans were depressed," he explains. "The war had beat the hope out of them. As we traveled north toward our camp, toward the 38th parallel, we went through areas where the Alliance had gone back and forth, north to south. People were living in their basements. There is nothing exciting about living like that. The people were doing what we had done in Holland: They were just waiting for the war to end.

"After World War II was finally over, we all worked so hard," Pete continues. "We had ambitions and dreams again. But during the war, there had been no thoughts of what you wanted to do later on. I never thought about what I wanted to be while World War II was going on. No one had any drive or ambition – that came only after the war ended, for everyone. It was like that in Korea. At first I thought the Koreans weren't very motivated and weren't taking good care of their farms and homes. I thought they were maybe kind of lazy. And then I remembered what it was like."

Pete got oriented to his new foreign home during the first few weeks of his stay. First of all, he made peace with living in a tent. Then he became friends with some of the men in his company. He removed old wiring as directed and avoided climbing poles whenever he could.

Then one day, he had a serendipitous opportunity to come down from heights forever, an opportunity he went after determinedly – and without a moment's hesitation.

"After a few weeks, my lucky day arrived," he says. "Our mailman had to make an emergency trip back home, to the States. I went to the sergeant immediately and asked him for the mailman's job. He didn't think I could do it, but said I could have the job temporarily. That was enough for me."

Once Pete got off the poles, he never looked back. With gusto, he took care of mail pickup and delivery, laundry drop-off and pickup, movie selection, and anything else he was asked to do. Sometimes when he drove to deliver mail to outlying, detached groups, he heard cannons shooting overhead, aimed toward North Korea. They did not deter him.

"The cannons didn't bother me much," he says. "I had been used to that in Holland."

As far as he was concerned, Pete had secured the best job in the Army. Proving his sergeant wrong, he turned in his lineman gear for good and started driving one of the unit's three-quarter-ton trucks. It was a big step for a man who had not known how to drive at all until he began working for the Poor Sisters of St. Francis a short year before. Now Pete was driving around Korea independently as the bearer of good gifts, basically keeping his own schedule. He quickly learned that few things mattered more to the soldiers than seeing him arrive with the daily mail.

"In the Army, there is no better life than being the mailman!" Pete says with a laugh. "Everyone is always looking forward to receiving a letter from home, from a friend, from their better half if they are married, from their Wilma. Let's not forget all the Wilmas of the world.

"I drove 25 to 30 miles south every day to the Army post office. Along the way, I dropped off our company's laundry, to be washed in a creek by several Korean ladies. I took a Korean interpreter with me to negotiate the price of the laundry. His name was Johnny and he was about 10 years old. He would wait for me to pick him up every day.

"We would turn off the main road and a little 8-year-old girl would be waiting for us, to ride in the truck," he continues. "She took my personal clothes to her mother to be washed, and, I must say, I had the cleanest and most well-pressed uniform in the company. One day the little girl was waiting for me, wearing a coat I had found for her. I'll never forget her standing there with the coat on backwards, all the buttons in the back, waving and grinning."

Along the route, Pete also dropped off film to be developed, and while he was at the post office he selected movies for the soldiers to watch at night. Because he didn't know much about the movies or the actors and actresses in them, and because he still couldn't read English very well, he relied on a long list of suggestions given to him by the soldiers back in camp. When he was done with everything, he headed back to his tented company as quickly as he could get there; he knew the importance of his deliveries. But he always stopped on the way back to buy a few fish to add to the rice pot for Johnny and his family.

Once Pete arrived back at camp, he immediately got to work sorting and distributing mail. He followed a foolproof system he devised after a short time on the job.

"First, I did a quick sort for the first sergeants, then all the officers, then the motor pool and the supply group – all places where a person might want to have a friend at one time or another," Pete explains. "The final sort was for everyone coming out of the field at the end of the day. My little post office was their first stop. It was just a great job to have, lots of fun.

"Every other day I left in the evening, sometimes with two or three friends, to deliver mail to groups attached to other companies," he continues. "One group I traveled to was an American detachment living in the British camp. Their quarters were not real clean and they did not have great food, but they had beer, which was a scarce item. The American troops got a beer ration once a month. You could drink it quickly or over a period of time, but once it was gone, it was gone.

It usually lasted only a few days. My friends and I always made the British camp the last stop of our day. We'd have a few beers and sit and play cards for hours. I didn't have to turn out for 6:30 a.m. roll call in the mornings, so it was no problem for me to come in late, though I wasn't supposed to come in real late. My friends had morning roll call, but it was worth it to them to go with me.

"Our return trips from those nights were usually uneventful, except for one rainy night. We always had to cross a river, driving across a makeshift bed of rocks. One rainy night, though, the river had risen and when we got in the middle of it, the truck engine drowned. I had to swim to the other side, walk a couple of miles, alert the guard, who let me pass, then wake the sergeant of the motor pool, who sent a friend back to the river with me with a tow truck. The two friends who had gone to the British camp with me stayed back in the truck, probably asleep. But everything worked out great. I was home for good sometime before sunrise. I was definitely not supposed to be out that late, but I was able to talk my way out of trouble the next morning."

☙❧

Ever alert to opportunity, Pete noticed that a soldier in one of the detached groups was constantly receiving packages in the mail. It was like Christmas every day for this guy, and Pete could not figure out what was going on. He watched and wondered and asked around until he eventually learned that the soldier was operating a little business on the side – and making a tidy profit at it. He bought men's and women's watches, necklaces, cards, etc., in Cleveland, Ohio, and had them shipped to his post in South Korea. He then sold the goods to his fellow soldiers, who turned around and mailed them back home to their loved ones. The entrepreneur in Pete was immediately drawn to the novelty of the business, and when the soldier-turned-businessman returned to the United States, Pete stepped in to fill his shoes.

"I bought out the soldier's inventory. I eventually got our supply sergeant to go in with me because he had a safe place, and the room, to store the goods. One of our most popular items, and the one that traveled the most, was a pillowcase soldiers often bought to send to their mothers. Embroidered on the cloth were the words, Greetings from Korea. But the pillowcases were made in Taiwan before being sent to our distributor in Cleveland. From Cleveland, they were sent to us in Korea, where we sold them to soldiers who mailed them back to the U.S.A.

"Outside sales went well for me, a traveling mailman. Soon I was selling items to Korean ladies for Korean money. I used the Korean money to pay for the laundry, film, etc. You could say I became an early millionaire, with over 1 million South Korean won in my possession. Too bad the exchange rate wasn't that good!"

❧

Toward the end of Pete's tour of duty, he worked – or he was supposed to work – as a mechanic, in addition to his mail duties. But the inner workings of automobiles and trucks have never come easily to him. He admired the many soldiers who hung around the motor pool because they liked – and understood – engines. He enjoyed watching them and wished he had an affinity for what they were doing.

"My only qualification as a mechanic was my toolbox!" he explains. "I've never been very good at what goes on inside engines. I would just put my toolbox down and after a while some soldier would wander over who knew what he was doing and he would fix the problem."

What Pete had an affinity for was meeting people and making friends; he eventually knew someone almost everywhere he went. He could talk himself out of almost any tight spot just by being himself. He was charming and casual, willing to admit what he did not know, willing to take the hit if his misdeeds were found out, willing to work hard if hard work would solve the problem. It was all about attitude, and while Pete's expertise may have been lacking, his attitude was contagious.

"I really enjoyed my life in Korea," he says, his eyes merry again. "I seldom made anyone upset with me, and if I did, I could usually talk my way out of it. One time I was in an area I wasn't supposed to be in. The first sergeant had come back from somewhere and was standing on a divider between a couple of rice paddies. He told me in a very military manner with a few choice words that I wasn't supposed to be there. I told him I had only stopped by because I thought he might be in trouble since a little further away, lying upside down in a rice paddy, was his jeep.

"Jeeps were personal vehicles, and you had to be pretty important to have one to drive," Pete continues. "I took the first sergeant back to the company, got my favorite driver and a tow truck, and we went back and pulled out his jeep. We did a fine carwash on it and parked it in front of his tent. Everything turned out fine, and I found this was a good way of making friends for life!"

☙

Although he's not one to dwell on hard times, there were problems for Pete and the other soldiers he lived and worked with, even if they were not involved in the terrible fighting taking place in other parts of the country. For starters, he was shocked with the way African Americans were treated while serving their country with the U.S. Army.

Pete never witnessed much overt racial prejudice growing up in Holland. No matter if you hailed from a crowded city or a small town, the Dutch prided themselves on making room for all kinds of people with all kinds of religious and political views. In reality, there existed some prejudice against Jews, and there was a real divide between the members of the Dutch aristocracy and ordinary citizens. However, the Holland of Pete's youth was fairly homogeneous, at least outwardly. Prejudice was not as malicious and easy to identify as white against black. The divisions separating people were subtler.

In contrast, the racial tensions that existed in mid-20th-century America broadsided Pete almost from the moment he stepped off the ship in Hoboken. He was not prepared for such a dark underside to life in the country of his dreams – the country that around the world stood for democracy, liberty, and freedom.

From the time he began working as a field hand in Missouri, Pete heard remarks and sneers toward blacks that surprised and disturbed him. He was once physically directed by a bus driver to move from the back of the bus, where blacks sat, to the front, where whites sat. Pete did not understand what the man was saying or why he needed to move, but he left his seat and did as he was told. Another time, standing outside after church, Pete commented that he had seen no blacks in the congregation, noteworthy only because he was working in the fields with many blacks who lived in the area. Were there no black Catholics in America? He was taken aback when a listener responded indignantly that he would not attend the parish if blacks were allowed to worship there with whites. Pete wondered if he had heard correctly. When he later learned it was illegal for blacks to stay overnight in one of the counties where he was working as a migrant, he was even more disturbed. African Americans could toil and sweat beside him all day long, but they were not welcome, as he was, to take their rest nearby.

Pete had carried all of this around inside himself since his arrival in America, trying to make sense of it. No matter where he went, the black man or woman was treated differently. Now he saw blacks being looked down upon and treated unfairly in Korea, though they were doing the same work as everyone else, though their lives were on the line like everyone else. They were even U.S. citizens, which he wasn't. Yet they received worse treatment just because of the color of their skin.

"I remember a big, black soldier from Texas joining our unit," Pete says. "When he walked into the tent, everyone stopped and just kind of stood there, and said nothing. I pointed out a bunk for him. 'Here, take this bunk,' I said. It was next to mine. I really didn't think anything of it, but I could tell the others did. Everything was tense at first. But after a few days, everything was OK. I think it was good for white Americans to have black Americans integrated into their units, but not everyone liked it."

The treatment of black soldiers bothered Pete even after he was released from the Army, and it greatly influenced his decision to be color-blind to those he did business with later on in his career. Struggling to gain a handhold in society was an experience he identified with. He says that poor, black Americans were some of the best customers he ever had.

There were also the real dangers of war: soldiers got sick, struggled with depression, were sometimes unfairly disciplined, betrayed people they loved back home, argued with each other, took unfair advantage of men they shared a tent with. It was still life, with its shared ups and downs, rights and wrongs. Most of the men in Pete's unit spent all of their time at work on the poles, or in the camp. They did not have Pete's freedom as a mailman, did not travel from one camp or small village to another. Once they came in from the day's assignment, there was nowhere else for them to go – no nearby town they could walk to, no possibility of getting away from the men they lived, ate, and worked with.

Shortly before Pete left South Korea, a good friend of his was killed when he stepped on a landmine while out in a field cleaning up old wires. He was just doing his job, a little ways off from the other troops when the explosion happened. His death reminded everyone that nothing could be taken for granted. It reminded Pete of his personal goal to make use of every opportunity he was given.

"Harry Stang was a true, quality friend, someone I spent hours with," Pete says. "His death was in an instant, without any good-byes. He left lots of friends behind. Harry was kind of different in that he didn't believe in God. That was surprising to me, but morally you couldn't find a better person.

"Korea was full of new experiences for me all the time," he continues, shifting to a different thought. "That's why I loved it. I traveled to Seoul my first and only Christmas there, to attend midnight Mass. The cathedral looked good from the outside, but once you got inside you saw that half of the building had a dirt floor.

"In the middle of my time in Korea, I traveled back to Japan for a five-day break. It was just great to get back to the real world. Everywhere, there was something new to see. As I was traveling to the hotel just before dawn, I saw a tangle of traffic, the bustle of people moving as fast as they could – walking, biking, motorcycling, riding in rickshaws, traveling in cars, trucks, and buses. And all of this was happening on the wrong side of the street! When I returned to Seoul, an old Army truck was waiting for me. What a world of contrasts.

"I know everyone did not have as good a time as I did while we were over there. No one really wanted to be there, including me. But World War II provided me with lots of experiences that made Korea easier for me to get used to. And Korea was a pretty country. I would travel along the hillside early in the mornings, as the sun was just coming up over the rice paddies: It was a gorgeous sight. I will never forget seeing the ladies at work out in the paddies, knee-deep in water and mud with their colorful clothes on. It was just unbelievable."

∾

Pete received word he would be leaving Korea for good after he had been there for about 18 months. It changed the way he conducted himself those last few weeks – where he went, the chances he took.

"After I was told I would be going back to the U.S., I didn't get off the main roads anymore when I was driving. When you get close to the end of a war, you so badly want to live. You get that close and you really become careful," he says.

It was a lesson he had learned during the Occupation. And his mind was there, back in his home country, with increasing urgency. For Holland was where his family and Wilma were. He knew he would receive a month's leave from the Army after he returned to the United States. It was leave he intended to make good on.

"The troop ship was waiting for us in the Yokohama harbor," Pete says of his last day in Japan, after leaving Korea and the tents behind. "Everyone was excited, now that we were on our way home. But I was already figuring out how, once we crossed the Pacific, I would cross the Atlantic. I was already trying to figure out how I could get home to Didam."

As eager as he was to see his family, Pete was even more anxious to keep a long overdue promise: He was on his way to get Wilma.

ೞ

Marriage

The day the troop ship arrived back in San Francisco was one of the greatest days of my life. I got the same feeling when I returned to America as I had when I first arrived in Hoboken, New Jersey. The great lady was not there, of course. Instead, we passed San Quentin – a place you want to stay away from – and sailed under the Golden Gate Bridge. A nice homecoming had been orchestrated for us: Speeches were made, a band was playing, and people were cheering for us as we got off the ship. We enjoyed it all for a while, then we took off to visit the big city. The sun was shining at its very best and the temperature was warm. There was no time to get warm clothing, but it was summer, and we didn't think we needed it anyway.

Except for those who were once again seasick, Pete and the other exultant troops returning home from Korea enjoyed their 15-day trip across the Pacific. They took in the nice weather on deck whenever they could, they talked and relaxed, and they played cards – lots of cards, so many games of cards that Pete arrived in San Francisco in debt. Losing substantial money at cards was unusual for Pete. As a rule, he didn't gamble for high stakes unless he thought he could out-smart his opponents. His goal was always to come out a little bit ahead; he preferred to fold his hand and watch if it was clear he was going to crash and burn. He had taught many friends in the 51st Signal Corp how to play cards. He loved the game, but he didn't want to throw away any of the hard-earned money he needed to get back to Holland.

Crossing the Pacific with hundreds of soldiers who were both relieved to be getting out of a war zone and jubilant to be going home was infectious, however, and Pete kept playing, one bad hand after an-other. He arrived in San Francisco thrilled to be there, thrilled with the city's welcome, and flat broke. A $25 draw against his next paycheck set him in good stead for a day in the city and the upcoming trip across the country. By the time the sun set in the cosmopolitan city known for its steep hills, the men who had hurried off the ship and into a day of freedom on American soil were getting chilly. By the time night was hard upon them, they were cold. Very cold. Pete remembers the tem-peratures dropped low enough to keep him awake in the early hours of the morning. He couldn't believe how cold it was or that he still had no coat.

⚮

The next day found Pete and his buddies and hundreds of other soldiers on a train bound for Chicago. As Pete traveled across the vast, empty western landscape, he realized that he, too, now thought of America as home. He loved Holland; it was where his family and Wilma were, and he was intent on getting back there as soon as he pos-sibly could. But America had become home to him during his stint in the Army. America was where he intended to stay.

It wasn't just that Pete now spoke and understood English well. More importantly, he now identified with and understood Americans well. The men he had spent almost every waking moment with in

Kentucky and Korea had been for him a living, breathing class on American culture. Paradoxically, being sent out of the country with the U.S. Army had immersed Pete into everything American: its language, popular culture, work ethic and belief in opportunity, system of government, food, regional differences, family and social structures.

As the train carrying the troops rolled across the desert, Pete found himself observing the landscape through an inner lens that was becoming more American- than European-shaped. America was no longer a country that just glittered in his imagination. Like any other country in the world, America had its own problems, social ills, and difficulties. Pete understood that now. But still, it was America, and to him and countless other immigrants, it represented opportunity. The difference for Pete as an immigrant and returning soldier was that he now felt he belonged. More than ever, he could imagine opportunity coming his way.

"I really felt like I knew America when I came back," he explains, "in a way that couldn't have happened for me in everyday life had I not left the country with the Army. I had been with men from so many different places, from all over the country, and we had talked so much about everything. It was very important for me that I got to know America in this way because this was where I was going to live. I had never seriously doubted it, but now I knew it for sure. I came back with a bigger vision of what I could do in America. It was a much wider world and held more opportunity than when I left.

"America just looked great when we returned from Korea," he continues, "though our trip back across the country took us through the desert. The desert was different. You can only stay excited about sand, cactus, and rolling weeds for a short time."

Pete and his companions began playing cards again as the journey stretched on. And Pete's luck finally changed.

"The cards turned friendly again and the $25 in my pocket turned into $250," Pete says with a grin. "After a few days we arrived back in the Midwest, which to me was still the best. A two-hour layover in Chicago turned into an all-night affair for a little group of us with drinks, food, and pool. Best of all, everything was on the house because we were soldiers back from the war! We enjoyed the refreshments to such excess that early the next morning, around 2 a.m., we had to start hitchhiking to Camp Atterbury to meet the rest of the train riders, who had gone on without us. But we got there before they did. No one had even missed us, and good friends had looked after our duffel bags."

Hitchhiking across America was safe and convenient when Pete and his buddies were doing it as returning soldiers in the early 1950s. Whenever possible, Pete opted to stick out his thumb and hitch a ride. He had learned as a migrant worker that taking a bus was slower than hitchhiking. He had also learned that bus fares ate up money he didn't have to spend.

"I would never spend the money on a Greyhound bus unless I absolutely had to," Pete says, "and anyway, I could hitch faster than I could ride a bus. People picked us up because we were soldiers and had our uniforms on. Drivers liked to talk to soldiers and ask us about what was going on in different parts of the world. I remember a driver asking me what I thought about the conflict between Truman and MacArthur, when MacArthur wanted to cross into China. I didn't know what to say, so I just said, 'The President is the boss and MacArthur has to do what he says.'

"Once I hitched a ride and when the car ran out of gas, the driver and his companion stopped, took their guitars out of the trunk, went into a beer joint, and started playing and singing. I passed around a hat and collected money until we had enough to get back on the road again."

છ્ગ

Camp Atterbury, Indiana – Pete's destination by thumb – was home for the next few weeks. He was there just long enough to recover from one trip and get ready for another. Located between Indianapolis, Indiana, and Louisville, Kentucky, Camp Atterbury was the home of Wakeman General Hospital during World War II, the largest convalescent hospital in the U.S. Army. The camp was shut down from the end of World War II until the onset of the Korean War, when it was once again utilized by outgoing and returning troops. Mothballed at the end of the Korean War, not too long after Pete's stay there, Camp Atterbury was later given to the Indiana National Guard.

Much to Pete's delight, his good friend John Kruis returned from Korea and was sent to Camp Atterbury the same time he was. Actually, Kruis beat Pete there and was waiting for him when Pete arrived. Kruis had been on the grounds for a week when Pete showed up. He had already discovered that Wakeman General served the best food around. Since he and Pete knew a few men who worked at the hospital, the two friends would head there first thing every morning after reveille. While new Atterbury recruits scurried around getting their work assignments for the day, Pete and Kruis enjoyed acclimating themselves back to life in America by eating good food and relaxing as much as they could get away with.

John Kruis was also planning to spend his four-week furlough in Europe and had gotten a head start on the logistics of getting there before Pete returned. He first advised Pete that he would have to get an extension on his passport from the Dutch consulate before he would be allowed to leave the United States. Next, he pointed out, they weren't going to have much time to spend in Europe if they weren't diligent about finding the quickest way possible to get from Camp Atterbury to the other side of the Atlantic. An ocean voyage would take too long, and soldiers looking to travel by air were already deep in line.

Pete realized he could not possibly get to Holland, marry Wilma, and return to the U.S. by the end of his leave unless he and Kruis pulled out all the stops. The situation made him uncharacteristically anxious. Though he had communicated with his family and Wilma that he was coming, he had not been able to give them specific dates – there were too many unknown variables in the mix. And he had been traveling too much for their return mail to catch him, so he didn't know their plans. He especially didn't know what Wilma was thinking. Did she still want to marry him? Was she still willing to immigrate? These and other questions filled Pete's mind as he made his way to the Dutch consulate in Chicago to get a passport extension.

ɞ

D o you have permission from the Queen to wear an American uniform?" was the first question the Dutch consul asked Pete as he stood before the official in his spotlessly clean and pressed U.S. Army attire. Surprised at the question and the seriousness with which it was asked, Pete fumbled his answer at first, but got the extension without "too much difficulty" after he explained the circumstances of his being drafted.

Looking back, the question seems timely and fitting, for before the consul stood a U.S. Army-clad Dutch immigrant with one foot firmly planted in each world, at least for the time being. In many ways, Pete was no longer Dutch. But neither was he a naturalized American. He was returning to his home country to visit and, he hoped, marry the woman he had loved for a long time. He was also planning to bring her to America as soon as she could get a visa and book a ship. Pete's life was in flux. The one thing he was sure of was that he needed to get to Holland. Soon. He left to work on travel arrangements as soon as the consul excused him.

"Kruis and I talked to the first sergeant as soon as we could and explained to him my situation," Pete says. "Thirty days wasn't a long vacation if you were hitchhiking to Holland, even by plane. The first sergeant gave us a few days' early start. He said he wouldn't turn us in as missing as long as nothing went wrong.

"We were off with his words."

Pete and Kruis easily hitched rides by car from Camp Atterbury to the Wright-Patterson Air Force Base near Dayton, Ohio. Once there, Kruis proposed that they hitch an airplane ride to Washington, D.C. to take in a performance by legendary American Gospel singer Mahalia Jackson. Given his urgency to get to Europe, Pete was not interested in delaying for Jackson or any other entertainer, and Kruis had to do a lot of persuading before Pete acquiesced. If for no other reason, Pete finally agreed with the plan because Kruis had done so much to get the trip underway.

"I had some difficulty understanding how Mahalia Jackson should figure in on this," Pete deadpans. "But she did very well, according to John."

❧

Following the singer's performance, Pete and Kruis caught a flight to Rhode Island, where their luck in the air temporarily ran out. Once again, they put out their thumbs and hitched rides on the ground until they reached their destination, Westover Air Force Base in Chicopee, Massachusetts. Their last ride, which got them all the way to the base's gate, was in a "beautiful convertible driven by two young ladies I can still recall," Pete says. He was most impressed with the vehicle.

Westover Air Force Base was full of soldiers coming and going when the two friends arrived there at the end of July 1952. The 2500-acre site had been used for training and sending off bombers during World War II, and was the launching point for millions of tons of food dropped by the Allies to the starving citizens of Berlin over a period of 327 days during the Russian blockade of 1948. By the time Pete and Kruis appeared on the scene, hoping to hitch rides to Europe, Westover was being used to transport troops and casualties to and from Korea. It was a busy place.

To their dismay, the friends learned they weren't the only soldiers who had traveled to Massachusetts looking for a free plane ride across the Atlantic: competition was stiff. They were told it might be several days, if not weeks, before they reached their journey's end. But Pete and Kruis were not about to accept defeat without a fight. They were also experienced enough to know there are more ways to win than by using bluster and brawn. As soon as they got their bearings, they sought out a base chaplain.

"Our sad story to the chaplain qualified us for an earlier flight," Pete says a little embarrassedly, "but we had to split up and wouldn't see each other again until the day Wilma and I got married. John left that night on a flight to Europe traveling by the southern route. I left traveling by the northern route. My plane had to stop to refuel in Iceland. The landing wasn't navigated very well, though, and the landing gear required a day-and-a-half's repair in a place that was cold and windy and rainy – I never even made it outside – before we headed to Edinburgh, Scotland, and, at last, Frankfurt, Germany."

Pete was finally close to home. But he was not close enough. He could not get there fast enough to suit him.

"I needed to get to Holland fast!" he says. "Because I had grown used to the American way of travel, the first call I made once I arrived in Germany was to check on getting a flight there. I became aware I was no longer in America when they told me there would not be a flight to Amsterdam for two days! I couldn't believe it, and I immediately called the train station, only to learn the train was leaving in about 90 minutes."

Time was running out, and with it, another day of Pete's leave. After a very quick discussion with the Military Police – who could not figure out how Pete was standing before them in the Frankfurt airport a day before his papers showed he was officially scheduled to begin furlough, and who did not know what to do about it – Pete headed for the door. He ran through the airport, desperate to hail a taxi that would take him to the train station.

"I went rushing for a cab, then realized I didn't have any German money," Pete laughs. "I explained to the driver that I would pay him as soon as we got to the train station and I cashed a traveler's check. We got there, and the driver went inside with me. I hurried over to cash a check, but I had forgotten that it was a Saturday, and there was a very long line of people waiting to cash their checks.

"Things looked bad for a few moments. I knew I would never get my check cashed in time."

The cabdriver was waiting to be paid and the train was loading passengers. Pete had to pay for the taxi, and he had to catch the train, but neither could happen without German marks. He stood there for a few seconds in the bustling Frankfurt station, racking his brains for a solution, until he suddenly remembered a $5 bill he had long ago hidden away in a secret part of his wallet to use in case of an emergency. He had completely forgotten about the money; no emergency had ever equaled the one he was now confronted with. There was a hitch, however: U.S. military personnel were not allowed legally to spend American dollars in Europe. They were not even supposed to carry dollars with them. Instead, they were issued special overseas money to use in Europe and the Far East. Such a technicality was not about to stop Pete at this point. He was too close to being reunited with his family and Wilma to be stopped by what he thought should be a simple currency exchange.

Pete started walking the line, the $5 bill in his hand, telling his story as he went, pleading for someone to give him 20 German marks in exchange for the greenback. Many of those waiting were soldiers themselves. Surely one of them would be moved to help him, he thought. Before he knew it, an American lieutenant stepped out of the long, snaking column. He told Pete very clearly that what he was doing was against the law. He needed to put the money away, get it out of sight, and get in line like everyone else. Standing in front of the lieutenant, Pete quickly assessed the situation and decided he had come too far to see his dream of getting home before another 24 hours passed go up in smoke. He was going for broke.

"I knew very well what the officer was telling me," Pete recalls, "but I did not immediately put the money away. Instead, I begged him to do his good deed for the year and give me 20 marks in exchange for the $5, so I could pay the cabbie and catch the last train home."

After a few moments of consideration – and to Pete's surprise and eternal gratitude – the lieutenant took the $5 bill, gave him 20 German marks, and sent him on his way. Pete made good on the 15 marks he owed the cabbie. The problem now was that he had only 5 marks left, which was not enough to get him across Germany, much less all the way to Didam.

"I purchased a ticket for as far as 5 marks would take me, all that I had in my hand," he says. "The lady at the ticket window kept telling me in German that she needed the name of my destination, but I told her not to worry about it. I said I thought I had enough money to get two stops down the line, and I'd be sure to check when I got there.

"Everything had fallen into place, or so I thought," he continues. "I was finally on the last leg of my journey, on my way home. But trains come with conductors, and I knew I had to stay away from the one on the train I was traveling on. I did well for a long time, until we were several stops down the line. And then suddenly I was face to face with a German conductor who just could not understand how he had missed me.

"Just as suddenly, I could no longer understand German at all. The conductor patiently tried to explain to me that I had missed my destination several stops back. He took me along with him and at the next stop got off with me. He tried to show me, the best he could, that I had missed where I should get off, and he tried to show me how to get back there. He got back on the train when he thought I sort of understood what he had said. He left me standing there on the platform, and when enough cars had passed between us, I got back on as well.

"Much further on down the line, the conductor and I met again. He couldn't believe I was still there. Miraculously, I regained some of my knowledge of German," Pete beams. "I told the conductor that I was only three stops from where I needed to be, and that I was desperately trying to get home. He let me know I would be in plenty of trouble when I got there – and that he was going to be sure I got off the train and did not get back on. But he let me stay on until we reached the stop, which was the first station on the Holland side of the border. I had to get off there, anyway. I had to change to another line in order to get to Didam.

"I knew a whole new set of problems were about to begin once I got off at the stop. But then something miraculous really did happen. The conductor made sure I got off the train like he said he would, and which I needed to do. I knew I was going to have to turn in my ticket, which made me very nervous, since my ticket was no good. And then I saw an old childhood schoolmate of mine. He was the person collecting tickets as people exited the platform! I needed to hand him my ticket as proof that I had paid for the ride from Frankfurt.

"'What a pleasure to see you!' I said. 'Listen, there is a long story that goes with me not having a ticket. When you're done here, we'll have to have a couple of drinks and I'll explain everything to you and you will understand.' After we spoke of old times for a few minutes, he let me through the exit gate without turning in my ticket. I was so relieved. My troubles were over. And I was within five miles of home."

❧

Pete was in Holland. Once he made it through the exit line and entered the station, he finally cashed a traveler's check. Then he called home to let everyone know where he was, and, at long last, bought a ticket to Didam. Pete's parents and several of his siblings were waiting for him when he stepped off the train a short time later.

It had taken him days, but he was finally as close to home as he could get without actually being on the farm. One wonders what other travelers thought about Pete as he stepped off the train wearing an American military uniform. Whoever he was, he was immediately enveloped in hugs, tears, and laughter by a large, obviously Dutch family. Collecting his baggage, leaving the station, walking home – it was all a blur to Pete. He had not yet caught his breath when Wilma walked in the front door a few hours later. Instead of going to greet Pete at the station, Al, one of his brothers, had slipped out and left by motorcycle immediately after Pete called to say he was in the country. Wilma was with Al when he returned. She was the best welcome-home surprise he could have possibly mustered for his big brother.

"There was no end to the joy and happiness of that day," Pete says, reveling in the memory of their reunion.

Pete was 26 years old when he returned to Holland for the first time. It had been three-and-a-half years since he had seen any member of his family or Wilma. He had not talked with any of them in all that time, had not heard their voices, laughed or cried with them. His younger siblings had grown so much he hardly recognized them, a situation he at first found disconcerting. His parents seemed as buoyant and hardworking as ever; Wilma was obviously a competent woman with a job she loved; and the farm had further recovered from the scars of World War II. But the younger brothers and sisters – Pete could not get over how much they had changed.

Pete knew that he, too, had changed since he waved good-bye from the ship in Rotterdam. He had worked as a poor migrant across the Midwest and with the Catholic sisters in Indiana, learned to navigate life in America, crossed two oceans, and become fluent in English. He had been to Korea and back. He had put on some weight.

"All the letters had not kept up," Pete says. "There was so much to talk about with my family, deep into the night. And Wilma and I talked for hours. I will never forget it."

There was so much to say, so much to ask, so much to learn.

He hoped there was a marriage to arrange. Regardless, his leave would end in 30 days, no matter what was left unsaid or undone.

❧

By the time Pete returned for her, Wilma had been working for a few years as a counselor and life-skills teacher at various boarding schools for young girls who had been in trouble with the law. She did whatever she could to help girls get their lives back together as she was transferred from one school to another by the Dutch government. Like most of her countrymen, Wilma had never traveled around the Netherlands very much, and she found every location to be interesting; one school was even housed in an old castle. She talked with the girls, taught them how to clean and care for their rooms, ate all of her meals with them. She taught them how to bathe a baby and do domestic chores. It was a job she very much enjoyed. Though she occasionally visited her family on weekends when she could get away, she no longer lived at home.

Twenty-five years old and independent, Wilhelmina Aleida Maria Zents did not envision herself becoming a typical Dutch farmer's wife like her mother. She loved her parents, but she wanted something different from their traditional, small-farm lifestyle. Born on January 22, 1927, in the small town of Vorden, Wilma was the middle of nine children. With four brothers and four sisters, she did not feel compelled to help with the farm; her parents had plenty of help from their other children. Besides, working in a more professional setting pleased her.

Wilma had spent several weeks helping an older-than-normal group of girls prepare to make their First Communion when Al unexpectedly showed up on his motorcycle and told her Pete was home. He wanted to take her back to the farm to surprise Pete and the rest of the family. It was, after all, a Saturday. Surely she could leave for the rest of the weekend.

"I went home to Pete's house the Saturday night he got back. Al picked me up," Wilma explains. "But once I got there, I had to tell everybody that I had to go back to my job, to the girls, on Sunday morning.

"It was so incredibly difficult for me," she continues. "All the time I had been waiting for Pete, I had a good job. He had written and told me he would be back in August to get me. But he didn't know when in August. And here he was, on August 2, the very Saturday before my students were to make their First Communion! I had not expected him so early in the month and at first I didn't know what to do. It was difficult to tell Pete I was busy and had to finish with my group – I hadn't seen him in three-and-a-half years. But I also couldn't tell my girls that my boyfriend, or fiancé, had come home and that I wasn't going to finish with them. I was like their mother. And they had worked very hard. Even Pete's parents – even his mother, who was always so understanding – I don't think they liked it that I had this big commitment the very next day.

"The next morning, Pete took me back to school on the motor-cycle. I stayed with the children until after they had made communion and had a nice lunch to celebrate. Then I quit my job for good and left. The school had known I would leave once Pete got back. I had told them so. But they didn't know – I didn't know – it would be so soon after he returned, and none of us knew it would be so early in August. I only went back once to get my things."

As thrilled as Wilma was to have Pete back in Holland, his return threw her into a state of turmoil that lasted far beyond Sunday morning Mass with her students. Who was this man who had suddenly reappeared in her life after such a long absence, and what kind of claim did he have on her? They had only gotten engaged the day before he left the country – what did that mean three-and-a-half years later? Pete had gained weight and didn't even look like the person she had said she would marry back then. It was obvious he had matured, grown up. He now moved with the confidence of a man who knew what he wanted in life and who had a good idea of how to go about getting it. And there was one thing he knew for sure: He wanted to marry Wilma and take her back to America with him.

Pete's certainty and the fact that he had to leave before the month was out overwhelmed Wilma. She loved him. She had waited for him, as he had for her. But now that he was back in the country, she didn't know what to think or do. Her father remained opposed to the idea of marriage if it meant she would leave Holland; he was afraid Pete would not be able to support his daughter across the ocean. Both of her parents were afraid they would never see her again. What if they were right? Many Dutch emigrated with promises of coming back to visit their families, but very often the promises could not be kept because of finances. Wilma couldn't bear to think of saying good-bye to her family forever.

"Pete said to me, 'We should get married before I go back to America,' but I wasn't even sure I wanted to get married," Wilma says. "Deep down, I wasn't really expecting that. We had never talked seriously about marriage or having children or any of that. And my father did not want me to marry Pete. He did not forbid it, but he certainly expressed his doubts."

ᜎ

"My father was a good man," Wilma says, "though he wasn't much of a farmer as far as crops went. He was good with livestock. Other farmers would ask him if this or that cow was ready to sell or if they should wait for a while before they sold it. He would buy it himself if he thought he could sell it for a profit. He would often leave on his bicycle and go do business on other farms in our area. If he bought a cow, he would hire someone who owned a truck to move it for him."

Bart Zents was what the Dutch called a *nood nober,* which literally means "emergency neighbor" or "neighbor for emergencies." It was a bestowed honorific that carried with it a number of responsibilities: Bart could be asked to do almost anything at almost any time by friends in need. One did not campaign to be a *nood nober* - one was asked, and accepted the role as a sign of friendship, honor, and respect. Bart performed his duties with pride in the farming community where he and Marie, his wife, had for many years lived, farmed, and raised their children.

The way Wilma and her siblings saw it, their mother was pivotal to their father's success in being such a good "first neighbor," another apt description of all the work Bart did for others. He always came through in a time of crisis – the community could count on it. Among other things, Bart was one of the first people contacted (if not the very first) whenever death or tragedy struck among the many farmers he regularly visited and did business with. Usually, a family would ask in advance if they could turn to Bart if they ever found themselves needing help. That way, they knew, and he knew, that he was the person they would lean on. If and when that time came, Bart would be contacted as quickly as possible. Just as quickly, he would hurry by bicycle to the family's side. While the family grieved or discussed their situation with doctors or in some other way tried to remedy what was wrong, Bart alerted the surrounding community to the problem. He and other neighbors then worked together to make those arrangements necessary to keeping farms and families afloat in a wide variety of circumstances.

If a neighbor became seriously ill and could not manage his farm duties, Bart would organize volunteers to keep the farm up and running. If a decision needed to be made regarding the sale of an animal, he made it. His expertise and honesty were trusted. Sometimes, when a cow was badly bloated with gas, a condition that could kill it, Bart was called instead of a vet, especially if the animal went down in the middle of the night. With a long, sharp instrument, he would puncture the cow's stomach, thereby releasing deadly pressure on the animal's heart and lungs.

There were no funeral homes or funeral directors in Holland in those days, and burials traditionally took place a day or two after death. When someone died, the windows of the house where the deceased had lived were tightly shuttered as a sign that there were mourners and death within. Bart would personally clothe the dead body in a white gown and place it in a casket that remained at home until the day of the funeral, when friends and relatives gathered for Mass and subsequent burial in the shadow of the church. Understandably, wrapping his friends' bodies in their death clothes was often emotionally taxing for Bart. Whenever she could, Wilma's mother stepped in to help him. They worked together to ease the pain of the living and extend love and kindness toward the dead.

Marie was occasionally more involved when children were born. Babies were traditionally born at home, the mother aided by a midwife. As was the custom, women who had just given birth stayed in bed for 10 days. Marie was not a midwife, but she was a neighbor and a friend, and she walked or biked the distance to nearby farms whenever she could to visit mothers and their newborns.

Wilma loved and respected her parents and the roles they played both at home and in the community. What they thought of Pete mattered to her. She wanted them to be more than comfortable with the idea of her marrying him. She wanted their blessings. What they thought of her immigrating to America also mattered, for she did not want to leave them in emotional turmoil, burdened with worry. What Wilma's parents did for others was done without pay. Their advice and help, Bart's especially, was held in high esteem by so many neighbors. Surely their opinions of her and Pete should be considered.

❧

As Wilma continued to struggle with the idea of marriage and immigration, Pete somehow got her mother to agree with him that a wedding should take place before he left the country at the end of the month. Before Wilma fully realized what was happening, both her mother and Pete's mother were making wedding plans. Wilma was sure she loved Pete. She was just not sure what to do about it. The mothers' involvement further complicated her thought process.

"It was an awful time for me," she says. "All of a sudden the mothers were making plans, while I still didn't know if I even wanted to get married! I was a nervous wreck. For the first time in my life, I truly could not eat. I could not swallow and I could not sleep. I lost weight. I was totally confused. Getting married to an almost stranger. Going to America. It was just a little too much.

"I did tell Pete I wasn't sure about marrying him," she continues. "I explained why. I told him I didn't know what to do, what to think. He told me not to worry. He promised he would be a good husband and that he would take good care of me. He said he would be the best husband and father possible.

"Finally, in the third week of his leave I told Pete yes. I would marry him. I told him I still was not sure about the whole thing, but I would go along with the program. We set the date for the wedding to take place the following week, and arranged for family pictures to be taken at Pete's house the day after the wedding."

❧

It was now clear the marriage would take place, but Wilma's father continued to try to talk Pete out of returning to America. "You do not have to go back there to live," Bart told him. "You do not have to take Wilma there with you."

Besides running his own farm, which was much smaller than the Veldmans', and buying and selling cattle, Bart occasionally bought and sold small pieces of land. He managed what he had conservatively, and he had more money in the bank to show for it than did the

Veldmans. Like Pete's parents, Bart did not own the land he farmed or the house he lived in. But, he told Pete as wedding plans progressed, he currently owned a small piece of property that Pete could buy for himself and Wilma. To this day, Pete believes Bart would have given him the land if doing so would have persuaded Pete to live in Holland.

"But I just wasn't interested in staying," Pete says. "Wilma's father could not understand that. He would have never immigrated, would have never considered it. Neither of Wilma's parents ever left Holland as far as I know. They never had a passport, never traveled even to Germany. They never came to see us in America, which they could have done, even though they eventually had two daughters living in Indiana within a short distance of one another. They were very traditional Dutch, and they just would never travel like that.

"Holland was already changing when I went back," he continues. "It wasn't where I wanted to stay. There were always so many more rules and regulations there. There had to be, because there were so many more people. It wasn't like that in America. If you think you can accomplish something in America, you can try it. No one will stop you. There was so much more freedom in America. Within a month of arriving here, I could see there were so many more possibilities for me. I never seriously thought of going back to Holland to stay.

"Plus, in small towns in Holland, everyone knew so much about everyone else's business, and I didn't know if I wanted that. In America, you could just walk into a store and wander around, looking at all the merchandise. I liked that. That would never have happened in a small town in Holland. If you entered a store, the storekeeper would immediately approach you and want to know what you were interested in buying. If you weren't buying something, you did not feel you could look around. You weren't welcome."

Regardless of Bart's entreaties and reasoning, Pete was not going to back down. His mind was made up. He promised Wilma's parents what he had promised her: He would take good care of their daughter. He would send her home to visit them as soon as he could.

He would not, however, make a life with her in Holland.

To his and Wilma's rapidly developing wedding plans, Pete added another weighty task. He had to get Wilma a visa.

ॐ

Pete and Wilma were married on August 30, 1952. Pete says it was a great day, a wonderful finale to his furlough. The sky was blue, the temperatures warm. A wedding Mass, for immediate family only, was held at 10 a.m. at Saint Antonius van Padua, a small, old church in Kranenburg, a small community near Wilma's hometown. Brunch followed the ceremony. Pete wore a tuxedo and top hat and Wilma wore a pretty dress. The wedding party consisted of the bride and groom and two bridesmaids, Pete's sister Mary, and Wilma's sister Ada. Wilma's niece, Margo, was flower girl. According to Dutch custom, Pete did not have an attendant. In the evening, a dinner-dance was held across the street from the church for about 150 friends and extended family.

"Everyone had a wonderful time," Wilma says. "Friends and family celebrated with us in the evening. It would have been too much for our guests to ride bikes to Kranenburg in the morning and in the evening, and there would have been animals and farms to take care of in between. The way we did it, with a Mass for close family in the morning and a party for more people in the evening, was traditional. It was a nice celebration, but certainly nothing very glamorous. During the evening there were many skits, and of course we danced the traditional Dutch polonaise.

"I was happy to have Pete as my husband," she continues, "but I truly had mixed emotions. I was very sad and nervous to know he would leave in two days – without me – and I still wasn't too excited about going to America. But I was in love. I had decided I was going wherever Pete was going. However, I had to wait for my visa and would travel to America on my own, which was another scary thought."

Al had loaned Pete his motorcycle for the duration of his leave, which had made it easier for Pete to go back and forth between his and Wilma's family and to visit his scattered aunts and uncles and friends. By the day of the wedding, Wilma's father had given up on trying to change Pete's mind; Wilma had convinced herself that if Pete could make it as an immigrant in America, she could, too; and Pete had concluded that "motorcycles are dangerous."

"It was too long," Wilma still says of the three-and-half years it took Pete to return to Holland to marry her.

Pete did not plan it that way; he did not plan on being drafted or sent to Korea. Wilma had waited from March 1949 to August 1952 to know whether she would live her life with or without him. But despite her fears and questions, she was anxious to take the next step after Pete left her in Holland a few days following the wedding. She had made her decision: She was going to live as Pete Veldman's wife, in America, as soon as her visa came through.

And she was ready to get on with it.

ɞ

Pete did not get married in time to meet his furlough obligations. August 31, the day after the ceremony, was the official end of his leave. He should have reported back for duty at Camp Atterbury on that day. Obviously, he was nowhere near Indiana, but was instead spending every last minute he could with Wilma. Family pictures were taken, luggage was packed, and good-byes were said to his parents and siblings.

Shortly before the scheduled day of the ceremony, Pete had started sending his company commander a daily telegram with the message "no space available," meaning he had not been able to hitch an airplane ride back to the States. The telegram had no return address. On September 1, he and Wilma traveled to Frankfurt, where they spent a two-day honeymoon outside the military base. Pete was joyously AWOL. Once again, he started looking for the quickest way possible to hitch a plane ride across the Atlantic Ocean. (He always mentions that while they were in Frankfurt, he and Wilma "enjoyed some of the best Army food available.")

By the time Pete caught a flight back to the United States, Wilma and Pete's sister Willemien, who had traveled to Germany with them, were back in Holland. Wilma was once again living with her parents. Pete was once again traveling with his buddy John Kruis, who had also "extended" his leave long enough to attend the wedding. Pete and Kruis flew back to Westover Air Force Base, then made their way across the country to Camp Atterbury, with brief stops in South Bend and Elkhart, Indiana (Kruis' home). By the time they reported back for duty, they had been AWOL for a week. They were happy with the decisions they had made. They were also afraid they would not be allowed back on base. To their great relief, they discovered their fears were unwarranted.

"Getting back on base was easier than I anticipated," Pete says. "I told the captain my story, which he took a great interest in. Within half an hour we reached an agreement that I would add the days I had been AWOL to the end of my stay. He said he appreciated the telegrams I had sent, but that next time I should be sure to include a return address.

"With credit for good behavior and serving in an area of 'dangerous duty' in Korea, which was not all that dangerous, I was honorably discharged three weeks later. I was once again a free man. I could have stayed in the Army for six more months and become a U.S. citizen then instead of waiting a total of five years for citizenship, but I wasn't interested."

Meanwhile, Pete and Wilma were back to writing letters. However, they knew that this time their separation would be brief. As soon as Wilma's papers were processed and she received her visa, she, too, would leave from Rotterdam by ship.

"I had to wait six weeks," Wilma says, "but I really didn't mind too much. I spent those weeks at home with my parents, getting them used to the idea of me leaving. It helped a lot for me to do that."

Pete carefully wrote how Wilma would travel by train from New York City to Mishawaka, where he had returned to live shortly after his discharge. Upon leaving Camp Atterbury, he had traveled to Missouri to spend a few days with the Seesings, his original sponsors. Then he had made the trip back to Mishawaka where he was once again working for the Poor Sisters of Saint Francis. True to their word, the sisters had been "extremely good to him" during his 22-month career with the Army. They now promised to provide him and Wilma with a small apartment as long as he worked for them.

Pete felt that his life as an immigrant had so far been exciting. He had very few complaints, even about the tough times. He was convinced – as he awaited news of Wilma's departure from Holland – that his life in America would only improve once she was by his side.

 co

Three Oaks

Wilma boarded the *Ryndam* in early November 1952. As the ship pulled away from the dock and she watched her family grow small in the distance, she couldn't help but wonder if she would ever see them again. She knew Pete would do his best to get her back to Holland as soon as they could afford it, but no one could say what the future would bring. It had taken everything she had saved to pay for her passage to America. Who knew if she would ever have enough money to return home for a visit?

Other than the two days she had spent with Pete in Germany, Wilma had traveled very little outside of Holland. Indeed, she had traveled very little inside her diminutive country. Pete was all about expanding his horizons, and she was willing to go along with that, but she never would have immigrated to America were it not for him. Like Pete, Wilma was strong and ambitious. She had goals and dreams of her own regarding the kind of life she wanted to live. But, at the end of the day, she was a small-town farmer's daughter. Everything about crossing the ocean by herself made her nervous – it was all so new.

She was greatly relieved when after 11 days at sea the ship docked in New York City. "I've made it this far on my own," she thought to herself as she stood on deck and briefly took in the sights of the harbor. Her gaze did not linger on anything – she was too anxious for that. She was focused instead on the next step. All she had to do now was follow Pete's directions and find the train station. From there she would buy a ticket and board a passenger car that would take her almost 700 miles into the heart of America. Though she might stumble here and there, she spoke English well enough to transact basic business. That alone gave her courage.

"When we landed in New York City, we were sorted by categories," Wilma says. "American citizens, visitors, and immigrants. The immigrants were way at the end of the line. I was very nervous because I was in a different country and I knew I would have to get to the train station and then travel alone. I was really nervous.

"All of the sudden one of the immigration officers walked right up to me. 'Don't say a word,' he said quietly. 'Just follow me.' I didn't know what was happening. I just did as I was told. He moved me up to the front of the line, checked me out, and sent me on my way.

"I followed the other passengers, and when I exited the room, there was Pete waiting for me."

∽

I had written Wilma with instructions about how she should travel," Pete explains. "Meanwhile, I bought a like-new 1949 black Dodge automobile. It was my pride and joy. I bought it on payments for $1,200 from a priest at the convent. It had enough chrome on it for two cars. I didn't tell Wilma about it, though. I decided I would drive to New York to pick her up. There's nothing like a good surprise. I drove to Hoboken, where I had landed as an immigrant, on the first day. It was my first out-of-state driving experience. I stayed overnight in Hoboken and the next morning drove to the harbor.

"Wilma had not, like me, come over on a freighter with 100 immigrants," he continues. "It looked like there were over a thousand people waiting to get off the *Ryndam*. U.S. citizens were off and through the line first, naturally. I finally spotted Wilma, way in the back of the immigrants' line. After a while, it became clear I was going to lose the better part of a day waiting for her to get to the head of the line. I was looking around, searching for some sort of a shortcut when I noticed people coming off with special help. As one of the fellows helping a passenger came along, I asked him what the charge was for early release. Twenty dollars was the answer. I handed him a $20 bill and he said: Follow me! I pointed out who Wilma was. Ten minutes later she was off the boat, and soon after that we were on our way home.

"Meeting her was a huge surprise. She was so happy, and then there was the car. It was one of the best surprises I could have come up with. It was America at its best. Wilma and I had so much to talk about. The miles rolled by pretty fast. The next day we arrived back at the convent."

Wilma was stunned – and thrilled – to see Pete waiting for her as she exited the immigration line. The worry that had so burdened her dissipated the moment she saw him standing there. His confidence and resourcefulness boosted her flagging spirits. As long as she was with him, she'd be OK, even in a foreign country. If Pete was up for the challenge of making a life together in America, so was she. Those were some of the thoughts that raced through her mind as she watched him collect her few suitcases and a portable sewing machine before leading her away from the noise and confusion of the dock.

And then there was the car, which completely floored her.

"The car surprised me even more than Pete being there," Wilma laughs. "It never occurred to me that Pete would have bought a car. My parents never had a car their whole lives. Pete and I traveled back to Mishawaka. And we started our marriage."

❧

Pete and Wilma quickly settled into married life, living in two rooms above the laundry at the Poor Sisters of St. Francis convent in Mishawaka. They did not own a stick of furniture and their "apartment" had no cooking facilities. The newlyweds ate their meals with a few other employees and guests in a small dining room where they were served by the sisters.

"We now went everywhere together as a couple," Pete says. "It was great. Life had been exciting when I first got to America – there was so much to learn. But it was even better once Wilma was here with me."

Wilma did not waste much time wondering how, when, or where she would fit into American life once her feet were planted firmly on the ground. Psychologically, she never allowed herself the option of returning to Holland if America didn't suit her; as far as she was concerned, she was traveling down a one-way street as a newly married immigrant. Likewise, thinking and worrying too much about the details of the future was a luxury she felt she could not afford once she had safely crossed the Atlantic and was living with Pete in Mishawaka.

Wilma was afraid, she readily admitted, but she was also determined – as determined as Pete was – to make life in America work for the two of them. She conceded one significant difference between her experience and Pete's, however: She was not alone. She was traveling down that one-way road with Pete. He had paved the way.

Within a few days of her arrival, Wilma went looking for work. She and Pete were both surprised at how quickly she landed an office job at the Ball Band factory in Mishawaka.

Ball Band, a subsidiary of U.S. Rubber, spanned the St. Joseph River in downtown Mishawaka when Wilma arrived on the scene. The company, locally named because of its trademark on rubber boots manufactured in the late 1800s, produced rubber self-sealing fuel cells for military aircraft during World War II. At the height of the war, Ball Band employed about 10,000 people, many of them first- and second-generation European immigrants. It was still known as a good place for an immigrant to find employment when Wilma showed up in 1952. Some years later, the company was bought by Uniroyal. The factory's doors closed in the 1990s, and in June 2000 the facility was imploded by the city of Mishawaka.

Ball Band was a good place for Wilma to begin her professional life in America: The factory was strategically located in what was then a vibrant downtown area; it was a huge complex, and offered countless opportunities for meeting new people; and, from her first day on the job, Wilma was pushed to expand and refine her English-speaking skills.

"Wilma went looking for work on her second or third day in America," Pete recalls, "and found an office job in the mailroom at Ball Band right away. She delivered mail to different departments in the factory. That she had done well as a student learning English served her well. It was easier for her to get work than it was for me when I first came. She was so excited when she was first hired she forgot to ask what her salary would be.

"This was a totally new life for both of us. Times were great. We found new friends. It only took Wilma about two weeks before she took over our family finances. She was just good at that kind of thing. And she was totally happy in her work at Ball Band."

Perhaps not surprisingly, Pete's evenly paced work at the convent began to seem dull when he compared it to Wilma's office job in a bustling factory. She was learning something new every day, surrounded by people wherever she went. This was no longer true for him. For a while, living and traveling abroad with the Army had quenched his deep thirst for adventure and challenge. That thirst now returned with a vengeance.

As good as they had been to him, Pete needed a bigger challenge than working for the Poor Sisters of St. Francis, and he knew it.

಴

Pete started thinking about a new job, work that would both stimulate him and bring in a bigger income. He wasn't sure what he could find, but he remembered hearing while he was in the Army that if you lived in South Bend or Mishawaka, "Bendix was the place to be." From its beginning in 1924, the Bendix Corporation had produced everything from brake systems for General Motors vehicles to instrumental equipment for military aircraft during World War II to radios, phonographs, and televisions in the 1950s. Pete's Army buddies had said repeatedly that Bendix offered the best factory jobs around.

Now that Wilma had found worthwhile employment, Pete couldn't get the prospect of something new and different out of his mind. Furthermore, the word on the street in the winter of 1953 was that "Bendix needed workers everywhere." He decided he might as well start his search at the top.

"My work at the convent just didn't satisfy me anymore," he recalls. "I knew I had outgrown it. All the stories I had heard while I was in the Army, all the opportunity the soldiers had talked about, didn't fit what I was doing. Working in the garden and the orchard, taking care of the milk cows, working in the boiler room, driving for the sisters – it was no longer enough. My restless nature got the best of me and I decided to give Bendix a try.

"I filled out an application, went for an interview, and everything went just fine," he continues. "I was going to be a Bendix employee. And then, at the very end of our conversation, the interviewer asked me something about my nationality. He couldn't believe it when I told him I wasn't a naturalized American citizen, couldn't understand how I could have an honorable discharge from the Army if I wasn't a citizen. He apologized over and over and said how sorry he was, but he couldn't hire me after all. It didn't matter that he had just told me I could have the job. He couldn't hire me once he knew I wasn't a U.S. citizen. I got angry and finally told him not to worry about it. As I walked out of his office I said to him over my shoulder: It will be your loss.

"From Bendix I went down the street to the second-best factory job in town, at Studebaker. They didn't seem to care if I was a citizen or not, and I got a job with them very easily. I started building cars on the line a few days later, as soon as I finished up things at the convent.

"It was a good thing, in the end, that I didn't get that job at Bendix," Pete adds after a pause, "though it was considered the best factory job around. I learned a lot about how not to run a business by working at Studebaker."

℘

Pete's employment with the Catholic sisters ended well, which was important to him. They knew their Dutch friend would not return to the convent to work, and they were sad to see him go. Pete left the convent grateful for the many ways the sisters had helped him over the years – from the time he quit migrant work through his stint with the Army to welcoming Wilma and providing them with a roof over their heads.

Pete and Wilma moved out of their two rooms over the laundry as soon as they found a place convenient to their factory jobs. By March 1953 they were cooking for themselves in a second-floor apartment located on 3rd Street in Mishawaka. It was, Pete says, the perfect location for them. He drove their car to work at the Studebaker Corporation in South Bend while Wilma walked 12 blocks to her job at Ball Band. She remembers friends pushing her to take the bus to and from work rather than walk so far. But she had grown up walking and biking and didn't mind the hike. She was, in fact, happy for the exercise. And she had more important things to do with her earnings.

"I would never spend even the little bit it cost to take the bus if I could walk," she says. "Bus fare wasn't what I wanted to use our money for."

It didn't take Pete long to learn he wasn't cut out for factory work, even when it paid well and the work was not the least bit strenuous.

"Working at Studebaker was the worst time in my professional life," he says. "Quite frankly, I hated the place. I worked on the line. Doing the same work over and over on cars coming through the line wasn't for me – it turned the American dream into a nightmare. I quickly figured out factory work wasn't what I wanted to do for the rest of my life. There was absolutely no challenge in doing the same work every day. There was a board at the factory where vacancies were posted if someone was ill and couldn't come in. I would take those jobs whenever I could, just for variety and to meet new people.

"I also didn't like the union way of doing things," Pete continues. "I worked two shifts whenever I could for the extra pay, but I couldn't stand being there. Studebaker totally neglected paying attention to management. They worked for costs, plus 10 percent. The more something cost, the more the company made.

"There were guards everywhere, while people came and went all day long. There were always so many people on the line and such little work. It was a horrible atmosphere to work in. I was on a line with maybe 100 other people and no one really did any work. And then one day someone tapped me on the shoulder and asked to see my union card. I had to stop what I was doing immediately. Two hours later I was a member of the union."

☙

What eventually became the Studebaker Corporation was begun in South Bend, Indiana, in the mid-1800s by two brothers, Henry and Clement Studebaker. With a modest amount of cash and a set of blacksmith tools, the brothers began building horse-drawn industrial wagons and carriages. (Abraham Lincoln rode to the theater in a Studebaker carriage the night he was assassinated.) For almost 20 years in the early 1900s, the company produced both wagons and automobiles. In partnership with the Everett-Metzger-Flanders Company of Detroit, Studebaker was unique in moving from horse-drawn vehicles to electric- and eventually gasoline-driven automobiles. Though the company struggled during the Depression, it did not fold. Sales rebounded during World War II when the company produced large numbers of military trucks and airplane engines.

After the war, Studebaker quickly introduced new car designs that were well-received by the public. But by the time Pete found employment at the large complex, which covered several downtown South Bend city blocks, the company was headed for financial disaster due to rising labor costs, poor quality control, and stiff competition from Detroit automobile manufacturers.

Though Pete had never before worked in industry and knew very little about American capitalism, he saw the handwriting on the wall. He told Wilma repeatedly that the company couldn't last, would never make it. Studebaker, he said, paid better than any other place he had ever worked, yet the employees were unhappy and many put in as little effort as possible, just enough to get by. Everything about the social and professional climate of the place struck Pete as wrong, so much so that he began looking for other work.

"I could see my work was coming to an end," he says. "It was very obvious Studebaker was not going to make it. The management was terrible and so was their product. They didn't even make a good car! With all these people working for them, they still ended up with poor quality. I could always get overtime, which paid very well. Sometimes I did maybe 10 minutes of real work in four hours of overtime.

"Nothing made sense to me," he continues, "but the pay was too good to just walk away from, and I decided I would stay there as long as I could. However, I began looking around for another job on the side.

"Then, in the summer of 1953, all in one evening, 8,000 people were laid off. I was one of them. I was working overtime that night, and it wound up being my last day on the job. When 8,000 people are suddenly out of work in a town the size of South Bend, well, it's an unbelievable sight. People were scurrying around everywhere the next morning, trying to find work."

Because of Pete's foresight about what would eventually happen at Studebaker, he wasn't one of the thousands hustling for any kind of job he could find to pay the bills. He had already found one, had, in fact, been working weekends and whenever else he could at Hummer Farm Equipment in Lakeville, Indiana.

Located 11 miles south of South Bend, Pete found Hummer Farm Equipment "a pleasant place to work, with good coworkers, but, sadly, no Studebaker pay." Pete drove there and began working full-time the day after his job ended at Studebaker. In particular, Pete liked Mr. Hummer, who took a heartfelt interest in both Pete and Wilma and who gave Pete some good advice on advancing his career. Wilma remembers Mr. Hummer as a congenial man who even visited them socially, something that would never have happened in more class-conscious Holland.

"Someone who was your boss in Holland would have never treated you in quite the way Mr. Hummer treated us," she recalls. "I was really very surprised. We were very poor and owned very little, but he treated us like we were friends. It meant a lot to us."

∽

Wilma continued to work at Ball Band through the summer and fall of 1953, while Pete got up every day and drove to Lakeville. Though their income took a significant hit when Pete was laid off at Studebaker, they were saving little by little for the next thing. They weren't sure what that would be professionally, but they knew personal change was on the horizon, for Wilma was expecting their first child before Christmas. They had talked about it, and together they had decided that it was important that they both bring in a salary for as long as they possibly could. They hoped to have a large family, which would probably mean less of an income for Wilma for at least several years. Between now and then, she needed to work as much as she could for as long as she could.

"I never could see myself or Pete being satisfied with factory work forever," Wilma explains. "But I didn't know what we were going to eventually do, neither of us knew. Pete would talk to Mr. Hummer about it. Meanwhile, we both just kept working."

Through her contacts and responsibilities at work, Wilma was rapidly becoming acclimated to America. She handled most of the cultural changes well, straightforwardly and with a work ethic that equaled Pete's in every way. Her fear of what the future might hold, especially with a child on the way, was not so overwhelming as long as she and Pete were facing it together.

"I was in America, and more than anything else, I wanted to be American," she says. "I did not want to be old-fashioned Dutch, like I thought my parents were. I wanted to work and get through the transition of becoming American. Working was easier for me than spending a lot of time thinking about it. That was my way of dealing with how difficult it was.

"Within a few days of my arrival, I had my job at Ball Band," she continues. "I had had four years of basic English instruction in school in Holland before I came, but I wanted to really learn the language. Ball Band was a great place for that.

"I was just ready to go to work right away. It never occurred to me not to work. Also, when we were living at the convent, we didn't even have a kitchen, and I had to have something to do with my time. By the time we left the convent, I was beginning to learn my way around on my own. By the time Pete was working for Mr. Hummer, I, too, was thinking about what our next step would be. It was clear Pete needed a better-paying job than what Mr. Hummer could give him. It was something we thought about together.

"From the very beginning, I found Americans to be so friendly, so generous with their time, so helpful. People immediately came to me and said, 'Can I help you go to an interview? Can I help you with this or that?' Maybe if I had not been so set on becoming American, our children would have learned to speak more Dutch when they were growing up. But Pete and I didn't even speak much Dutch to each other – we spoke in English so we would both get better at it. And, then again, immigrant children need to become American.

"The hardest thing for me about immigrating wasn't learning the language or figuring out the American culture. I started working on those things right away. Pete helped me. The hardest thing for me was missing my family. I was homesick. I just missed them so much. I never even talked to my parents on the telephone. It would have been much too expensive. It also would have taken two days to put a call through. My parents and I wrote letters back and forth, usually once a week, for many, many years. I missed lots of events along the way, births and deaths and weddings and funerals and illnesses. But we did the best we could."

જી

Assembling farm equipment in Lakeville got Pete to thinking seriously about farming. He and Wilma had been talking since before he left Studebaker about what he could do next that would set them up financially. His options were limited: Working for Mr. Hummer did not pay well enough, and Pete never again wanted to work in a factory if he could help it. Should he and Wilma go into some kind of business together? Operate a dry cleaner? Run a small store or restaurant? What about farming, his original plan? Whatever it was, he could not undertake anything that required a large outlay of cash, since "money was the one thing lacking in the equation."

But farming – Pete's mind kept going back to it. The work was varied, the seasons different, he knew a thing or two about crops and animals and orchards and land. He doesn't recall Mr. Hummer "advising him to give farming a try." The older man probably had a better idea than did Pete about the unique difficulties facing small-time American farmers; he also knew from their conversations just how badly Pete wanted to make a profitable living. But when the possibility of leasing a 220-acre dairy farm in Three Oaks, Michigan, came up, Pete and Wilma decided to give it a try. Besides milk, the farm produced hay, wheat, and corn. Pete was convinced that farming could be what he and Wilma were looking for. Farming could be their ticket to the American dream. The owner of the farm assured them that if all went well – as everyone expected – the farm would one day belong to the young immigrants expecting their first baby.

ॐ

Pete quit his job working for Hummer Farm Equipment in November 1953. Wilma left Ball Band; they said good-bye to their friends in South Bend and Mishawaka and to Saturday night social events at the YWCA; and they moved about 25 miles west into a tiny, two-bedroom farmhouse across the road from a large dairy barn in Three Oaks, Michigan. The house, a stove, and a refrigerator were included in the lease. The little furniture Pete and Wilma owned fit into the back of a borrowed pickup truck.

Pete was characteristically optimistic about the future. From his perspective, both he and Wilma had some experience with dairy cattle. All they had to do was make a go of it, and for the right price the operation would be theirs. The owner had promised them that neither of his sons, who were both in the military, would ever want the farm as their own. His boys were not interested in living the hardscrabble life of an American farmer. Pete knew that it would be hard work, but that did not scare him, for both he and Wilma were hard workers. Besides, farming was in their blood.

Wilma, too, was hopeful about what the move would bring. She was also a little anxious. As farmers, their income would always be uncertain. Their profit would likely fluctuate from year to year. It would depend on the economy, the price of milk, the health of the cows – even the weather. The child she was carrying was due in about six weeks. She and Pete were about to become first-time parents; they were setting up house in a small, tight-knit community; they were beginning a new career. It was all a little too much for someone who craved stability. Truth be told, she knew Pete was more nervous than he let on.

The day Pete and Wilma vacated their apartment in Mishawaka the weather was cold and gray. Wilma remembers riding along, wondering if their house in Three Oaks would be adequately heated. Much to her relief, the farmer whom she and Pete were leasing from lived in a large farmhouse across the street, next to the dairy barn. After she and Pete began emptying the truck of their belongings, the farmer's wife came over with a meal to welcome them. She had also cleaned the house and turned on the heat. It was a kindness Wilma has never forgotten, one of many that continued as long as she and Pete rented from the couple. Though she and Pete did not keep a vegetable garden, the owners did, and Wilma remembers the wife periodically showing up with fresh vegetables or other small food items. She had a knack for appearing, gifts in hand, whenever Wilma was especially pressed for time, taking care of babies or trying to relieve Pete of some of the burden of running the place by himself.

Immediately after Pete's arrival, the farm owner took him to the barn and began teaching him the nuances of running a dairy. Their business agreement was a 50/50 split. The farmer owned the land, the house, the barn, and all of the equipment. He made any purchases necessary and paid all of the bills. He bought and sold the cows and paid for hay, corn, and other seed. These and any other expenses he covered – fertilizer, pesticides, medicine for the cows, occasional veterinarian visits, etc. – were deducted from the overall profit.

"The owner took care of the business side of the farm," Wilma says. "Pete did all the physical labor. We went into it with that understanding. Whatever profit was made after all the bills were paid was split between us and the owner."

No matter what they thought they knew beforehand, the reality of running the farm was a shock to both Pete and Wilma. They quickly discovered they were no longer in Holland, where hired help was inexpensive.

"Thirty cows kept us working seven days a week," says Pete. "It was not like milking a few cows for family use or to bring in a little extra cash. The American way of farming was just so different from the Dutch way. In Holland we worked a variety of intensive-care crops on a 100-acre spread. We had two live-in helpers and five or more hired workers coming in on a daily basis. Plus, there was my dad and me and some of my brothers as they got older. In Three Oaks, it was Wilma and me. We occasionally traded a little outside work with a neighbor who also farmed, but not much. We had tractors and some other more modern equipment, but none of it really made up the difference in the long hours we put in every day.

"In Holland, we worked hard, but farming never interfered with our social life," he continues. "In Three Oaks, we had no social life. You can't trade off milking with another farmer if you run a dairy. Milk cows aren't very agreeable. They don't like having strangers come in. Basically, there was never a day, or morning, or evening that we really had off.

"Milking cows comes around twice a day, whether you want to do it or not. The cows are there – waiting for you, no matter what – at 5 o'clock every morning and again at 5 o'clock every evening. They are always looking for you. You can't not be there. They have to be milked by someone, which was me or Wilma or both of us. And milking 30 cows takes quite a bit of time. Neither Wilma or I had anywhere near this many cows when we were growing up."

❧

It was during their time in Three Oaks that Wilma and Pete's work-life became inseparably entwined with their marriage and family life. Working together on the farm was a matter of necessity: It took two of them to keep up with the dairy. That they have worked together ever since has had much more to do with love, respect, and expediency. Today, they recognize and applaud the unique strengths the other brings to the table, strengths first glimpsed in a cold barn blanketed by Michigan darkness.

"Wilma and I became true business partners on the farm," Pete says. "When I later went into the automotive business, there was no question but that she was going to be right in there with me. She was always right back in a week or two after she had a baby. You couldn't keep her out!"

In reality, Wilma never wanted to milk cows – it was something she had watched her mother do every day when she was growing up – but she was willing to do it if she must because it was so important that Pete find work that both satisfied him and kept them financially afloat. Her mother had milked their few dairy cows by hand, which Wilma knew how to do. She and Pete used a milking machine the owner taught them to use. Even so, milking was a chore that could not be shrugged off, a chore that ate up a large chunk of time at the beginning and end of every day.

"My mother never went into the fields. Most women in Holland didn't," Wilma says, "but she helped with feeding and milking and anything else that needed to be done in the barn. Of course, my father never had 30 cows at a time! I did not work on the farm much at home. I wasn't crazy about farming. I knew I liked business more. But I needed to help Pete. We needed to make a living that would support a family."

❧

Pete and Wilma's first child, a son they named Tom, was born on December 19, 1953, not long after they moved to the farm. Before Tom arrived, one of Wilma's sisters, Ans, came from Holland to help her. A nurse, Ans was single and adventuresome. After spending a few months with Pete, Wilma, and baby Tom, she moved into the home of an elderly man in Three Oaks to help care for him. From there, she moved to Goshen, Indiana, to work in a nursing home. As much as she could, she spent her free days with Wilma. At one point during what turned into a yearlong visit to America, Pete tried to teach Ans how to drive. He gave up after she stopped the car so forcefully that his shoulder cracked the car's windshield.

"I was sitting sideways, without a seatbelt, instructing her," Pete says. "I taught many people how to drive over the years, but I gave up on Ans."

"Pete told her to 'Stop right now!' She did what he said," is Wilma's explanation of her sister's lack of skill.

Wilma cared for Tom and milked the cows pretty much on her own from the time Ans moved out. She would run across the road and begin milking in the wee hours of the morning while Tom slept. Every 30 minutes or so she would run back to the house to check on him. Every minute she spent milking by herself freed Pete for other chores that could not be done with a baby in tow. When Tom outgrew infancy and slept less, Wilma bundled him up, placed him in a stroller, and took him to the barn with her.

"Milking rooms have to be kept sparkling clean," Wilma says. "So it was no problem to take Tom with me. But when he was about 18 months old our second son, Dave, was born. I had no choice after that – Pete had to help me more. Working together, with two babies in the stroller, we managed to get it done.

"Looking back, I don't really know how I did it, but I did. Ever since Three Oaks, I've always worked with Pete, often out of an office at home, and sometimes for only a few hours a day, but there has never been a long period of time when I haven't been involved in what he is doing."

While leasing the farm, Pete took some evening agricultural courses on the G.I. bill. He enjoyed both the learning and the little bit of extra income the bill provided after the classes were paid for. He wasn't bringing in much money when he considered all the hours he worked. Nonetheless, he remained optimistic about his future as a farmer. Occasionally, however, he and Wilma questioned other decisions they had made together, decisions that had seemed right at the time but left them wondering afterward. More than once, they wondered if they had badly misinterpreted the American culture. For instance, as a matter of principle, they bought only what they could pay for with cash. Because cash was always in "short supply" for them as a young couple, the owner of the farm continued to purchase whatever was needed to keep the operation up and running. Periodically, Pete and the owner sat down and settled up their accounts. It was a painless way to do business as far as Pete was concerned: The farmer was an honest man, no time was wasted on unnecessary paperwork or trips to the bank, and Pete was not in debt. But as a result, he and Wilma never established any credit with local institutions.

"The few things we had to buy, we paid for with cash," Wilma explains. "We were so excited when we bought our first couch, which we paid cash for, that we sat on it for about 24 hours straight! We thought we were going about this the right way.

"But then, when Pete wanted to buy some items for the farm without going through the owner, no one would loan us a very small amount of money, not even the bank in tiny little Three Oaks. That's when we began to learn that you have to buy some things on credit in order to establish credit."

Living within their means – paying as they went – did not create a lot of conflict for Pete and Wilma. It was the kind of example their parents had lived out before them, especially Wilma's father. But Pete began to wonder if strict frugality was always the best practice. He needed to see a greater monetary return on the hours he and Wilma were putting in if he was going to buy the farm, and he was ready to begin personally investing in its operation in order to do so. But he was caught. He couldn't ask the owner to fund new ideas or equipment that might not yield an immediate profit, he and Wilma had little cash of their own to spend, and he couldn't get a loan. Despite the long days, Pete liked farming. He just couldn't figure out how to make it work financially.

"Farmers have such demands for their money," he says. "Farmers are always in need of money. Even if they are rich, their money is in the farm, in the land. It's not in the bank. I kept trying to come up with something Wilma and I could do that would help us financially. We were working very hard for very little money. The land itself was poorly drained and difficult to work, but I was sure we would make it somehow. We just needed a lucky break and the place would be ours."

❧

The year 1955 marked the beginning of Pete and Wilma's second winter on the farm. Before the season was out, Pete's sister Dolly and her husband, Henk, came to visit. Their stopover was a welcome respite for Pete and Wilma. Dolly and Henk helped with baby Tom, who was now a year old, and with the daily milking responsibilities. But they had not just come to America to renew family ties. They were immigrating to Canada, where they also planned to buy a farm and carry on the Veldman family tradition.

After several days of catching up on family news, Dolly and Pete drove to Ontario to look for possible jobs and housing, while Henk stayed behind in Three Oaks to help Wilma with the dairy operation and other farm responsibilities. The two couples had decided to put "all of Pete's immigrating experience" to good use. His knowledge of what kinds of jobs might work for his sister and brother-in-law and his proficiency with English were superior in every way to that of the new Dutch immigrants. That and the fact that he had a car made him their natural point person. Who better to turn to than Pete? He had been where they now stood, had struggled on his own to gain a foothold in a completely new culture. Pete stepped easily and willingly into the role of family leader, a position he would hold for numerous family members over the next several years.

Pete was personally disappointed with Canada. He returned to Three Oaks, the farm, Wilma, and Tom convinced that he had made the right decision about where they should live. He still needed to figure out how to make more money as a farmer, but he was convinced he was in the right place.

"As time passed, it always looked to me like we had made the better decision," he says. "America was, to me, the better place to live. I never got the urge to move across the border."

❧

Another family member, Pete's brother Ben, arrived in Three Oaks in early spring 1955, just as Pete was preparing for his second season of plowing.

"He came to see what America was like," Pete says, "and he showed up just in time. He was a great support to me on the farm. Between us, plowing and planting went into overtime."

Ben knew how to plow, plant, harvest, and everything in between. But he was also fairly well-educated and had a good mind. Before long he was trying to figure out how to remain in the Midwest as a college student, a move Pete strongly encouraged. Meanwhile, the two brothers began a new venture, injecting anhydrous ammonia into cornfields for use as fertilizer. Pete bought the specialized equipment required for the job from an independent distributor in New Carlisle, Indiana. The agent supplied Pete and Ben with a list of farmers who were interested in trying the product before they invested in the equipment themselves.

"Tom Lake, the man we bought the equipment from, needed additional sales. I needed the extra income. And Ben needed to pay for school," Pete says. "I've always liked win-win situations, and this was a triple win.

"Three Oaks was a very pleasant community and it seemed like we were well-accepted," he continues. "With great local support, Ben began summer school at the University of Western Michigan. He did the anhydrous ammonia work on the weekends and during school vacations. He traveled to farms all over the area. Then, in the fall, he enrolled as a full-time student, eventually earning a degree in mechanical engineering.

"In July 1955 Wilma and I had another son, Dave. Things seemed to be going smoothly for us. It seemed like we were doing everything well. But it was a very dry summer, and we just weren't making enough money. We were working hard, and with Ben's help, we were doing well enough on the farming side. But the price of milk, our largest product, wasn't very high. A farmer's character is really tested when the weather and falling prices cause an already low income to go down by the day. Still, we were determined to keep at it.

"But then, when we had been on the farm for almost two-and-a-half years, something very unexpected happened. One of the owner's sons came home from the military and told his father that he wanted to run the farm after all.

"We couldn't believe it. We had been promised this would never happen. Meanwhile, the price of an acre of land had gone up tremendously since we had first moved to Three Oaks. We knew there was no way we could buy the farm – not that farm or any other.

"I could see I was not, after all, going to be successful at farming in America. It was really very disappointing for both Wilma and me. After two-and-a-half years of hard work and little money, we knew we needed to do something different. We weren't sure what that would be. But as confusing as it was, we never considered going back to Holland."

Pete and Wilma started looking for new work before the spring of 1956. Their original agreement with the farm owner had been that Pete could stay on the farm long enough to harvest any spring crop he planted. He and Wilma knew there would be no planting that spring. The owner was not going to toss them and their two young boys out of the house without a place to live, but they needed to find work and move out as quickly as possible. They had no idea what they should try next. Once again, they began casting about for various, inexpensive business opportunities. They considered everything they came across, including running an ice-cream shop, but nothing seemed to suit their likes, abilities, and bank account until they stumbled upon a service station for rent in South Bend.

At the time, Pete says, there were service stations on the corner of every South Bend city block – and almost anywhere else one happened to look. They were all full-service, which appealed to Pete's friendly personality. He had received a minimal amount of automotive training in the Army, enough to convince a gasoline supplier that he could run a service station, but not enough to really know what he was doing.

"I'd been interested in trucks ever since I'd been in the service," Pete explains, "but I still didn't know a thing about engines. Mechanical knowledge did not come easily for me in the Army or anytime afterward. I was better at sales.

"However, nothing else seemed right as Wilma and I looked around for new work, and we finally decided to give the service station a try. If you had just a little bit of money, a supplier would put you in a station. I knew I could pump gas in cars, check oil and change tires, things like that. And Wilma liked the idea of a business."

Standard Oil owned the service station that caught Pete and Wilma's eye. The company reviewed Pete's application, sent him for two weeks of bare-bones automotive training, and set him loose running the small, new-looking site on Western Avenue.

"Looking back, it was good that the decision about leaving the farm was made for us," Pete says. "It was out of our control – we couldn't stay in Three Oaks. We were forced to look for a different opportunity. I guess you could say that, in the end, it was our lucky day.

"Of course, we didn't think that at the time."

There were details Standard Oil failed to divulge. For starters, the service station Pete and Wilma rented was in an extremely competitive part of town, with 24 stations in a five-mile stretch. Pete realized as soon as he opened shop that another station directly across the street was going to be a fierce opponent.

"A man had run the place across from us for many years," Pete says. "Although his son had taken over for him by the time we signed on, it was clear he would be an aggressive competitor."

Wilma found the move and Pete's new job unsettling. She was alone for long stretches of time with two small boys in a house she and Pete had rented around the corner from the service station. Running the station, Pete says, was like taking a crash course in Money Management 101. And the long hours he worked were like "being on the farm all over again."

They had been warned, Wilma thought to herself as she waited for Pete to come home late every night. They had been warned by a complete stranger right after they signed the rental agreement. She and Pete had gone to a discount appliance store one night to buy a stove for their small kitchen. When the owner of the store asked where the stove should be delivered, Pete gave him the address, adding that the house was close to a service station they had just leased. The owner had thrown back his head in disbelief.

"You suckers!" he had said without apology. "Don't you know that everybody goes broke at that station? Nobody makes it past a year." Night after night, the words rang in Wilma's ears as she waited for Pete to come home.

❧

IV

South Bend

Brothers, Sisters, Service Stations

From 1956 to 1959 Pete pumped gasoline, cleaned windshields, checked oil, and balanced tires – always with a smile – at 3520 Western Avenue in South Bend. The station limped along for the first several months, with Pete putting in longer and longer hours. He walked to work early in the mornings and walked home late at night. Alone for long stretches of time, he patiently waited on customers who stopped by primarily to check out the new immigrant owner. Occasionally, Wilma strolled over with the boys for a visit. She handled the station's bookkeeping from her kitchen table while the little ones napped or slept at night. It was a simple enough task, one she greatly preferred to milking cows.

"I did the little bookkeeping that we had," Wilma says. "I could do it in an hour or less, there was so little money brought in. I remember Pete calling me one day to say he had just filled up a Buick. That was a big deal. A $100 day in sales was a good day. A $200 day was a great day. Out of that, we had to pay our lease and pay for the gasoline when it was delivered to the pump. I worried if we would make it."

While Pete concentrated on getting the service station up and running, his brother Ben continued injecting anhydrous ammonia into

Indiana and Michigan cornfields whenever he was free from school. That small side-venture was the first of many for Pete and his siblings. Over the course of the next few decades, Pete grew adept at pursuing anything that might benefit himself and help a brother or sister get established in business, reach an educational goal, or simply have authentic, paying work. His entrepreneurial gaze sharpened as one sibling after another followed what became a well-worn path to South Bend's west side.

From the time Ben moved in with Pete and Wilma in Three Oaks in 1955, to 1965, when Pete's last brother, Ted, left Holland for the United States, Pete scrambled to find work for his extended family. His siblings faced their own hurdles with language, education, and culture, but they arrived in America knowing they had a job and a bed if they needed it. Most importantly, they knew they had Pete and Wilma's pragmatic, unshakable support. Some of the siblings worked for Pete temporarily. Some became business partners and worked with him for years. At one point, a service station and its many spin-off businesses were owned by four Veldman brothers and a brother-in-law. Even then, Pete remained on the lookout, scanning the horizon for new opportunities that would help support the many families and individuals looking to him to lead the way.

From urging his father to buy a tractor for the farm in Holland to acquiring the "keepsake" business when he was stationed in Korea to considering how to increase his profit as a dairy farmer in Three Oaks to living today as a successful, semiretired business owner in South Bend – Pete has always had his eye on the next best thing. He has also always been a realist. No one – then or now – would describe Pete as ruthless, but from his beginning days as an entrepreneur, his acumen and instinct for self-preservation made him willing to cut loose any side-business that was no longer making a profit. During the years he leased one service station after another, he never held on to any side-venture longer than it was financially viable. Not paying attention to the bottom line was an indulgence he felt he could not afford.

There were no guarantees. Back in the summer of 1956, when Pete was starting out in business for himself, he was not sure he could hang on to the 3520 Western Avenue station. He hoped he had left farming behind for good, but only time would tell. Meanwhile, Ben paid for college via the anhydrous ammonia side-business until farmers began buying the equipment for themselves, convinced of the product and its results. Once Pete saw what was happening, he quickly sold the fertilizer applicator that had served Ben so well. But now there was a new problem: Pete had, by this point in the summer, hired a few part-time employees to help him during odd hours at the station. Ben, however, could not make tuition payments on such a meager income, and Pete could not afford a full-time employee other than himself. Searching for ideas, Pete eventually decided to keep the station open 24 hours a day – and he hired Ben to work every night he was home from college. Besides helping his brother, being open all night was an inventive move that sharpened the station's competitive edge.

"Being open 24 hours put us on the map," Pete says, "and it helped Ben pay for college."

Though he returned to school in the fall, Ben continued working the night shift on weekends and during longer breaks until he moved from Western Michigan University to the University of Michigan to get a degree in mechanical engineering. U of M was too far away for weekend commuting, but Ben returned to South Bend to work with Pete between semesters and every summer until he completed his education.

❧

As the days and weeks and months passed, it became clear to Pete that running a successful business was not going to be a simple matter of determination or hard work. No matter how long his days were or how late the station stayed open, it would never be enough. He had to find a way to improve the odds that were stacked so heavily against him. He had to do something to bring in more business. About this time, two serendipitous events happened that saved him from becoming another name in a long list of hapless owners of the Standard Oil service station at 3520 Western Avenue: Pete's brother Al decided to give working with his eldest brother a try, and the Indiana Toll Road was opened as far west as South Bend.

By Christmas 1956, Al and his wife, Liesbeth, had rented a small house about three blocks from the station. They moved from Canada, where Al had tried unsuccessfully for a few years to find dependable work. Their relocation to South Bend was prompted by mutual need – theirs and Pete's – for Al brought with him the kind of automotive mechanical skill Pete so sorely lacked. Though Pete was confident he could eventually bring in enough work to make the move worthwhile, he had told Al before he left Canada that he could not guarantee his salary. The move was a big commitment for both brothers.

"My personal mechanical knowledge was such a failure," Pete says. "I couldn't believe how little I really knew once I started running the service station. I got along fine with the basics of full service, but when it came to mechanics, I was lost. I just wasn't suited for it, and I didn't know what I was going to do to keep the business afloat. I was searching for ideas. There was only one thing I was sure of: I was not going to fail.

"Meanwhile, Al had been in Canada for a few years, trying to get established," he continues. "But because he was an immigrant and did not know the language, he was doomed to low-paying, labor-intensive jobs. The last job he had there was working in tobacco.

"Al's personality is more lighthearted than mine. He's always had lots of fun. He wasn't as affected by the Depression or World War II as I was. Whenever there were German troops staying on the farm during the Occupation, Al could be found on top of the trucks, between the soldiers, evaluating what to steal from them next. He was too young for them to think of him as anything other than a pleasant little brother. Fortunately, he never got caught. He missed several years of education because of school closings during the war. He never did get caught up on his education, but he has always had lots of street smarts, which have served him well.

"Al came down from Canada to visit us and to take a look at the station. He thought it was heaven on earth. He loved to work on cars and had great mechanical skill though he had not been to school for it. He saw right away that working as a mechanic in a service station could be a great opportunity for him. He got all excited and said, 'I don't know how long it will take, but I'll be here.' A couple of months later, Al and Liesbeth moved to South Bend for good."

Between the two farm-bred brothers, a kernel of hope that the business would survive took root. With patience, attention, and the right conditions, they hoped to grow the small Standard Oil station into a viable full-service operation. Thus began a close business partnership that would last for 18 years.

"Although we were only four years apart by birth, it took us many years to figure out that our age difference wasn't really that great," Pete says. "We worked together for so many years. It was great. Al had his area of expertise, and I had mine.

"One big problem was solved," Pete continues. "I had no trouble bringing in mechanical work that needed to be done, and Al enjoyed doing it. I did most of the selling and service at the pumps. Al did his work in and outside the station's two service bays. And until he graduated from college, Ben was with us when he was home from school, working at night. He got a lot of studying done that way."

Meanwhile, the Indiana Toll Road opened an entry/exit ramp in Roseland, a small, incorporated town near downtown South Bend and the University of Notre Dame. The toll road is a major highway artery that runs 157 miles across northern Indiana, connecting the Hoosier state to Illinois in the west and Ohio and beyond in the east.

In the late 1950s, drivers from all three states were waiting for the road to open near them.

Pete knew that Western Avenue businesses would not benefit from toll-road traffic in Roseland; the access ramp was too far away to do him or his numerous competitors any good. He was, therefore, stunned by the bonanza of his station being first in line for Chicago drivers coming in from the west in search of the new highway. They were as eager to drive across South Bend and pick up the toll road in Roseland as Pete was to service their vehicles, give them directions, and send them on their way. It was an unforeseen, fortunate development for Pete, and he seized the opportunity for increased sales with renewed energy and vigor. Suddenly, the service station that had been leased and re-leased, opened and closed so many times before now had "customers galore." And along with service with a smile, it now had a good mechanic.

"Our sales went through the roof, which created a lot of excitement for us," Pete says. "We still didn't charge enough, but we gradually worked up to having lots of business. Both Al and I were now working long days, and the variety of what we were doing increased. I did most of the selling – tires were my favorite. Al did the mechanical work. As time went on, he was able to keep both bays full. His skills became a great cornerstone of the business."

❦

Pete and Wilma's family grew during the three-and-a-half years they remained at the 3520 Western Avenue Standard Oil service station. A daughter, Connie, was born in 1957, followed by Sharon in 1959. In addition to caring for four young children, Wilma continued her work as bookkeeper. She still worked from her kitchen table, albeit from slightly larger spaces as the family outgrew one small house after another.

In 1956, the house that Pete and Wilma had rented after leaving

Three Oaks was sold. Tired of throwing away money on rent and eager to begin investing in a place of their own, they scraped together enough cash for a down payment and bought their first home at 505 South Wellington. Within walking distance of the service station, the house had two bedrooms and no garage. It cost $5800.

By the time Sharon was born in 1959, the family had moved to a three-bedroom house on Grant Road where, theoretically, the two girls shared one bedroom and the two boys another. The house was on a lovely lot outside of town, nestled under tall trees. It looked so inviting, Wilma recalls, until they moved in and realized there was no one around for their children to play with. They disliked the isolation so much that within a year they moved again, this time closer to town, into a larger house on State Road 2 that was within walking distance of a neighborhood with playmates, a school, and a church. (Western Avenue becomes State Road 2 at the edge of South Bend. The house was also within walking distance of Pete's second service station, an important fact as the children grew up.)

No matter where they lived or how many bedrooms they had, there were often family members moving in for long visits (Wilma's siblings) or to work for Pete as newly arrived immigrants (his siblings). The extra adults helped fill each successive house to capacity. A sister of Wilma's, Ada, once lived in South Bend for a year while she worked as a nanny for the children of a couple who owned a furniture store. Ada had a room in her employer's house during the week and lived with Pete and Wilma on her days off.

"I was a little jealous at Christmas, when Ada came home with several presents from the family she worked for," Wilma says. "She even had gifts from the children's grandparents! We had so little money at the time that we really didn't do anything for Christmas. We certainly could not buy new sweaters or scarves or toys or things like that."

Gifts or no gifts, even Wilma saw that there was room for hope as far as the business was concerned. Due to Pete's pluck and ingenuity, and his and Al's hard work and dependability, the service station at 3520 Western Avenue was growing.

"Every year at the station was a little bit better than the year before," Pete recalls. "Our incomes were still small, but we knew we were headed for success. We never added a sign with a name for the station – we didn't want to spend the money it would cost – but we listed it as 'Al and Pete's Service Station,' or something like that, in the yellow pages of the phone book. We put Al's name first so our address would be near the top of a really long list!

"Within a few years, we added a U-Haul franchise to the business. We rented U-Haul trailers. Some years later, when U-Haul expanded to renting trucks, we rented trucks as well. We were at another location by then. I always liked working with the rentals. We would get a call whenever a U-Haul truck broke down, and we'd drive another U-Haul over, unpack and repack all of the goods, and tow the truck in need of repair back to our station.

"Transferring the load was my favorite part of the job," he continues, "because by the time Wilma and I had been married five years, we had moved seven times. I was an expert in moving! Almost always, U-Haul customers would be driving a truck that was much too big for what they were moving. We would arrive with a smaller truck, and they couldn't believe everything would fit. But it almost always did. We rented U-Hauls for at least 20 years. It was a great fit with us, from the days Al and I started renting trailers from 3520 Western Avenue.

"It took a while, but the small station gradually became known for good work. We were honest, we did quality work, and we gave endless friendly service. Nothing was ever too much to ask of us, and we did it all with a smile."

☙

Day in, day out, Pete and Al kept at it, and the service station stayed in business. Pete was increasingly confident he had found a job he could stick with. He liked what he was doing: He wasn't working in a factory, doing the same thing over and over; he wasn't assembling and selling farm equipment for someone else; and he wasn't milking another man's cows on land that wasn't his, dependent upon the rise and fall of commodities or the vagaries of the weather, worried that someone's son would push him out of his job. He was working with one of his brothers full-time (Al) and another brother some of the time (Ben). Best of all, his aptitude for innovation and entrepreneurship was being honed with each successful stroke across the whetstone of small-business ownership.

Pete and Wilma didn't have much money to spend after they paid their monthly bills, but they were making ends meet. He was working such long hours every day of the week that neither remembers much about the day they became U.S. citizens. Pete had put it off for some years when a friend finally talked him into taking a few hours off to complete the process. By that time, Wilma had been in the country for five years and was also eligible for citizenship.

"It wasn't that big of a deal to me," Pete says. "I was working in my own business. I had been in the U.S. Army. I already felt like a citizen."

"I do remember that we only had to answer a few very simple questions, like giving the name of the current U.S. president," Wilma interjects. "I don't recall that we had any kind of celebration afterward. Maybe we bought a hamburger at a diner in town. That would have been a pretty big deal for us. Whatever we did, if anything, Pete went back to work that day. I'm sure of that."

Working hard, looking ahead, pleasing the customer with skill and affability – Pete has always believed there is room for a business to grow if the owner does his or her job well and is willing to take a risk. With Al riding shotgun as mechanic, the 3520 Western Avenue station was doing good work as a full-service venue. But expanding the business beyond automotive repair, towing, and U-Haul rentals seemed almost impossible due to Pete's unmitigated lack of financial resources.

It had nothing to do with lack of will or effort on his part, nothing to do with fear or poor planning. Pete was more than willing to venture into new territory, but he lacked the kind of financing that would help swing open the door of expansion. However, he was not to be deterred – what he lacked in capital he made up for in stamina. Pete stood before the door with determination and vision and very little else, and he kept pushing until it yielded.

"I had had my eye on the corner of a fairly busy intersection on the far-western edge of town for quite a while," he says. "There wasn't a station on any of the intersection's four corners, but I could see that there should be. I used to tell Wilma that someone needed to put a service station on one of those spots. I thought I should be that someone.

"Evidently, Standard Oil came to the same conclusion about putting a service station there, only I wasn't the person they had in mind," he continues. "Because one day, after we'd been at the first station for about three years, I was driving by and saw that new gasoline tanks were waiting to be installed on one of the corners I had dreamed of having. I had not been able to do anything about opening a station there because I didn't have the money.

"I thought it was great when I saw that the tanks belonged to Standard Oil. As we had a good business relationship with the company, I went to them and told them how much I'd like to have that station, the new one on the corner. They, however, did not think my credit was good enough to operate two stations, and they weren't going to give me the new one. They said I should just concentrate on the station I had; I should continue to build up the business and do well where I was. But I told them the new station was going to be in a much better place and that it was the one I wanted.

"I had lots of discussions with the district manager. We went back and forth, but I was determined. After a lot of arm-twisting, they finally agreed to let me be the owner of the new station as well as the first one. And although they didn't want to, they eventually said they would finance both of them.

"The new station was on the southeast corner of Mayflower Road and Western Avenue. It was a huge turnaround for us because it was a heavy traffic area. Plus, a new housing development that would bring in a lot of business was being built behind the station. It was truly the place to be."

✲

In 1959, Pete left Al to manage the first station while he poured himself into getting the new one off the ground. But the two brothers missed working together. As soon as Ben came home from school, Al turned over the 3520 Western Avenue station to the college student while he moved down the street to work with Pete at the new place, Veldman's Service Center. Pete did not hire a mechanic to replace Al at the first station; Ben sent everything that came to him there in need of more than basic service to the new site at 5316 Western Avenue – on the corner of Mayflower and Western – which had been built with two service bays. Less than a year after the move, the lease on the first station came up for renewal, but Pete let it go. He had learned enough about the business by then to know he was pumping gasoline and changing tires on the corner of Mayflower and Western with a winner on his hands.

Very early on, Pete added an additional service bay to Veldman's Service Center. Soon afterward, two more bays were built. As the bays were added and new mechanics were hired to work under Al's supervision, Pete stepped up to "the real challenge" of selling. But, he says, it was always a soft sell. He never tried to talk people into car repairs or batteries or tires they did not need. The mechanics were instructed to do whatever was necessary to keep a vehicle running; anything optional was left to the owner's discretion.

Because South Bend's west side has long been populated by working-class residents, many of Pete's customers took months to pay for work that was done on their old vehicles. But Pete has always identified with the underdog, and as long as their debts were honest, he treated those who struggled with their payments as fairly and generously as he could. His children say a hallmark of Pete's style was that he showered his customers with respect. Such frankness and honesty, combined with his good humor, contributed greatly to his early success as a salesman.

"Dad was always unfailingly kind to his customers – all of them," his daughter Connie says.

In Pete's opinion, many of his poorer customers were his better customers. But Pete is not naive, and he has never been a pushover. He admits, somewhat sheepishly, to towing *back* to the station some cars that were worked on successfully – and driven home – but for which the owners refused to pay. Pete threatened to keep the vehicles until at least part of the outstanding bill was taken care of.

"Dad would always let our customers pay as they could," explains son Dave, "so much so that some of our customers would not even get one bill paid off before another was added onto it. If you were honest and couldn't pay, Dad honored that. Not so, if you could pay, but didn't."

"Business truly blossomed at the new station," Pete explains. "Many of our former customers started coming to us on the corner of Mayflower and Western. Al couldn't keep up with it all and we suddenly had a great need for more trained mechanics. When a well-known automobile repair shop closed, we added two mechanics from there to our growing group.

"We truly turned a new leaf in automotive repair with some very fine mechanics," he continues. "One of them, Herb Thorpe, did incredible work tuning up engines and rebuilding carburetors. When he first came to us, he looked at our setup and announced, 'I'm not going to work in a service station.' So we agreed to hire him temporarily, until he found a place to his liking. Twenty-seven years later, when his eyes had become too bad to continue, Herb retired."

Characteristically, the station, which remains in the family today, became known for doing some types of automotive work that few others in town could or would do. This is not because Pete learned new skills. He readily acknowledged – then and now – that he does not know how to do lots of things. But Pete is a great facilitator with an almost uncanny ability to find the right people to do what he cannot or does not want to do. *You do the job well that you know how to do, and I'll do mine,* has long been his modus operandi. Ultimately, Pete's style allowed those who worked with him to flourish. It allowed for success on both sides of the street. For example, not many service stations worked on Corvairs, a sporty car with the engine in the back that was made for most of the 1960s. Veldman's Service Center took a little success with Corvairs and ran with it.

"We became well-known experts on this car, which brought in quite a lot of work for us," Pete says. "We worked on Corvairs until Chevrolet quit making them."

❧

The 1960s were a time of rapid expansion for Veldman's Service Center, with Pete and Wilma's family keeping pace. Three more children were born to them before the decade was out: Audrey in 1961, Marcia in 1963, and the last of the seven, Mark, in 1967. By the time the older children could begin helping their father as young teenagers at the station, most of Pete's siblings had joined him in South Bend. There was growth everywhere one looked – aunts, uncles, cousins, service bays, and new spin-off businesses. The corner of Mayflower and Western was busier than Pete or anyone else had ever imagined it could be.

Of the eight siblings who eventually joined Pete in the United States, half came as unmarried young adults: Ben, Willy, Fran, and Henry. The other four siblings came with their partners: Al and

Liesbeth, Mary and Hank, June and John, and Ted and Theresa. They were all drawn by the idea of going to a country where opportunity still existed, and they were greatly encouraged by Pete and Wilma's example of emerging success. Pete had done the hard work of learning the language and getting established on his own, they reasoned, with no family around to champion his cause. He had taken the initial business risk, and as long as they were willing to work hard, he would bend over backward to hire them. Why stake out territory of their own when they could work together and make Veldman's Service Center a success for everyone involved? On the other hand, the siblings were equally assured of Pete's support if they took a look at the station and decided they wanted to pursue some other goal.

The brothers and sisters traveled straight from Didam to Pete and Wilma's house, where they were welcomed with a bed for as long as they needed it and a job or the opportunity to go to school, or both. Pete's sister Mary and her husband, Hank, were the only couple who never worked with Pete at all, though they, too, landed next door to Pete and Wilma's house for a while. When Pete's much-younger brother Willy moved in with them in 1960, Pete concluded that the young man needed a high-school education as much as he needed employment. Willy had his misgivings, but he complied with Pete's clearly stated wishes and enrolled in Washington High School as a junior. Willy was 20 years old and spoke very little English when he began Washington High, but he enjoyed the students, who couldn't believe that someone his age was willing to sit in classes with 16- and 17-year-olds. Willy kept at it. He attended school and worked part-time at the service station until he graduated two years later, at which time Pete put him to work full-time.

"I really looked up to Pete as my big brother," Willy says. "He was almost like a father to me, which at times was good and at times was bad! Pete is a very disciplined, determined person. He sets himself to do something and he sticks to it, whether it is exercise or work. He really carried as much power as our parents did.

"Pete also has a business mind that doesn't quit. At every corner he finds an opportunity," Willy continues. "He is the oldest and has Mama's perseverance. He will put pressure on you to make the right decisions. Do not hang out in the wrong places. Do not do anything you are not proud of. He is an extremely generous person, but you know not to take advantage of him. He always said, 'You're never too good to do anything, and you lead by example.'"

Pete's youngest sibling, Henry, was 8 years old when Pete left Holland. He remembers waving goodbye as Pete boarded the ship in Rotterdam, the ride home in a flatbed truck, and being treated to ice cream. It wasn't until Henry was 19 that Pete entered his life in a way that shaped not only who he was then, but who he would become as a grown man.

"As the baby of the family, I had not given my parents any reason to think I would do anything useful with my life," Henry says. "I was basically doing as little as possible, playing as much soccer as possible. I had been asked to leave high school when Pete came into my life, and that made a huge difference. I had applied for a factory job in Holland but was turned down after I took an aptitude test. The person who was going to hire me looked at my scores and said I really should finish school.

"Pete told Mama and Papa to let me come over to America," Henry continues. "He said he would put me to work and they wouldn't have to worry about me. I arrived on a Wednesday in 1961 and on Thursday I went to work at the service station. Four of my brothers and a brother-in-law were working there by then. I looked around and it was family.

"I thought America was wonderful – the cars, the music, all of it. Plus, it wasn't farm work. If I wanted to buy something, I earned money for it. If I didn't earn the money, I didn't buy it. There were no handouts, although Pete, in an underhanded way, helped me out. He told me I needed to go to an Indiana extension university, but I didn't have a car or the money for one. So he gave me an old car to use.

"Without Pete, I would have been just another immigrant who struggled even harder than I did," Henry continues. "When people ask me what it was like to be an immigrant, I say, 'Don't ask me. Ask someone who came here like Pete did, all alone. Someone who didn't have family and who didn't speak the language.'"

When you ask Pete about the role he played in his siblings' lives as they immigrated to America one by one to work with him, he shrugs his shoulders, laughs a little, and says, "I wasn't pressured into helping my family, but I had the opportunity to do a lot for them. I made Willy go to high school because by the time he got here I really regretted not having an education myself. And I pushed Ben and Henry to go to college because I knew they could do the work. None of the brothers ever made it as farmers. We really weren't that good at it.

"Wilma was also very good to my family," Pete adds. "For many years, we had one small house after another, and she was willing to have my brothers and sisters come in. Many of them were single when they came. They worked with us at the service center, some took classes locally, some went away to school and came back to live with us on their breaks. There were always extra people around. Eventually, there was more of my family here than there was in Holland."

❧

Sometime around 1962, Pete built a lawn- and garden-equipment business next door to the service center. "It had a real small showroom and two service bays," Pete explains. "We sold and serviced lawnmowers and lawn tractors in the summer and snowblowers in the winter."

A similar lawn-equipment business had closed before Pete built his; from there he hired an experienced mechanic. Pete's sister June and her husband, John Wynen, had immigrated about the same time as Willy. Pete says that John and Willy both played a major role in the success of the Lawn and Garden Center.

"They made running this entirely new business possible," Pete says. Under their care, the center eventually expanded to installing underground sprinkler systems. John concentrated on the irrigation business, Willy on lawn and garden equipment. Both men also continued working at the service station as they were needed. Wilma remembers John coming by the house late at night with the service station's bank deposit, standing in the doorway and talking for a few minutes before he headed home to his own family.

Veldman's Service Center continued to grow until it included 10 to 15 service bays. Most of the additional bays were attached to the Lawn and Garden Center building, which meant that Pete did not have to pay Standard Oil an increased leasing fee. Everyone connected with the service center worked long hours. Pete and Wilma's children remember their mother regularly holding supper until Pete could get home to eat with them at night. Wilma very often gave up, put Pete's supper in the oven, and she and the children ate without him.

The service center was officially closed two days a year: Christmas and New Year's. The family, especially the younger children, would wait for Pete to get home on Christmas and New Year's Eves for special church services or family events. Because Pete and his brothers would not leave the station until the service bays were as empty of cars as they could possibly be, the waiting could stretch on for hours.

"Our customers needed their cars, especially on the holidays," Pete explains, "and we wouldn't leave until they got them."

Moving from her kitchen table to a small room in the basement, Wilma continued to manage the service center's books during the years Pete's siblings were arriving one after another. Pete's sister Fran immigrated the same time as Henry. They were both single and Fran "didn't have anything else to do" when she agreed to leave Holland and travel to South Bend with him. She found a place helping Wilma, while Henry eventually went to college, as Pete thought he should. The bookkeeping job grew larger and larger until another helper was added. Eventually, a part-time accountant, Bob Stephan, joined the team. When the job grew beyond part-time work for anyone, especially as new side-businesses were added, Stephan's job went full-time. Today, more than 30 years later, Stephan still works with Pete and Wilma and several of their children.

"Bob is now over 75 years old and is back to working part-time for us," Wilma says. "He handles the payroll. He is officially retired, but I think he just likes coming in."

ও

By 1962, all of Pete's siblings who would immigrate were in South Bend, minus one brother, Ted, and his wife, Theresa. They had taken over the family farm outside Didam and lived in the large homeplace with Pete's parents. With so many of their children and grandchildren living in Indiana, Bernard and Wilhelmina, now called Opa and Oma (grandfather and grandmother), came for their second visit to the United States. Much to everyone's surprise, they decided to stay. They did not even return to Holland to pack their possessions, but sent word of their decision to Ted and Theresa.

"Would you ship our furniture and belongings to Pete's address?" the retired couple asked.

"Looking back, it seems like all we ever did was work," Pete remembers, "and I guess that's about right, though our kids did play a lot of soccer as they got older, and we went to their games as long as they were close by. About the time all of my siblings were coming over and helping with the service center, Wilma and I had moved to a larger house on a one-acre lot on State Road 2. Besides the house we lived in, the property had an old, large, two-story home on it that we thought we would eventually tear down. We filled up our house with our seven kids and anyone else who was living with us at the time. Everything was within a few blocks of where we lived: the service station, Holy Family Church, and Holy Family School. Our children walked to school in the mornings and from school to the service station and then home in the afternoons. It was the perfect location for us. We lived there for over 30 years.

"We never tore the other house down," Pete continues, "because my parents came to visit us and liked the situation so well they never left! They liked the old house with its large rooms and high ceilings. I think it reminded them of their farmhouse in Holland. So we fixed it up and they moved in. The house needed a lot of work."

ↄ౩

Wilhelmina and Bernard were in their mid-60s when they joined their children in South Bend. They never second-guessed their decision to immigrate, but moved as quickly as they could into the house next door to Pete and Wilma and their grandchildren. Their unmarried children, those living with Pete and Wilma, moved out of Pete's house and back in with their parents. Pete's sister Mary and her husband, Hank, were already living in the garage apartment next door to Pete and Wilma's when her parents moved into the house that went with it. Appropriately enough, Oma and Opa's new place came to be called "the immigrant house" by several of their grandchildren.

"It was nice having Oma and Opa live next door," Wilma says. "In all the years they lived there, they never interfered with our family's life. I'm sure Oma saw things going on at our house – with our children – that she wondered about, but she never said anything to me. She was a special lady and we had a great relationship. Pete's dad, too. He was just very easy to be around. He would walk over sometimes just to chat. Not so much, Pete's mother."

True to form, Wilhelmina enrolled in English class as soon as she and Bernard were settled in their new home. While his mother studied, Pete taught his father how to drive, which thrilled the retired Dutch farmer. Bernard slowly learned his way around town and before long he, too, was working at the service station. He spent three to four hours a day stocking soda and candy machines, writing out credit card purchases, and making bank deposits.

"Mama did fairly well with her English," Pete says. "Papa went to class with her, but he pretty much went along for the ride. He didn't put much effort into it. I don't think it bothered him that he spoke only minimal English. With his characteristic charm and good humor, he got along just fine. He charmed all the ladies at the bank with his Dutch accent, poor English, and big smile."

෴

In 1964, Ted and Theresa sold the farm inventory in Holland and joined his parents and eight siblings in South Bend. Of Bernard and Wilhelmina's 12 children, only two daughters, Willemien and Rieka, now remained in Holland; daughter Dolly was over the border in Canada. Pete quickly found Ted a place at the service station, and Ted and Theresa moved into Pete and Wilma's first purchased home on South Wellington, which they had hung on to as rental property.

By the time Pete was 40 years old, almost all of his family was working with him at Veldman's Service Center in one way or another. Some worked full-time and were involved in all areas of the business. Some worked part-time and were students as well as employees. Some worked only as long as they needed to pay school tuition. Some moved on after they finished school, some stayed. Some of the sisters quit working once they married and had families of their own. For a while, as the business grew, some were shareholders in the various enterprises. Some were not interested.

Everyone worked to adjust culturally to life in the United

States. Families, cousins, and grandchildren grew. The corner of Mayflower and Western was sometimes a chaotic place to be. Sometimes the cousins argued. Sometimes the adults disagreed; they approved what worked politically and hotly debated what did not. But everyone worked hard, and everyone was willing to take Pete's lead as the business expanded.

"When you have that many people from one family working together, you sometimes have to agree to disagree," Pete says. "I always felt that at work, we should work. But when we left work at the end of the day, we should leave our disagreements behind."

℗℞

Building a Business, Raising a Family

F rom the early 1960s until the late 1970s, Pete concentrated on growing the business and keeping his extended family gainfully employed for as long as they chose to work with him. As his brothers and sisters married and began families of their own, as they became citizens and homeowners with "American" expectations and hopes and dreams, the pressure on Pete increased. It was one thing to help provide housing and jobs for newly arrived immigrants who were just trying to get their feet on the ground. To come up with enough work to reasonably support several families, including his own, was a much weightier responsibility. But harking back to the days when he planted his feet in the schoolyard and put up his fists rather than walk away from a fight, Pete loved the challenge. He never backed down, never ceased looking for new business opportunities for himself or his siblings.

"I always wanted to make enough money to be financially secure," Pete says. "We all did, and we were willing to work together for it. We worked for ourselves and we worked for each other. I would have tried many of the same things as a service station owner even if my brothers and sisters had not immigrated, because that's what I wanted to do. But because they were here, we did it together. They spurred me on."

Finding viable ways to expand the business beyond Veldman's

Service Center was the hard part, for Pete was too financially conservative to risk wrecking what so many people were working to build. Filling leadership positions once he had decided to move ahead in a new area was the easy part. If one of the brothers was suited to managing a new spin-off business, the job went to him. If not, Pete looked outside for another qualified person. Occasionally, he was approached by salesmen or other individuals looking for a partner with whom they could form a new business. Occasionally, the owners of established businesses sought him out because they were ready to sell and they wanted him to be the buyer. Pete considered all offers.

By the middle of the 1970s, Veldman's Service Center had spawned several new businesses that were owned by Pete and his brothers. An incomplete list includes some natural offshoots of the increasingly successful service station: 10 to 15 automotive bays, located on-site and off, provided quality repair work; the U-Haul franchise, which had moved with Pete and Al from the first station; a towing service. Other spin-offs ventured into new territory: the Lawn and Garden Center and its spin-off underground irrigation business; pop-up camper rentals and sales; Vel-Mac Distributors, a wholesale tire, battery, and accessory enterprise that was established with the help of a new business partner, Jim McIntire; W.A.R. Equipment, a former Mishawaka company that sold automotive equipment; an artificial Christmas tree store, to help tide over the Lawn and Garden Center during the fall and winter months; and, toward the end of the decade, a store that sold mail-order tires out of Indianapolis, The Tire Rack.

Some of the expansion businesses were short-lived; some lasted for years; some died quickly once it was clear they were no longer profitable; some remain profitable today. As haphazard as a few of the ventures seemed, they all had a connection – however slim – to the service station. And they all had a connection to Pete.

✂

The task of establishing and overseeing the many businesses fell largely on Pete's shoulders. While his brothers ran the service station and the lawn and garden store and worked on cars, while his father filled candy and pop machines and his children helped pump gas after school and during summer vacations, while Wilma spent mornings and afternoons working on the books at the station and, after hours, hired additional employees from her favorite interview site – her dining room table – Pete tracked the progress and needs of the various businesses and searched for new ones. He walked to the corner of Mayflower and Western early every morning and helped at the service station as needed and whenever he wanted a break from his desk and the many details that lay upon it awaiting his attention. His "office" moved from a desk in the service station to a cramped corner in the Lawn and Garden Center to, eventually, a dedicated room in a warehouse that housed Vel-Mac Distributors.

As much as he enjoyed the challenge and variety of all the enterprises he and his brothers were involved in, Pete never tired of the service station and working there with his family. He loved the customers and considered many of them to be friends, but he especially trusted and understood his siblings. They had all been shaped by World War II. In many ways, they were all looking for the same thing.

"Our lives would have been totally different if it had not been for the War," Pete's youngest brother, Henry, says. It was a perspective shared by all of them.

Of all the work Pete and his siblings did at the service station, he always liked tires best. He liked selling them and he liked the hands-on work of putting them on and balancing them. But no matter what he was doing – from cleaning a windshield to selling snow tires to negotiating a delinquent payment – Pete treated every customer the same way.

"We grew up kind of color-blind," Pete and Wilma's children say when they speak of growing up on South Bend's west side. They remember Pete listening to customers with deference and respect, trusting that he would be treated in kind. They also recall the value their father placed on maintaining a good relationship with his siblings. There was not an inept or weak-willed one among them, Pete included, which sometimes made for a lively mix.

"I was tired at the end of every day," Pete admits. "We put in long hours. With such a large group of family and associates, there were bound to be disagreements. Fortunately, I could usually leave them behind when I finally went home at night. I tried to abide by the philosophy that what was left unfinished one day could be dealt with the next day."

The brothers and brother-in-law who continued working with Pete as the years progressed were shareholders in the various enterprises for an extended period of time; Pete bought them out in later years as they made the move to owning and operating their own businesses. But they worked together for a long time before that happened, and they all worked hard. They kept their fingers on the pulse of the business they were most involved in and regularly contributed their insights to the group. Once a month, Al, Willy, Ted, John Wynen, and later, Jim McIntire, met at Pete and Wilma's house to discuss business issues and make decisions. Wilma was consistently the only woman in the room, for she was the only woman with a continued presence at the service station and other business sites as the years went by.

Wilma's professional life grew along with the businesses. She started spending more time at the service station as her children grew up, though for years she worked as many hours from a table or desk at home as she did from the corner of Mayflower and Western. When her youngest child, Mark, was old enough to start school, she hired a woman to come in for a few hours in the late mornings to feed him lunch and help him get out the door for afternoon kindergarten. Every afternoon Mark and his siblings walked to the service station after school to greet their father and uncles and to pick up Wilma. The older children often remained on site to put in a few hours' work while the younger ones continued the short journey home with their mother.

Wilma's continually shifting role suited her and was appreciated by Pete. It gave her insight into his multifaceted business world, and it allowed her to remain closely connected to their children. Strong, determined, and capable, Wilma was charting her own course at a time when many women were just beginning to consider the complications of managing both a career and a family. But Wilma didn't spend much time fretting about how, if, and when: She worked out of necessity, and she worked because she liked it.

$$\infty$$

The explosion of Veldman-run businesses on the corner of Mayflower and Western came as no surprise to anyone who knew Pete and his siblings. As a group, the Veldmans were highly motivated, quick learners who did good work. For the most part, they enjoyed what they did. Pete especially enjoyed the diversity of people he and his brothers worked with. It all made for a successful work environment as far as he was concerned: different work, different people every day. As long as he liked what he was doing and the people with and for whom he was working, long hours were acceptable. He found boredom much more deadening than hard-earned fatigue.

"As a service station we were doing well," Pete says. "We were open 24 hours a day and we had many fine employees. I always heard lots of service station owners complain about their employees, but we happened to have the best. Working at the station was something I really enjoyed. If we got 250 different people a day, I knew about half of them. It was fun to do business there. You were there from morning to night with all these different people. To keep most of them happy was quite a challenge."

In addition to basic car service and car repairs, Veldman's Service Center sold tires at an astonishing rate, more than any other service station in northern Indiana. At one point, Jim McIntire, a Standard Oil regional salesman, told Pete that Veldman's accounted for at least

30 percent of his area's total tire and battery sales. Pete and McIntire worked closely together for so long that they struck up a real friendship based upon mutual respect and trust.

"Jim would come to me with some new sales promotional program he was trying to sell," Pete says. "We'd go have coffee and I would ask him if the new program was really an improvement and something that I needed. Jim knew me really well, knew what I was after, and sometimes he'd say, 'No, this isn't worth it,' and sometimes he'd say, 'Yes.'

"Tire sales were much simpler in those days," Pete continues. "We sold Atlas tires, a brand supported by Standard Oil. A good product was all I needed. Our mechanics also used Atlas batteries and accessories successfully in our service bays."

❦

Pete and Wilma's children began working at the service station for a few hours a week when they were around 10 or 11 years old. Pete paid them a small wage for each hour they spent helping him, their uncles, and other employees. The children cleaned tools, helped Opa stock snack machines, and watched the meter as someone older pumped gasoline into cars. They were not tall enough or strong enough to open hoods and check oil or clean windshields when they first started working, but in time those tasks and others were added to their list of responsibilities. They especially liked moving cars from one part of the station to another.

Like their father, the children thought working at the service station was great. They considered it to be an extension of their home and family. Growing old enough to help out on the corner of Mayflower and Western was considered a rite of passage. The girls did the same work as the boys; with Pete's encouragement, the older girls pumped gasoline, which was unusual for the time. The younger boys and girls admired their older brothers and sisters – they seemed so knowledgeable and confident as they performed their tasks and interacted with customers. It was a badge of honor to be given new jobs by the adults.

Young or old, "the cousins" were all welcomed by their uncles, who joked around with them and with each other, arguing world events and politics, determined to change each other's minds. Pete's children listened well as they went about their tasks, for they were certain their father would have one of the last words.

"Dad was some kind of a champion on the debate team in Holland," Pete and Wilma's youngest daughter, Marcia, says with a laugh. "And he practiced that skill regularly!"

For several years, all of the aunts and uncles living in the area gathered at Oma and Opa's house every Sunday after Mass for coffee, conversation, and endless card games. Cousins of all ages played soccer and ran around outside while the adults sat inside. In the summer, the children spent entire afternoons swimming in a pool Pete and Wilma installed in their backyard next door.

Wilma had one nonnegotiable rule concerning the use of the pool: The cousins had to have an adult member from their family with them, even if they could swim. No one ever abused the rule, she says, "because they didn't want it (the pool) to be a burden." The pool is often mentioned by Pete's siblings as an example of his and Wilma's unfailing generosity. Nothing could replace the lake on the family farm in Holland, but the pool came close.

"We played with our cousins more than with friends when we were younger," says Pete and Wilma's oldest daughter, Connie. "Mom was very easy about that. Perhaps because we were so tied in with our family, we were not aware that it was different. We never thought about the fact that we had so many aunts and uncles and that they had all come over from Holland. That's just the way it was in our family. There was always somebody coming, somebody doing something.

"When we were young," she continues, "people would ask us,

'Where are your parents from?' Sometimes I would think, 'Why do they ask that?' I was so used to talking to so many people with accents that I didn't get it. When we were older, in our teens, and worked at the station, people often complimented Dad to us. 'Your dad is such a great guy. He did this for me. He did that for me,' they would say. People always talked about how Dad or one of the brothers had treated them.

"I remember feeling proud about coming from good people."

ري

Some of the spin-off businesses, like renting and selling pop-up campers, came about simply because Pete recognized opportunities that others were oblivious to. For example, he and Wilma took their seven children on very few vacations. If and when they did leave town, it needed to be affordable, which narrowed their choices considerably, and it needed to be fairly close by, a further constraint. Camping was an activity they could do as a family that met both criteria.

Though Pete has never really liked camping – not since he was an Army recruit freezing in a tent at Camp Breckenridge – he was willing to go with his family. It was inexpensive and not all that difficult and everyone had a good time, barring a few mishaps, like the time they lost Marcia in a campground only to eventually find her across a small stream, though she could not swim and hated the water. Or the time Pete went to bathe and was gone for so long – hours, according to family tradition – that Wilma finally went into the men's shower house to be sure he was still alive and found him deep in conversation with a complete stranger. But that was Pete, so genuinely interested in everyone, so conversational. He had not even begun to shower.

Once, to make his family's camping experience a little easier, Pete decided to rent a pop-up camper. He knew it would be a tight fit for everyone, but it seemed like an idea worth trying, and he could always put the older boys in a tent. He started looking around and, to his great surprise, learned that renting a camper was not an easy thing to do, at least not in South Bend. Families bought pop-ups; they did not rent them. Armed with this information, Pete traveled to Cincinnati, Ohio, to find out more. He returned with five Nimrod pop-ups, which he promptly started renting from the service station. Business went so well that Pete soon added more campers, and then more. For some years afterward, pop-up campers could be rented from Veldman's Service Center. In classic Pete style, the campers were also for sale – new or used. All a customer had to do was make an offer.

Dave, Pete and Wilma's second child, was truly interested in camping, and he took over the camper-rental business as a young teenager. He quickly became skilled in all areas of the job, from working with customers to managing the paperwork.

"There was such an entrepreneurial spirit going on around the station," Dave says. "I think that sunk in when we were kids. I worked with the campers when I was young, during the summers. I think I was 14 or 15 years old at the time, and I was totally in charge of the business. We had at least 30 or 40 campers as I recall, all pop-ups. I set up the leases, showed customers how to put up and take down the campers when they came to pick them up, put on the trailer hitches and connected the trailer lights, and cleaned out the campers when they were returned. I was also involved if a customer wanted to buy a camper.

"We kids all had a high level of responsibility early on in our lives," he continues, "partly because both of our parents were working, but also because they trusted us and were never afraid to let us make mistakes. I think they understood that making mistakes is part of the learning process."

Pete lost Dave as a manager in 1973 when Dave graduated from high school and moved on to Indiana University (IU). No one shared Dave's enthusiasm for the small business and the work was so seasonal that Pete didn't think it was worth hanging on to without him.

"Renting the campers was never a stand-alone business," Pete explains. "We began selling off all the pop-ups the summer before Dave left."

Dave and older brother Tom, an IU sophomore, roomed together that fall. The following semester found Tom in the Netherlands, living with one of Wilma's brothers and working in the engineering department of a milk-tank factory. But Tom's time in Holland was cut short when he learned that Opa had been diagnosed with cancer; Tom hurried home to spend as much time as he could with his beloved grandfather.

Hunting the most profitable work he could find until he returned to college the following fall, Tom realized that it would be difficult to improve upon the family business. He talked with Dave about it and the brothers decided they would together manage a service station in South Bend that had been closed for some time, on the corner of Western and Lombardy. Tom opened the station in March 1974. Dave completed his freshman year at the university and joined Tom in May. From there, Dave sold the last of the pop-ups – a raggedy old unit that a customer wanted to restore.

ಆ

Tom was 20 years old when he opened the service station at Western and Lombardy. He says he would have never gotten his foot in the door if Pete had not signed the lease for him. He had no history at the bank and was considered too great a financial risk without his father's backing. But Pete believed that Tom, and a few months later, Dave, knew what they were getting themselves into and that their work experience – for him, their uncles, and others – would serve them well. Experientially and intuitively, Tom and Dave knew what was required to run a service station; they had lived and breathed small-business values since they could remember; they knew how to be family business partners; and though they had no intention of doing so, they knew they could ask their father or one of their uncles for help if they found themselves in a real pinch. They also knew that Pete expected them to make it financially. If Pete wound up owing the bank money because of them, Tom and Dave would be expected to pay him back.

"Pete left us to do our own deal," Tom says. "Our understanding was that if we lost money, it would be our own money."

Tom and Dave ran the station on the corner of Western and Lombardy only until the end of August, when they sold it and split what turned out to be a sizable profit. They had been in business for less than six months.

"Because of a national gasoline shortage, we did very well in those few short months," Tom explains. "Gasoline was allocated by location for several months during 1973-74. Our location had been closed for quite some time when we leased the station, and it had built up a significant gasoline allocation that we were able to sell. While other stations were selling gas for only a few hours a day, we were pumping all day, six days a week.

"Dave and I also did light repair work – oil changes, tire sales, new batteries, windshield wipers, things like that," Tom continues. "We did the work ourselves, with one other employee. We bought the inventory we needed on credit from Vel-Mac, and paid off our bill as we went. Our goal was to sell enough accessories and do enough automotive work to pay all our expenses, which would allow us to keep the profit we made from gasoline sales. And we were able to do that.

"We spent a lot of time pumping gas, but we knew it was opening doors for us to do other things. We washed every car window and mirror, checked tires, did all the things service station employees had done a few years before. Most operators weren't pushing that kind of service as much as they had in the past; they knew their customers would be back because they could only buy so much gas at a time. Customers weren't filling up their cars and

Wilma, third from right, on board the Ryndam, *November 1952. One of her few pieces of luggage was a sewing machine.*

Pete and Wilma's house in Three Oaks, Michigan.

Veldman's Service Center on the corner of Mayflower and Western.

From left: Dave; Tom, pushing jack; Wilma holds Connie in background.

Tom and Dave get in on the action. Tom, seated. Dave, standing.

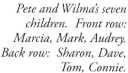

Opa and Oma (Bernard and Wilhelmina), possibly before they immigrated. Their decision to remain in the United States while visiting surprised everyone.

Pete and his brothers at a farm show in the United States.

Pete, his siblings, and his parents at a family gathering in South Bend, after Opa had been diagnosed with cancer.

Pete and Wilma's seven children. Front row: Marcia, Mark, Audrey. Back row: Sharon, Dave, Tom, Connie.

From left: Mark, Audrey,
Pete, Wilma, in Monaco.

Audrey in Mexico.

Marcia's wedding.
From left: Connie,
Marcia, Sharon,
Audrey.

Audrey on horseback
with niece Julie.
Audrey was devoted
to her many nieces
and nephews.

Pete and Wilma in Tanzania, 18 kilometers
from the school named in Audrey's honor.

Village residents near the school.

Students of the school.

From left: Pete, Wilma, the bishop, Tom, Dave, at the school dedication.

A short biographical sketch of Audrey, written in Swahili and English, hangs inside the school.

Audrey Veldman

Audrey alizaliwa huko mji wa South Bend, jimbo la Indiana, Marekani tarehe 18 mwezi wa kumi 1961. Alikuwa mtoto wa tano wa Baba [...] Wilma Veldman.

Baada ya kuhitimu masomo ya [...] kazi ya uhasibu kwenye biashara ya [...] Alikuwa mwenye furaha nyingi na [...] akafurahi kusherehekea na kuwa na [...] hali ya hewa si baridi kama katika ji[...]

Audrey akaaga dunia tarehe 9 [...] ya kuugua kwa siku nne tu. Kifo c[...] kubwa kwa familia na marafiki yake [...] kila siku.

Tunafurahi kwamba Audrey a[...] wanafunzi wote wa Chuo cha Aud[...] hakika kwamba Audrey anawaomb[...] hiki na wakristu wote wa Parokia y[...] Brendan Kitete.

Tunampenda Audrey na h[...]

familia ya V[...]

Audrey Veldman

Audrey was born in South Bend, Indiana U.S.A. on October 18, 1961. She was the fifth child of Peter and Wilma Veldman.

After college, Audrey worked in the family business in accounting. Audrey was always happy and had many friends. She enjoyed parties and vacations in warm climates, since Indiana gets very cold in the winter.

Audrey died on January 9, 1996. She was sick for only four days. This was a very sad day for our family and her friends. We miss Audrey every day.

We are very happy that Audrey will always be remembered by the students of the Audrey Veldman School. We are certain that Audrey prays for the students and for all the members of the St. Brendon's Parish.

We love Audrey and will never forget her.

The Veldman family

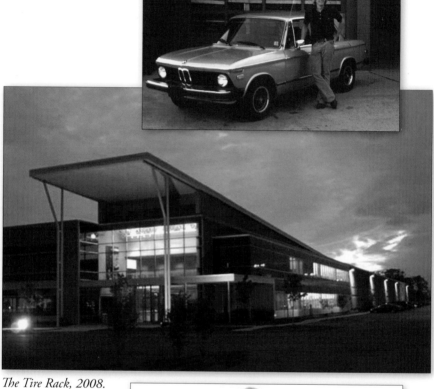

Mike Joines in front of the original Tire Rack in Indianapolis, 1979.

The Tire Rack, 2008.

Pete and his Jaguar.

*Pete and Wilma's 50th wedding anniversary cruise with
their children and grandchildren.*

*From left: Marcia, Dave, Pete, Tom, Wilma, Connie, Mark,
Sharon, at the 2008 wedding of Tom's son, Peter (not pictured).*

Anniversary party. Standing, from left: Steve, Anita, Anne, Mark, Dave, Linda, Mike, Matt. Seated, from left: Marcia, Tom, Wilma, Pete, Connie, Sharon.

Pete and Wilma, 2008.

Pete and Wilma and several of their granddaughters on the occasion of Pete's 80th birthday.

such attentive service seemed unnecessary.

"Our idea worked. Dave and I closed the station before returning to IU that fall, having met our goal. We each paid for two full years of college from our earnings."

ↂ

Standard Oil became Amoco in the early 1970s, which affected only the name of the gasoline on the sign at Veldman's Service Center. But changes in the automotive service industry were under way, changes that would impact Pete and his brothers and service station owners all over the country in the coming years. Most of the changes, such as the move to convenience-store stations and self-service gasoline pumps, were driven by economics and customer demands, but some were the result of an evolving social landscape, especially in the country's urban areas.

"We were still doing good business as a full-service station, but we began having problems in the deep part of the night, between midnight and 6 a.m.," Pete says. "After experiencing a couple of robberies, we decided to close the service station during those hours to prevent something more serious happening to our employees or anyone else. Standard Oil, now called Amoco, did not want us to change our hours and they let us know it."

In addition to Amoco's pushing Pete to keep the service station open 24 hours a day, the company kept raising the rent Pete and his brothers paid for their corner location. It got so bad, Pete says, that he and his brothers and Amoco "agreed to disagree" about staying open 24 hours a day. The Veldmans simply turned off the lights at midnight. But Pete had no recourse when it came to the escalating rent. Amoco had him over a financial barrel and he had to pay, like it or not.

Meanwhile, a new Sinclair service station located across the street from Veldman's Service Center – on the southwest corner of

Mayflower and Western – went through several managers in a short period of time. The Sinclair station kept changing hands because no one could compete with Pete and his brothers. At the height of the Veldmans' tensions with Amoco, Pete quietly approached Sinclair and asked about signing on with them. Sinclair responded by offering him a very low lease and enough money to stage a spectacular grand opening.

Sinclair's package deserved serious consideration. It was risky: Pete had no idea who would move into his and his brothers' spot if they severed ties with Amoco. On the other hand, Sinclair's offer had teeth. If Pete would commit to moving across the street, the underdog company would bend over backward to help him get established. The rest would be up to Pete and his extended family.

Pete did not struggle with the decision for long. He sized it up as a fight he could not resist.

"It was a little like David fighting Goliath," Pete says of the situation. "Sinclair had never had success with that corner, but together we turned it into one of the best corners in the city. They gave us an incredible lease and they put up the same amount of money as the first year's lease to fund a grand opening that was hugely successful. Cars were literally lined up at the pumps. We were immediately pumping more gallons of gasoline a day than we ever had. Tom was attending a Catholic college-prep school near Lake Wawasee at the time, and he and a few of his buddies came home for the weekend to help us out. It turned out to be quite a special occasion.

"I instructed every one of our employees to say nothing negative about Amoco," Pete continues. "For starters, Amoco had, over the years, been very good to us. Second, Jim McIntire, the Amoco salesman we had always bought our tires and accessories from, had decided to leave Amoco and join us at our new location. Jim and I had worked together for several years by then. We had sometimes talked about starting a wholesale business, but I had decided that wholesale was not for me – I didn't have the experience or the patience. But I knew Jim could do it. He was great at selling tires and accessories and at training service station operators. I knew he would do an outstanding job.

"From the very beginning, Jim and I didn't like the Sinclair tire program, nor did we like their other products. We approached Amoco about buying the Atlas brand from them, like we'd always done, but they didn't want to sell to us. However, a little investigation on our part led us to the discovery that we could buy the Atlas supplies we wanted from a distributor on the East Coast for at least 15 percent less than we had been paying for them! We jumped at the opportunity and were soon selling Atlas products to mostly local and regional Amoco service stations, even though we were officially a Sinclair station. We did not make huge profits, but it worked for us. Jim knew how to give good support to our customers and we delivered orders quickly. We were in the wholesale business. Eventually, we added a line of Cooper tires, which also worked well for us and for our customers.

"My brothers and I managed both corner stations for a few months, until our old lease ran out at the Amoco station. We did everything we could to encourage our former customers to move across the street with us. I think we were the only Sinclair station ever that for a while accepted Amoco credit cards!"

Dave says that his father's move across the street was "one of the biggest business coups Dad ever staged."

"Dad and the uncles had had the Standard Oil/Amoco station for years and were doing famously there," he says. "They had the Lawn and Garden Center on one side and Dad owned the land on the other side. But they didn't own the station, and Amoco just kept raising the rent. When Dad moved across the street, he left a brother at the Amoco station, but he barely turned on a light and after a few months the old business closed. Across the street, at the Grand Opening, we all wore red and white striped jackets, and straw hats, and we carried canes. We gave away prizes and had special sales.

"It was really something."

❦

Almost unbelievably, Amoco and Pete eventually made amends. Under new management, the Veldmans' old station on the southeast corner of Mayflower and Western had opened and closed at least twice when representatives from Chicago came by to see for themselves what was happening next door. After observing how well the brothers were doing at the Sinclair station, Amoco offered Pete a much better lease than they ever had in the past. They also offered him an Atlas distributorship for tires, batteries, and accessories for 80 to 100 service stations, a shrewd move on their part that sealed the deal.

"There was no fanfare this time," Pete says with a twinkle in his eyes. "We quietly moved back to our original spot on the corner next door, beside the Lawn and Garden Center and our detached service bays. The Sinclair station went out of business again; it was eventually torn down and a restaurant was built in its place.

"Jim McIntire, however, did not go back to working for Amoco," Pete continues. "We officially formed a new company, called Vel-Mac Distributors, that specialized in selling tires, batteries, and accessories to service station operators. We added three salesmen and a couple of delivery trucks to the corporation. Jim coached the salesmen so they could help him not only with sales but also with training and supporting service station operators, though he preferred to do most of the training himself. Vel-Mac was really a success because Jim knew what he was doing.

"We built a 10,000-square-foot warehouse on land we owned directly east of the service station. The warehouse had two floors and was used to store automotive accessories and lawn and garden inventory. It included some fine office space. Vel-Mac's offices were on the second floor."

The warehouse also had enough space to house inventory for W.A.R., an established automotive equipment store that Pete and his brothers had bought about the time business was booming back on the original Mayflower and Western corner. The owners had decided to sell and had come looking for Pete. They wanted him to buy the business and keep it running.

"W.A.R. was a small, old company. Over the years, we had had lots of contacts with the people who owned the business, and lots of their customers moved over to us when we bought it. It seemed to be a natural fit with our other businesses," Pete says. "The company sold engine hoists, equipment for automobile tune-ups, things like that. We operated W.A.R. mainly out of our lawn and garden building. I never liked the name, which we inherited with the business. We never sold machine guns or anything like that, which is what it sounded like!"

കൗ

Winter sales at the service station were generally strong for Pete and his brothers. Many South Bend residents still talk about the blizzard of 1978, a three-day whiteout event that dumped 36 inches of snow on the city in 10- to 20-foot snowdrifts. Newscasters and hospital personnel were stranded in their places of work for days, city and outlying schools closed for up to two weeks, and grocery store shelves emptied of basic food items. Pete proudly says that Veldman's Service Center, the Lawn and Garden Center, and the warehouse parking lots were plowed and cleared of snow days before the roads surrounding them were, thanks to snow removal equipment stocked by the Lawn and Garden Center in the winter months. Snow blowers and small tractors flew off the showroom floor in the aftermath of the blizzard. It was a winter sales bonanza that rivaled the sale of snow tires.

Several years before the blizzard and its windfall, the Veldmans had stumbled upon the idea of opening an artificial Christmas tree store in the Lawn and Garden Center during the fall and early winter months, to boost sales in the off-season between lawn care and snow removal. With lawn equipment stored elsewhere (this was before the warehouse was built) and a minimal amount of snow-removal equipment on display, there was enough space in the Lawn and Garden Center to create a Christmas wonderland.

Veldman's Tree and Tinsel Center was a particular love of Wilma's. She enjoyed shopping for decorations with Pete at Chicago's Merchandise Mart; she enjoyed helping in the store when needed; and she greatly enjoyed the trees' beauty.

"We had the most beautiful store," Wilma says. "Two local ladies, who were very creative, decorated 40 artificial trees each fall, each tree in a different theme, with a lot of attention given to detail. The walls in the showroom were covered with black cloth, which showed off the trees and their lights. The store became the talk of the town, and we did very well with it. We especially sold a lot of trees to churches and businesses. Our daughters helped at the store part-time during the busy season. We had a lot of fun working together. The girls would work for us all day on Sundays and then we would go out to eat, which was a very big deal for us.

"Unfortunately, we were hurt by the 1973 energy crisis," Wilma continues. "I remember it very clearly. President Nixon came on T.V. and urged everyone to conserve energy, and he announced that the lights of the national Christmas tree would not be turned on. The energy crisis hurt the Christmas tree business badly, so much so that we were eventually forced to close. We had a total of 26 employees in our various businesses by then, and we let all 26 take home a tree of their choice. We still gave away a lot to charity."

೦ン

Pete sometimes jokes that in order to be successful in business, every man or woman needs a spouse like Wilma. Only, he isn't really joking. For as determined and driven a businessman as Pete has been all these years, Wilma has kept pace with him. From selecting decorations for Veldman's Tree and Tinsel Center to sorting the mail for their many businesses to hiring employees to paying the bills at work and at home, she's matched him step for step. Even when she was primarily at home with small children, Wilma kept abreast of Pete – his ideas, dreams, and schemes. She has said they needed each other too much early on in their marriage to let each other down. Looking back, their raw need as young immigrants to keep the wolf from the door bound them inextricably together and made their survival as individuals and as a couple easier. They lived through the early decades of their marriage fully aware that success or failure for one of them meant success or failure for both of them – and for their children and, at least initially, for Pete's extended family. No one would make it without greater hardship and difficulty if Pete and Wilma did not make it first.

Pete unabashedly admits that Wilma's presence in his life has been pivotal to his success. She has always been there – encouraging him, prompting him, asking difficult questions – keeping one eye on their finances and the other on their family, using her peripheral vision to peer around as many corners as possible. That Wilma is naturally more cautious than Pete is has added ballast and stability to his full-steam-ahead character. That she has always worked as hard as he has, though perhaps in different venues, has added to her stature as house-wife, mother, and business partner.

Wilma was as invested as Pete was in the success of the various enterprises emanating from the corner of Mayflower and Western. She never considered passing off her work to someone else and stepping out of the picture. At some point it became clear to everyone involved that she wasn't working with Pete only because she needed to; she wanted to be there, right in the middle of all that was going on. Her interest was genuine and her business intuitions were substantial. It would have been as useless for Pete to try to stop her as it would have been for Wilma to try to keep Pete from dreaming and looking ahead. Wilma's role was to keep Pete's dreams anchored in reality. To that end, she unflinchingly interpreted the critical numbers and Pete's ideas through her own growing expertise.

"Even today, Pete comes up with more ideas than anyone I've ever seen," Tom says of his now semiretired father. "He is the consummate salesman. He's always thinking about how to sell something new. It's pretty safe to say that without Wilma, Pete would have crashed and burned many times over."

"Wilma just knows how to think about business," Pete concedes. "Her family was always more business oriented like that."

Wilma broke her leg badly when she was 53 years old, playing soccer on a team coached by Tom. She wound up in a cast for several months afterward, admonished to keep her leg propped up for much of each day. Mark, the last of the seven children, was a young teenager at the time. There was very little Wilma could do in the house for him or for his siblings who still lived at home. As determined to put her recuperation period to good use as she had been to win the game, Wilma started spending more time at the service station. The hours of her workday stretched as her leg mended – and never changed after the cast came off.

"Well, we were playing to win," is how she recalls the incident.

☙

According to Pete, no one could stop Wilma from working at home and in the business when their children were growing up. He certainly couldn't stop her, and he doubts anyone else would have fared better.

"Mom's work was never done," Dave recalls. "I had a room down in the basement. At 5 o'clock in the morning, the dryer would be on. And she'd be folding clothes in the kitchen at 8 or 9 at night, after having been at work all day.

"Mom is very conservative financially," he continues. "The traveling she and Dad have done in recent years because of winning so many business trips has maybe encouraged her to raise her standards a bit. But Dad doesn't make any waves. He's not going to tell her to get a better hotel, because it doesn't matter to him. I remember, as a child, that there would be a lot of discussions between Mom and Dad after we went to bed, not so much arguing as having strong differences of opinion. They were both relatively unrelenting. Dad would maybe have a new business idea and Mom would be saying, 'No, you can't sell go-carts.' And Dad would be saying, 'I think we can sell those things!'"

Pete and Wilma's bottom line improved little by little as their family grew up. However, as the chief household manager, Wilma always shopped cautiously, cutting corners wherever she could. But though frugality ruled the day, Pete and Wilma have never been misers, and their generosity to their parish and the wider community made an unforgettable impression on their children. (Pete once stepped in and helped a priest organize and keep to a budget for the sake of their parish. The kindly man kept giving everything away, Pete says, to the extent that it was creating operational difficulties for the church.) It is fair to say that the children observed their parents being generous precisely because they were frugal.

"Even before there was financial success," Dave says, "there was generosity. Mom and Dad would give to the church and to various causes. They always had foreign exchange students over for Christmas. They've always been very giving people, whether there was money there or not."

"The way I look at it," Wilma says, "you have to teach your children to be generous and to see the needs of others. Even talking to and listening to people who are having a hard time requires effort. It doesn't just happen automatically."

⁂

Wilma had been in the United States for four years when she returned to Holland to visit her family for the first time, Tom and

Dave in tow. Thanks in no small part to her discipline, she and Pete had managed to gradually put aside enough money for an Atlantic crossing. Cash-strapped as they were at that point in their lives, they had been intent on keeping the promise they had made to Wilma's parents, especially to her father: Wilma would go home. She would see her family again.

Wilma and her parents had not spoken with each other since she had left them standing on the dock in Rotterdam. She knew her mother and father had waved good-bye until she had disappeared from sight, fearful she would never return. They had certainly not visited her and Pete in America; it was understood they would never travel so far outside of Holland. Such a journey was inconceivable to them. For four long years, Wilma had assessed the situation clearly: If she wanted to see her parents again, if she wanted them to meet her children, she would have to go to them.

Finally, after endless scrimping on more immediate needs, she and Pete had saved enough money to send her and the little boys home. The three of them traveled as economically as possible; each trip across the Atlantic took 10 days. They were gone for a total of six weeks.

"I was always so homesick," Wilma says. "I never talked to my mom or dad in all those early years; it was really hard when our children were young. And it was hard later, when my father died, and then when my brother died in a car accident. But Pete and I had decided that we wouldn't even try to go home for funerals. Then, we couldn't do it financially. Now, we prefer to visit family while they are still alive. But still, it was hard to miss those times with our families.

"The first time I went home with the boys, my parents were impressed that I could cross the Atlantic again. Pete and I could hardly come up with the money for the trip, but we did it, like we had promised. My dad asked me a lot of questions about our finances. Pete and I had very little at that point, but I answered my dad's questions, and he was finally satisfied."

By the time Pete and Wilma's daughters were old enough to

travel overseas, it had become less expensive to fly. Wilma once flew home to Holland by herself with all four young girls. As she recalls, their return trip was one of the worst travel experiences of her life. She and the girls had completed one long leg of their journey back to South Bend when trouble caught up with them in LaGuardia Airport in New York City.

"I had all four girls with me," Wilma says. "They were very small. One was in a backpack, one was on a tether, and two were holding hands with each other, with one of them holding my hand. We were trying to get through customs in New York when Connie came to me crying, 'Sharon won't hold my hand.' I looked around and I could not find Sharon. I went into a complete panic, trying to hold onto the other three little ones while at the same time trying to look for her. It was awful. Pretty soon some airport personnel started helping me, and we finally found her wandering down a big hall. I felt like collapsing.

"Those minutes that we searched for Sharon and the extra time it took us to get through customs caused us to miss our flight to Chicago," Wilma continues. "We had to wait four hours for the next plane to O'Hare, and we had nowhere to go during that time. Airports didn't have as many conveniences then as they do now. Finally, some United Airlines personnel let us into an office of theirs. By the end of the workday – when it was time for us to catch our next flight – all four girls were sound asleep on the floor.

"We somehow made it to the plane to fly to Chicago, but then we encountered an electrical storm as we flew across the country. It was the scariest flight ever, and by the time we landed in Chicago, we had missed the last flight of the day back to South Bend. It was pretty late in the evening, but I remember calling Pete and telling him I couldn't stay overnight in Chicago, couldn't take any more, and he came to pick us up.

"It was the worst trip I ever took. I lost 10 pounds getting home, it was so awful."

❧

Although Wilma eventually spent most of every school day working with Pete, she remained the parent in charge on the home front. She kept abreast of all seven children and their activities and made the numerous daily decisions required to keep everyone moving ahead. She cooked nightly for the brood; she did copious amounts of laundry; she drove; she cleaned; she coaxed and pleaded and demanded respect and obedience; she established curfews; she paid attention to who her children's friends were; she bought school uniforms and supplies for class projects; she fanned the flames of faith to the best of her ability. And, as the seven grew older, she learned to let them go. It was not always easy, but, with Pete's urgings, she encouraged the children to make their own decisions and live independently of her and their father.

"Mom took care of everything," Sharon says. "Dad never helped in the house at all. The only thing he ever did was vacuum the floor on Christmas Day. He still does that."

"He didn't help in the yard or in the house," Connie adds. "And he missed a lot of dinners. Mom always had dinner ready, and we waited. And we waited. And then Mom would try to get hold of Dad. It's been a habit of his forever that he doesn't communicate where he is. And we often couldn't get hold of him because he'd be out on a tow truck or something. Eventually, Mom would give up and we'd eat without him."

"That's right," Sharon interjects. "We didn't realize, at the time, how hard it was to make a living to support seven children. It wasn't like we patiently said, 'Oh, he's busy.' It was more like, 'Where the heck is he!?'"

Like many parents, Pete and Wilma look back on their children's growing-up years with a mixture of good humor, thankfulness, and relief that the hard work is over. That four of their six surviving children and three of their children's spouses work with them today is testimony to how tightly woven the family fabric is. Of course, Pete and Wilma say, they had no guarantees that everyone would turn out so well; they just did the best they could as parents, with Wilma most often taking her position on the front lines and Pete ready to step in when she needed reinforcement. The two often talked in bed late at night, after Pete had come in from work and Wilma had put aside her chores in the laundry room and kitchen. She filled Pete in on the day's activities and what each child had going on in his or her life. Because of her, Pete remained connected to the daily life of the children. He also saw them regularly at the service station. Their arrival was a break in the day he always looked forward to.

"I look back and can't believe how much I cooked!" Wilma says of those busy years. "Maybe that's why I don't like to do it now. As the kids got older, we seldom had all seven of them at home at the same time. Tom went away for high school when Mark was about a year old.

"Keeping everybody under control and motivated was the hardest part. But I don't think it was as hard then as it would be now. Children today want more material goods, want to go out more and stay out later. It's probably harder now – and it wasn't easy then. But the children all wanted to learn. And they wanted to work and earn money. We didn't have much to give them, so they did jobs to earn spending money."

☙

The children themselves recall lots of freedom. By the time the older ones were teenagers, the family had long since moved to the house with the large lot on the edge of town. Oma and Opa lived next door. There was enough space outside so the children could sleep in a tent every night in the summer if they wanted to; they could grow vegetables with Opa or flowers with Oma; they could play soccer; swim in the pool; drive an old car in the field; invite friends over and make a mess while fixing lunch; keep a small fire smoldering for days just to see if they could.

But with the freedom came a fair amount of responsibility. All of the children started working when they were young (Connie remembers working 30 hours a week the summer she was going into the eighth grade); all were expected to abide by their parents' rules; all were expected to get good grades in school without much parental involvement with homework and test preparation; all were expected to graduate from college – and to pay for it themselves.

Though there were some bumps along the way, Pete and Wilma say that all seven children lived up to their expectations as children and as young adults. Six graduated from IU with an undergraduate degree in business or marketing. Some earned advanced degrees from other institutions. They all learned to be dependable employees.

"We always believed in education," Wilma says, "and we were willing to make whatever sacrifices we could for it. We talked college all along, from the time the children were young. But the children had to work for much of what they wanted, which was probably better for them in the long run."

Though Pete and Wilma instilled a desire to excel in their children, they were not, as parents, overly involved in the minutiae of everyday schoolwork. In their way of thinking, the work of becoming an educated person rested largely on the shoulders of each individual child. What they provided as parents was the encouragement to keep at it and a constant, look-at-me reminder regarding the fundamental value of education. The children knew Pete had quit after one year of high school. More importantly, they knew he considered himself handicapped by his lack of formal education. Quitting school as a young teenager was not an option for any of the seven: They knew they would never convince their parents to go along with such a decision.

"Mom and Dad were not real involved with our homework and grades, though they expected good grades," says Connie. "If we showed them all good grades, it was like, 'OK.' But we cared. We all wanted to make good grades and get straight A's. It was much more our responsibility. It was up to us. I suppose if we hadn't cared, it would have been different, but we did."

"Wilma and I wanted the children to care," Pete explains. "I had to teach myself as I went along, and I certainly made a lot of mistakes. I guess you could say mine was a pretty expensive education!"

"Looking back, our lives were fairly simple," Connie continues. "We played at home a lot, with each other. We didn't have a lot of neighbors; we played with our cousins more than with friends. Our lives were busy then, but in a simpler way. We didn't have as many scheduled activities."

"And what activities we had we kept track of," adds Sharon. "We kept track of where we had to be, even though Mom had to get us there. We even kept track of our library books. She never wrote anything down. She never had a book to keep track of everything we were doing. I think maybe that's why we're so independent."

"That, or else she had a really good memory," says Connie.

"Another thing," Sharon throws in, "we never went out for fast food. But Mom drove a station wagon, and every now and then she would call out, 'Oh, the car wants to turn!' And we would turn into a fast-food place and get French fries. That was huge for us! Mom would always make a big deal of the car wanting to turn on its own. It was fun. I often wish my kids could experience that because it was very exciting."

❧

If Pete and Wilma's children were spoiled by any excess, it was the best kind possible: They grew up surrounded by their many relatives who offered them love and security, no matter what. Every one of the children knew that even if they were in minor trouble with their parents, someone at the service station would be glad to see them walk in after school. But home was where love and security were brought into balance. At home, they knew they were loved and they knew a line had been drawn that they dare not cross unless they were willing to accept the consequences.

"There was a line," Marcia says. "Mom absolutely had to know where you were. And there were curfews."

"I agree," adds Dave. "Of all the people I hung out with in high school, I had to be home the earliest. There was a line, and it was drawn hard and fast. Dad could reach three rows back in the station wagon and smack me from the front seat – even though I was in the back. You'd think it was physically impossible until it happened a few times. But it was deserved.

"Mom and Dad were like one-minute managers," he continues. "They could take care of it, whatever the problem was, and then it was over. I do remember getting grounded in my room a few times."

℘

They were disciplinarians, they set high expectations for their children, and they both worked hard at everything they did, but Pete and Wilma could also be innovative and fun when their children were growing up. Wilma remembers Pete saying unscripted evening prayers with the children well before Vatican II ushered in liturgical changes for the worldwide Catholic Church. Connie and Sharon were the first females they ever knew of to pump gas. Pete hired one of the first female mechanics in South Bend, a move Wilma calls "disastrous" because the woman was not very good at what she did and Wilma, not Pete, had to let her go. (Other than when he once fired Dave for refusing to get up early for work, Pete has never fired an employee. He lets Wilma do it.) Pete also hired a female to work the front desk in the service station, which raised quite a few eyebrows at the time.

"She did a great job," Pete says. "You know, men just act different when there is a woman around, especially in a service station. Hiring her was a good move on my part."

In a reversal of traditional roles, Wilma became a crazy University of Notre Dame football fan, not Pete. She cultivated a love for the hometown team while Pete worked on football Saturdays.

"I never really had any hobbies," Pete explains. "I always liked playing soccer and riding horses, but for many years I did not have health insurance and I was conscious of the fact that I should not get hurt. I always worked – that's what I did. Wilma worked all the time, too, but she developed a real taste for sports along the way."

The four girls – Connie, Sharon, Audrey, and Marcia – shared a bedroom for a while when they were young. They also shared a fervent desire that Notre Dame win each and every football game it played. From childhood on, the girls looked forward to Saturdays when the games were televised nationally. Usually, one of Pete's brothers stopped by the house to watch part of the game with Wilma, who never missed a chance to cheer on the Fighting Irish.

"My sisters and I would line up all of our dolls and stuffed animals on the couch," says Sharon. "They were our student body. Mom would turn beet red during the games. Everything was let go in the house; she never paid any attention. If Notre Dame won, we could raid the cupboards, which we could never just get into otherwise. We could never have sweets and junk food just when we wanted it, but if Notre Dame won, it was a different story. Usually Mom had bought something extra special in case they won. If they didn't win, we didn't get it."

"I think it was Mom's way of making us Notre Dame fans," Connie adds with a laugh. "For bowl games, Mom would buy quite a bit extra. We watched the games and cheered with her. We desperately wanted Notre Dame to win!"

"Dad, on the other hand, could care less," explains Sharon. "He only wanted Notre Dame to win for Mom. He supported her, I think. He still does. Even now he goes to the games because of Mom."

The children also knew their parents could have fun with other adults. They watched them interact with the aunts and uncles on Sundays over coffee. They watched them with their employees. And they watched them with their friends, like the time they threw a big party to celebrate their 25th wedding anniversary.

"At that time, ladies wore long dresses to parties, even though it was summer," Connie says. "I can remember Mom's dress. It was green and white and had a flower on it. The guests were doing a Dutch train dance out on the patio, and Mom was leading the group around the pool. And to our amazement, she went up the slide and into the water! With her long dress on and everything! We couldn't believe it. All of her guests did not go in the water with her, but some did. That was a little out of character for Mom. She was a little wild that day!"

໑

If Pete and Wilma modeled anything for their growing children day in and day out, it was a continuing sense of loyalty to their marriage, their family, and their faith. The children observed firsthand Pete's loyalty to his siblings and to his parents as they immigrated and worked to establish themselves in the United States. And Pete and Wilma's loyalty to their faith was unquestioned. But even more closely, and with far greater implications, the children observed firsthand Pete and Wilma's loyalty to each other.

Like most married couples, Pete and Wilma have had their share of conflict over the years. Both of them are strong, goal-oriented people who are committed to what they think is right. But though they are different in many ways, they share many of the same fundamental beliefs. If – and when – they do disagree, one thing is certain: They will ride out the tempest. Their children grew up with that surety before them, and its impact upon their own lives and marriages and families should not be undervalued.

"To begin with, it's extremely important that you feel trust in your marriage," says Pete. "Once you lose that, you're on a slippery slope. One thing Wilma and I always had in mind was that a commitment had been made and that it wasn't going to change. When things weren't going well, we worked hard at it, because, for us, there was no other answer. Divorce would always be out.

"Why should people think that when they get married, their lives are all of the sudden going to be perfect," he asks, "when they didn't get along perfectly with their own parents and siblings? Marriage isn't perfect, and you have to have the ability to weather some of that. Usually, if couples will stick with it, they'll find that there's just as much love there after the hard times as when they got married. I think we helped our children develop a lot of common sense when it came to thinking about marriage. From early on, we made them think realistically about romance.

"However, it's true that Wilma and I were very fortunate. We had a common goal in many ways. There was never a day in the business that Wilma wasn't there or involved in some way, and that made a lot of good things happen. It also made it easier for her to understand the hours I worked and what I was going through."

"I would add that you have to be honest with each other," interjects Wilma. "Marriage is not automatic and everything isn't always fun. It's something you always have to work on, even when you've been married for a long time. Always keep communicating – silence is not the way to go. You don't always have to agree, but keep communicating and trying to work it out.

"Pete and I would go out to dinner once a week or so when our children got older," she continues. "And for many years – after some of the children had left for college – we went away for one weekend a year with two other couples. We went with John Kruis – Pete's friend from the Army – and his wife, Ida, and another couple, Joe and Ciel Bauters. Every month we saved a little bit of money for our annual weekend trip. There were 23 children among the three couples, and we had so much fun. You have to work to keep your marriage fun and to keep romance in it.

"It's true that Pete and I needed each other very much, too. We didn't have parents we could go back to or family that could take us in. We just really needed each other, for many years. Being able to manage money was a great help to us. A lot of marriages fall apart because couples cannot manage their money. We see it all the time – couples who are immediately in a bad situation when anything unexpected happens in their lives.

"It's true that money can often be a burden on young married people, and even people who have been married for long periods of time, if they never learn to manage it. You can have constant disagreements over money. It's hard when you can't buy things you need and want."

"I don't think it's the lack of money as much as it is the mismanagement of it," Pete clarifies. "That should be one class everyone is required to take in high school: basic money management, how to balance a checkbook and pay your bills, practical skills like that. I've seen people inherit lots of money and within a few years be more in debt than they were before. It's so sad."

"We've had a good marriage," Wilma summarizes. "It's not that we never had a problem and never had a disagreement – and the children know that. But life is easier now. We get along fine. We have nothing financial to worry about, though it wasn't always that way. And I have to say that, in some ways, it's easier after your children are gone, because when you are raising a family, you just naturally have more stresses and disagreements, and they are often about the children.

"Also," she says in a final afterthought, "prayer and religion help a great deal in raising a family. We used to kneel and pray with our children every night."

"It's not that I always got so much out of every Sunday morning's sermon," Pete hastens to add, "and some of that was surely my own fault. But think about it, if you continue to go to church – even if you wind up spending that one hour, just one hour a week, thinking about a whole lot of other things you haven't thought about during the week, and some of those thoughts maybe relate to your family and to other people who may or may not still be in your life

– you simply don't have many hours like that. That is valuable time, and it makes a difference."

Today, Pete and Wilma are both in their 80s. They have been married for more than 55 years, but their marriage seems fresh. They still talk about working to understand each other and about reaching compromises, about new places and new people they have been exposed to, about new business ideas. Their children often mention that their parents seem as much in love as ever, if not more so.

Pete and Wilma's children, their children's spouses, and their grandchildren have watched the couple adjust to an active life with only the two of them living in the house. They travel abroad regularly, eat out for breakfast and most other meals every day of the week except Sunday (Wilma cooks only for family celebratory events or holidays), walk together in the evenings or work out at home, stay abreast of world politics, keep close tabs on their children and grandchildren, and entertain visitors from all over the globe. They have on several occasions offered a room or other tangible help to newly arrived immigrants trying to get a foothold in America. They are involved in community events. And after all these years, they still drive to work together every morning and return home together in the afternoons.

"One of the things I most appreciate about my parents today is how close they are," Marcia says. "They are still in love with each other. And they are tolerant of each other, for they are really different in a lot of ways."

☙

Out of such a tightly knit environment, it was not hard for the children to develop a sense of loyalty toward each other and toward their parents. Loyalty was part of the air they breathed at home or at the service station, family standing up for family, in good times or bad. Once – when Tom had just gotten his driver's license and was the proud owner of an old Volkswagon Beetle – Pete, Wilma, Tom, and Dave when out for pizza. They went, clearly by Pete's design though the boys did not know it then, to a pizza parlor where the manager owed Pete and the brothers money for work done on his car.

"When the bill came," Dave says, "Dad sent it back to the kitchen with a message to the manager that he'd deduct it from what the manager owed on his car."

"The manager called his wife and she came in a taxi with the money," Tom interjects. "He asked us to meet him outside to get it. Tensions were very high. A crowd from inside the restaurant had gathered to watch. It was clear the manager was preparing for a fight. He handed Dad the money with one hand, and took a swing at Dad with his other hand. Dad ducked and the swing missed. When Dad came up he kicked the guy."

"The manager doubled over and I jumped on top of him," says Dave. "Mom was over on the side yelling, 'These boys can protect their dad!' The guy was really mad."

"I don't know why Dave did that," Tom still wonders, "because we had the money by then. But we were only around 15 and 16 years old at the time. Anyway, the guy was yelling that someone should get the kid off him. He finally got away from Dave and went to his car and pulled out a handgun."

"We bolted for Tom's car," Dave takes over. "Tom's got this piece-of-junk VW locked and he can't get it opened. And we're all hunched down, waiting for gunfire. Finally, we get in and race home. We kept the lights off in the house and stayed huddled down under the windows.

"I don't think we ever paid for our pizza," he continues. "But that was Dad. The only move he made was nothing fancy, but it was highly effective. I think he was very aggravated that this guy had not paid his bill. There were lots of people who didn't pay and Dad let it go. But this guy was different. He had lied, cheated, or stolen in some fashion and Dad didn't have a lot of tolerance for him."

"It seemed like we were in the house with no lights on for hours," Pete dryly concludes.

☙

During the mid- to late-1970s, Pete's brothers left the corner of Mayflower and Western to own and operate their own businesses. (Brother-in-law John Wynen had left earlier to further develop the irrigation side-business that had at one time been connected with the Lawn and Garden Center.) The brothers had worked together successfully for many years; they parted company with each other on good terms as suitable opportunities arose. Of all the siblings and their spouses who had once worked with Pete in one capacity or another – short-term or long-term – only Willy remained with the Lawn and Garden Center.

Dave graduated from college and took over Veldman's Service Center toward the end of the decade, while Pete focused on the other spin-off businesses. But Dave never intended to make a career of running the corner service station. Once he reached a pre-established financial goal, he and his wife moved to Colorado.

"Mom could not believe I would leave the level of security I had at the service station," Dave says. "I owned the station, had several employees, and was making good money. My wife was a teacher at a parochial school. Mom couldn't believe I'd walk away from that. Dad was more understanding. After all, he chose to leave Holland."

"It was hard – and I hated to see him go – but I could understand that Dave wanted something different with his life," Pete concurs.

About the time Dave moved on, Pete's reasonably secure business world began to teeter. One by one, the various businesses he and his brothers and Wilma had labored to build lost their footings. It started with the phenomenon of traditional, full-service stations closing all over the country. Gone were the days of numerous service stations on every city block, with a host of attendants and mechanics poised to meet every possible customer automotive need, from engine tune-ups to replacing batteries and brakes to gauging tire pressure. Customer loyalty deteriorated as drivers pumped their own gasoline and cleaned their own windshields. The idea of numerous service bays affiliated with a single service station became passé as drivers began taking their vehicles to more specialized automobile repair shops where they did not necessarily know the mechanics. The few service stations that survived were gradually replaced by gas-and-go type centers.

Every change in the service-station landscape had a tremendous impact on Veldman's Service Center. For the first time since he had started as a businessman, Pete needed fewer general employees and mechanics, not more.

"Telling dedicated employees that there was no more work – it was the worst of times," he says.

Pete's sense of vertigo was severely compounded when Amoco announced they would no longer award distributorships to service-station operators and altered the agreement they had used to lure Pete back across the street. The subsequent loss of several thousand dollars a month in tire, battery, and accessory sales was a significant blow to Vel-Mac Distributors. Try as they might to bridge the gap, Pete and Jim McIntire could not find a way to replace the lost revenue. Pete lost the W.A.R. business to a former employee; the Christmas tree store and underground irrigation businesses were long gone; U-Haul rentals were less robust than they had been in the past; towing cars to the service station for repair work declined along with the number of viable service bays – the downward spiral seemed bottomless as one small part of the business after another declined. The changing landscape left Pete severely demoralized. Unable to anticipate the next punch, he fought to remain upright.

"All of a sudden, it seemed like I had lost my touch," Pete says. "I really had to find a way to make it work, but I wasn't sure which way to turn. For so many years, everything I had done had seemed to make things a little easier. If some idea or new business didn't work out, there was always plenty of other work to cover for it. But that was no longer true, and it was scary."

Pete was so depressed by his inability to stop what was happening – and so in need of a game plan – that he started listening to Dale Carnegie tapes on salesmanship, self-confidence, and self-improvement as he walked to work each morning. He also mulled over speeches by legendary professional football coach Vince Lombardi, who had reached iconic status in the eyes of the American public by the time of his death in 1970.

"Winning isn't everything; it's the only thing." Lombardi may not have said it exactly like that, but the quote famously summarizes his football and life philosophy. He was known for demanding absolute dedication from his players. Nothing less than one's sacrificial best would do. Pete wondered what that kind of dedication should look like in his situation.

From the sidelines, Wilma watched Pete get knocked down time and again, to the point that she grew worried for him. But Pete took to heart Carnegie's and Lombardi's insistence to keep putting one foot in front of the other, even against the greatest of odds. He was not sure how his business situation would improve, but he willed himself to believe that it would. As long as there was any hope of a turnaround, he would not give up. He would not quit.

"We were so worried about financing the businesses," Wilma says. "Before, we had always solved problems together, but I started pushing more that we go out of business. I told Pete we could sell everything, pay everyone off, and get out from under the burden of it all.

"Pete tried to act like he wasn't worried, but I knew him better than that. And I was worried. I was worried about him and the business. I would stop by his office on Sunday nights and he would be sitting there, surrounded by endless paperwork. He really didn't know what he was going to do, and neither did I."

ೞ

The Tire Rack

Pete had been here before – in a new place, unfamiliar with the land-scape, unsure of his future. As a young teenager growing up in the Netherlands, his world had been turned upside down when he awoke to the deafening sounds of an invading army. For five long years, he had not known what to expect of the ubiquitous German troops who, with a punishing grip, commandeered every aspect of Dutch society. Later, as a newly immigrated, non-English-speaking migrant worker, Pete had literally and figuratively crisscrossed new territory as he chased the harvest and his dreams of personal independence and financial security. He had served as a U.S. soldier in the Korean War, though he was not yet an American citizen. He had worked for the convent sisters, worked in a doomed factory, worked for an equipment dealer, worked on a dairy farm with Wilma. He had signed a lease on his first service station because he had few other options for supporting Wilma and their young sons. And then – even before it was clear that the service station would make it – he had begun searching for something more, something that would both firmly establish himself as a busi-nessman and provide work for those family members in Holland who wanted to join him in South Bend.

Difficulty was nothing new to Pete. In many ways, adversity

and hardship had from the very beginning pushed him forward. Pete was comfortable with that. As the years had passed, he had come to recognize that trials bring their own scratched luster to the winner's trophy. But this time was different. This time it seemed more possible than ever before that he might not rise above the melee. He might not be left standing after the dust settled.

Despite his admiration for Wilma's business sense, Pete decided to put off her advice for the time being. He would not sell what was left of their business enterprises, pay off his debts, and hang up his gloves. He, Wilma, and his extended family had worked too hard for him to walk away now. Pete's older children were beginning to launch careers of their own; he knew they and their younger siblings were watching his every move. Quitting had never been part of Pete's working vocabulary, and he couldn't bring himself to quit now. He couldn't bear modeling defeat to his children. He could tolerate fighting and losing. To not fight, or to fail to give it his all – that was intolerable.

Pete admitted that he was on the ropes. But he was still standing. He was not yet down for the count.

ॐ

In 1978, Pete and Wilma's oldest daughter, Connie, married a fellow Indiana University student during her senior year. Mike Joines was also a senior when he and Connie said "I do" and began thinking seriously about how they were going to support themselves as a married couple. They both graduated from IU with degrees in finance, and Connie was quickly hired by an Indianapolis bank. Mike also had opportunities in the financial industry, but he was unsure of what he wanted to do. He kept coming back to the idea of starting some sort of automotive-related business on his own, but exactly what that should be was anybody's guess. That, combined with the fact that he was young and inexperienced, seemed to be an insurmountable obstacle.

He really liked cars; he even raced on weekends when he could. But racing was a hobby, and Mike was looking to start his career.

Connie and Mike would discuss possible business ideas whenever they drove up to South Bend to visit Connie's parents. Wilma listened and offered the young couple her encouragement and support. She believed Mike would find something that worked for him. Meanwhile, Connie had a job, for which Wilma was thankful. They were both college graduates, Wilma reminded them. They were so far ahead from where she and Pete had started.

Pete also listened to his son-in-law. He asked Mike questions and discussed business ideas with him. Pete understood what Mike was going through. Young or old, he knew how hard it was to formulate a business plan with real staying power, how scary it was to take the first step, how difficult it was to arrange financing. The truth was, Pete was still casting about for a new, winning proposal of his own. He told Mike how after decades of steady progress, several of his businesses had stalled or lost ground. Even worse, some had closed. At the moment, Pete was particularly worried about Vel-Mac: He and Jim McIntire desperately needed something to shore up the once-thriving tire, battery, and auto accessory business. Amoco was in the process of severing ties with Vel-Mac. It was a severe blow to the corporation, and to Pete's confidence. He wasn't sure what could be done to replace the lost revenue.

As much as his own business situation was on his mind, Pete wanted to see Mike succeed. He didn't believe that success of any kind would – or necessarily should – come easily to Mike, or to anyone else, for that matter. Success certainly had not been handed to him and Wilma or to his brothers and sisters. But Pete had not been hardened by the difficulties he had endured as a teenager living in an occupied country or by his experiences in the United States as a lonely, poor, minimally educated foreigner. He had been toughened by his tenure as a businessman, but he was not calloused.

Pete was not bitter over what he calls his years of "expensive business education" because he had never thought that success was owed him and his siblings. Success was something they had pursued. Pete was now over 50 years old. Thinking about Mike reminded him how grateful he was for his and his family's accomplishments and for the possibilities that remained as long as he was willing to go after them. Another person's victory would not undermine what Pete had achieved. Rather, lending a hand and seeing a much younger member of the family make it would validate what he had learned along the way.

"I was already successful, as far as I was concerned, though we were definitely in a downturn with our businesses, especially with Vel-Mac," Pete says. "My siblings and I had done far more than I would have ever thought possible. We had worked well together, and those who had gone out on their own were doing well for themselves.

"I wanted to help Mike find something that would work for him," he continues. "It seemed natural to me that he do something with cars. I think people should always look for a job that they like, not just one that will make them money. Mike has always been interested in cars, ever since he was a little boy, according to his family. He can look at just a small fragment of a car's bumper or fender or trim, curve of the hood, just anything real small, and tell you what kind of car it is and all of its particulars. It's amazing.

"Mike kept looking and I kept encouraging him to go out on his own. But he didn't have the experience or the funds to start something new. Finally, because we needed another business and because Mike loved anything that involved cars, I suggested that he open a small, retail tire store in Indianapolis. It would be my business, but he would run it. You could say that Mike was my employee, which was true, but I've always preferred to say that I work *with* others, not that they work *for* me. Mike agreed to give tire sales a try. I took out a loan, rented a building, and helped get some tires on the floor. But from the beginning, it was really up to Mike. And he did a good job. He completely immersed himself in the product details. It was a natural fit for him, and he poured himself into it."

༄

Pete and Mike modestly hoped that the Indianapolis store, cleverly dubbed The Tire Rack, would become known as "the place" in the city to purchase quality tires for a good price. The small store, which opened in 1979, did well from the start. Mike ran the operation alone at first, but other employees were soon added to help him install new tires for customers who wanted the job done on site. About once a month, Mike and Connie drove an empty truck to Kokomo, Indiana, a town less than halfway between Indianapolis and South Bend. There they met Pete and Wilma, who had driven a similar truck that was filled with tires from Vel-Mac. The two couples would enjoy a cup of coffee and maybe a quick bite to eat before Pete and Wilma returned to South Bend with the empty truck and Connie and Mike returned to the store with a new load of tires.

"I did everything for a while," Mike says. "We had rented a former service station in a rough part of town. The station had three service bays. I was technically Pete's employee, but I was running the business. Pete was excited about it. He could envision it working because trying something new has always been his passion.

"Pete has always trusted and invested in people," Mike continues. "He gives advice and inspiration. He does not dictate or micromanage. Even then – as young as I was – he was willing to trust that I knew what I was doing or that I would learn how to do it. From the time I started working with him, he gave me the freedom to buy inventory and run the business as I saw fit. He was just very encouraging.

"That's not to say that Pete is not determined. He has his own ideas. When Connie and I graduated from college, Pete and Wilma offered us some cash toward the purchase of a car. It was a gradua-

248

tion gift to Connie, who had paid all of her own college tuition and expenses. The only catch was that Pete said we had to buy American. At the time, there wasn't an American car out there that I wanted. I researched them all and told Pete that I couldn't find an American car that I wanted to drive – and we didn't get the money, at least not at first. In the end, Pete relented, but only halfheartedly. Connie and I bought a used Opel that cost less than half of what Pete had originally offered us. But we didn't buy it until after Pete and I reached an understanding that he wouldn't give us the rest of the money. He never changed his mind about that. I guess the story says something about both of us."

Sales at the former service station remained steady. As Mike got the hang of the business, he started talking to Pete about selling some of the kinds of specialty, high-performance tires and wheels that he personally bought as a mail-order customer. Because the items Mike wanted for weekend racing were not readily available, he ordered them from advertisers listed in the back of automobile magazines. Mike told Pete that he was eager to try running a similar mail-order business out of Indianapolis: The Tire Rack would stock and sell not only regular tires and wheels, but some specialty tires and wheels as well. The merchandise would be shipped to customers who phoned or mailed in their orders from wherever they lived.

Pete was dubious about the idea, but he listened anyway. He had just liquidated Vel-Mac's inventory of alloy wheels by selling them off by the pound. Mike's proposal sounded good, but Pete's experience had proved otherwise. "Luxury" tires did not sell well, at least not in South Bend, and not to Vel-Mac customers. To begin selling high-performance tires around the country would swing Pete in the opposite direction of his current course. Worse, Vel-Mac would not be Mike's supplier because the corporation did not carry the kinds of items Mike would be pitching to automobile enthusiasts.

"As far as the product went, what I was suggesting to Pete was similar to what he had just gotten himself out of at Vel-Mac. But he listened anyway. That has always been one of Pete's strengths: He listens to new ideas, even when they seem opposite of what experience has taught him," Mike says. "I explained how I thought we could create a niche for ourselves. We could sell tires that customers couldn't find anywhere else, and ship them UPS. Pete and I talked more and he kept listening and asking me questions, until he eventually gave me the go-ahead. He said I could give mail order a try and we would see what happened."

℃℈

Mike began selling mail-order specialty tires in 1982 by placing a very small advertisement in the classifieds section of AutoWeek, a weekly magazine for auto enthusiasts. Customers would call in their particular tire or wheel order (Mike answered the phone), and Mike would ship the items as quickly as he could from Indianapolis (Mike prepared, strapped, and labeled the packages). Meanwhile, in the store, he continued selling – and installing – regular, quality tires that were supplied by Vel-Mac. He and a small crew of employees also occasionally installed high-performance tires for local customers who bought them from The Tire Rack. The specialty tires that Mike needed to fill orders came from several suppliers, many of them foreign. Gradually, he began building a small inventory of tires from around the world.

"Even without an 800 (toll-free) telephone number, Mike had a great response to that little ad," Wilma recalls. "The initial response was repeated over a period of time, until it became apparent that he needed a much better tire inventory. Meanwhile, our other businesses still were not what they once had been; we couldn't make up for the Vel-Mac loss. But Mike had clearly outgrown the space we were renting in Indianapolis. We started talking about the possibility of him and Connie moving back to South Bend."

Pete had not expected much from Mike's mail-order idea, but

the small, Indianapolis tire store quickly became a psychological bright spot in his business portfolio. In 1981, he had sold the service station on the corner of Mayflower and Western to Willy, the last of his brothers who was working with him. It had been a big moment for Pete when he officially handed over the keys to Veldman's Service Center. Everything that he and Wilma had, everything they had done, every one of Pete's family members who had come from Holland to join him in America – it had all gathered momentum when he and his brother Al moved to the corner site.

For 25 years, since he had started pumping gasoline and cleaning windshields, Pete's life – and the lives of his brothers, sisters, parents, wife, and children – had been circumscribed by the opening and closing hours of one service station or another. Veldman's Service Center had been the hub; what was happening there had factored into every other business decision he had made.

"By the time Willy took over, service stations were closing all over the country," Pete says. "Those that survived changed drastically. Willy did a great job implementing the changes needed to keep the corner station alive. We still had Vel-Mac, with Jim McIntire, and the Lawn and Garden Center. We also had the warehouse and another business we were trying to bring to life, IMO, which sold automotive service equipment such as wheel balancers and engine analyzers."

Pete liked the Indianapolis store because it involved tires and because his son-in-law was there. He was intrigued with the emerging mail-order side of the business. He wasn't sure how far he and Mike could go with it, but he was pleased with the way it had begun. He was even more pleased with Mike's ingenuity. Pete was willing to give the fledgling business more time to develop. From his point of view, he had nothing to lose. But the more he and Mike and Wilma and Connie talked about it, the more he thought his son-in-law and daughter should relocate to South Bend.

"Mike knew from the beginning that mail order could work because of his own experience using it. He had bought tires that way simply because that was the only way he could get what he wanted," Pete says. "He felt that he must not be that different from other customers.

"We weren't sure how far we could go with selling specialty tires, and we had enormous competition selling regular tires," he continues. "But the little ad in AutoWeek had produced remarkable results, surprisingly so. The specialty tires that Mike sold were mainly for foreign cars, which were becoming more and more popular. Some were for weekend racing.

"While we were considering what we should do, Mike and I visited a company that ran several very large advertisements for mail-order tires in automobile magazines. It was a big operation – and it was the most disorganized business I had ever seen. I couldn't believe it. But regardless of their total disorder, the company was still doing a lot of business. They were selling a lot of tires. I became convinced – as Mike and I talked on our return trip – that we could find success with a mail-order tire business that was run well. But that could not begin to happen in the small space we were renting in Indianapolis. If we were really going to give the business a try, Mike and Connie needed to move to South Bend."

ɷ

Connie and Mike and their one-year-old son moved to South Bend in the summer of 1984.

"We set up a desk for The Tire Rack inside the Lawn and Garden Center, put up our name, and I went to work," says Mike. "I handled all of the orders by phone. I also mounted new wheels and tires on cars, and I handled shipping."

"Mike did it all for a while," agrees Pete, "the buying, the selling, packaging the tires to be shipped, putting on tires if a customer wanted. He even helped load the UPS truck. But he didn't work by himself for long. Our second-oldest daughter, Sharon, had returned to South Bend after graduating from IU a few years after Connie. She was already working with us when Mike and Connie moved here – at the Lawn and Garden Center, for Vel-Mac, and for IMO, which ultimately failed. As soon as the tire-order business got too big for Mike to handle alone, Sharon stepped in to help him. Wilma was also helping with all of the businesses, of course. She helped Mike place ads in automobile magazines and did whatever else he needed her to do. I continued with the Lawn and Garden Center, lawn tractor sales, the warehouse, and Vel-Mac."

"I think that Sharon sometimes wondered if she was in the right place," Wilma adds. "She had worked as an intern in some nice, upscale stores when she was a college student. But she threw herself into her work with us. She worked hard to become acquainted with the kind of equipment we sold at the Lawn and Garden Center and with the tires, batteries, and accessories we sold through Vel-Mac. She would always get very excited when she saw new business opportunities on the horizon."

Connie accepted a job at 1st Source Bank in South Bend as soon as she found someone whom she and Mike could trust with the care of their son. (Twenty-five years later, Mimi is embraced as a member of the extended family. She has helped watch over Connie's and Sharon's combined 10 children since they were born. She still helps out one day a week at each house, as each family has in recent years adopted a daughter from China.)

The Tire Rack quickly outgrew its space at the Lawn and Garden Center and next moved into the Vel-Mac warehouse. But before that move ever took place, Jim McIntire let go of his interest in Vel-Mac, which had continued to decline regardless of his and Pete's efforts to restore it to vibrancy.

"The warehouse had everything we needed," says Pete. "Ten thousand square feet of space, a computer system, good phone lines, and office space. There was plenty of room for The Tire Rack to move in without Jim leaving, but he was ready to get out of Vel-Mac and try something new. He couldn't see staking a whole business on mail-order tires. He felt like I had earlier on – that it wouldn't work. Jim had been a wonderful business partner for several years by the time we parted ways professionally. We remained good friends."

ഗ

From the time The Tire Rack opened in Indianapolis, until today, 30 years later, the business has experienced nonstop growth. In 1985, a year after the business moved to South Bend, Pete and Wilma bought their first full container of high-performance tires and wheels. It was the largest single inventory purchase they had ever made. Fittingly, the shipment came from Holland.

"At the time, the U.S. dollar was so strong that buying a whole container of tires from Europe made sense. We got a better price that way," Wilma recalls. "But it was still a little nerve-racking. The tires were made specifically for the many foreign cars that were on the U.S. market. My sister, Ada, helped us with the transaction in Holland. The container was a few hours late getting to us in South Bend, which made both Pete and me nervous. We were on pins and needles until it got here. We had taken out a large personal loan to buy the tires. It was a very big step for us."

Pete nods his head in agreement. "The hours that we waited seemed like forever. It was terrible."

The shipment did not last long. The months passed. Mike continued answering the phone, buying and selling inventory, and mounting and shipping tires and wheels. Sharon became an expert in phone sales and customer service. In addition to handling his other enterprises, Pete took out additional loans for The Tire Rack, worked in the service bay putting on new tires, helped Mike package tires and wheels – and never stopped pushing everyone to think creatively about potential and growth.

Over the course of the next few years, it became apparent that Pete needed to concentrate with Mike solely on expanding The Tire Rack. Once he felt sure enough of where mail order was headed, he let go everything else. It was a risky move, but Pete didn't flinch: He had spent his entire life preparing for just such an opportunity. Though Pete says repeatedly that luck was on his side and that he was in the right place at the right time, he was clearly primed to reach for the next rung on the ladder. It was now or never – even if it meant he was momentarily suspended in midair. One by one, the spin-off businesses that had taught him so much and had employed so many people changed hands or closed. The Lawn and Garden Center was bought by a longtime employee. Vel-Mac was dissolved. Willy eventually bought the warehouse.

From the warehouse location – next door to Veldman's Service Center – The Tire Rack moved to a former South Bend Toy Company building on Sample Street. For the first time since he had tried dairy farming in Three Oaks, Pete found himself not working with or next door to any of his brothers. Though the brothers occasionally lent Pete a hand as The Tire Rack moved from one building and set of offices to another, their lives were equally full. Several were working with their families in automobile-related businesses around town. Others were using their college degrees in fields of their choosing. All of the siblings remained close friends and saw each other whenever they could, gathering usually at Oma's house, who was now well into her 80s.

"We had completely outgrown the warehouse when we moved to Sample Street," Pete says. "We had also completely outgrown the computer system and our offices. And we were once again in the position of needing to hire additional employees on a regular basis. Advertising soon became our second largest expense, after payroll. Looking back, it was probably good that we had experienced such a hard time with our other businesses. It helped all of us really enjoy the turnaround.

"We eventually expanded the space we occupied in the Sample Street building," he continues. "When we outgrew that, we relocated to part of South Bend's Studebaker Corridor – though not where I had worked on the line! – to an old building on Chippewa Avenue that had been a truck factory. In 2001 we moved for the last time, this time to a building designed and built specifically to meet our needs. It is our flagship tire distribution center and office facility – a very large, spacious, modern building that is located near the airport and is also right beside the Indiana Toll Road. Our location expedites shipping and receiving tires and wheels by air or on the ground.

"Including our South Bend building, we now have a total of five warehouse distribution centers strategically placed around the country, so that our customers never have to wait long for their tires to reach them. We still sell high-performance tires for car enthusiasts, but we sell even more quality tires for regular use. Most orders are shipped within a few hours of when they are placed; our customers never wait longer than two days for their tire or wheel delivery. Combined, our distribution centers have about a million tires in stock.

"Our South Bend site is a very busy place; it houses our largest warehouse team and all of our sales representatives, administrators, and office employees. It's hard to believe, but we now have over 500 employees when you combine all five of our locations. We have a sophisticated computer system that facilitates exceptional use of Internet ordering, dedicated salespeople, and a staff that does everything from credit checks to tire testing – on our own test track. Our warehouse management system is top-notch. We ship out thousands of tires every day. It's unbelievable.

"We install a small number of tires at our South Bend location as a service to customers who buy directly from us, but we don't advertise that we do so because we don't wish to compete with local businesses that we sell to. Tires are not installed at our other distribution centers. Another service to our customers is an arrangement we have with over 5,000 independent tire installers around the country. If a customer doesn't know where to go to have their new tires put on, he or she can make an appointment with one of our recommended installers. Our tires can even be shipped to the installer if the customer prefers. The installers charge their own fees for their work. We benefit by knowing that the tires have been put on properly.

"Wilma and I now drive down Vorden Parkway to go to work. Vorden was the name of Wilma's hometown. Didam Boulevard, named after my hometown, runs behind the building, at the edge of the property," Pete summarizes. "I have a desk in a big office with a row of windows, but I prefer working in the warehouse. I can be found most days installing tires or helping with shipments. Wilma works at a desk in a huge room with many other employees. She is right in the middle of the office pool. Naturally, she knows everyone around her. She directs incoming mail, making decisions about who in the company should handle what piece of information. She does a host of other jobs as well, including interviewing every prospective warehouse employee. All warehouse hires are still done by Wilma. Some of our employees were hired by her over 20 years ago."

ॐ

Once, when Dave was a teenager working for his father and uncles at Veldman's Service Center, he asked Pete, "Dad, can I just work here?"

"No. You can't. You have to be an example," Pete replied.

That sentiment has not changed; the bar remains high. Despite the success of The Tire Rack, Pete and Wilma remain committed to the ideal that members of their family should set an example for other employees. Even grandchildren have not mellowed Pete and Wilma's resolve.

"We don't want to be easy on our grandchildren because of who they are, no more than we would have been easy on our children when they first started working with us," Wilma says. "I really think our grandchildren should work very hard and be very good at what they do. They have to dress and act appropriately, and we tell them that. They need to be a good example, whether they are working here in the summers when they are students or coming to us as college graduates – and they are. Frankly, we don't give them a chance to goof off."

Early on, when the business was still moving from one warehouse to another, Connie quit the bank and joined forces with Mike, her parents, and her sister. Sharon's husband, Matt, was the next family member to throw his hat into the ring. Audrey had been working with her parents and siblings for a while by the time Mark, Pete and Wilma's youngest child, graduated from college and came on as a full-time employee. Tom was the last to deliberate returning to the kind of family business atmosphere he had grown up in.

"No one is going to be in the business because he's a son or a daughter or a son- or daughter-in-law," Pete says. "They are going to be here because they are needed, and because they want to be here.

"I had given up on Tom ever joining us," Pete adds after a brief pause. "He had been away for quite some time and had made partner early in a Dallas law firm. I thought we would never get him back. But Tom decided he liked the idea of working with us. He also liked the idea of his children growing up around their aunts and uncles and cousins, like he did."

Pete says that he gave up, but according to Tom, his father never really threw in the towel. Instead, Pete bided his time, patiently waiting for the right moment to approach Tom, who has both an M.B.A. from Indiana University and a law degree from the University of Notre Dame.

"In May 1989, Dad took me with him on a trip to Monaco, sponsored by Road & Track magazine," Tom says. "I was happy to go along, although I wondered why he invited me. I had never been on a business trip with him before, because I wasn't in the business. Everything about the trip was first-class – the flight over, the hotel, everything. The first morning we were there, Dad said to me as we were eating breakfast, 'Well, Tom, what can you do for The Tire Rack, and when can you start?'

"I was completely surprised by his boldness. But it worked. We started talking about the possibilities that week, and we kept talking for several months afterward. The conversations involved all of my siblings who were already in the business. I talked to them individually, and we all talked together. After 11 months, my wife, Anita, and I decided to move to South Bend with our three small children. When I first circulated a memo to my partners at Johnson & Gibbs that I was leaving the firm – after having made partner just 18 months earlier – to go to work for the family tire business, they thought I was joking."

Tom says that he liked his work as a corporate and securities lawyer, but somehow it wasn't enough. He missed the stimulating mix of family, ideas, and business that he had grown up with. And Texas was far away.

"The more I thought about it, the more I knew I wanted to be in business, not just advising businesses," Tom explains. "That's the climate my siblings and I grew up in. Coming back, working here, was a good decision for me professionally and personally. I have enjoyed being part of the tremendous growth The Tire Rack has experienced in the last 19 years. We've all worked hard at it. But the success we've witnessed since I joined my family in 1990 was set in motion by a decade of hard work by my parents and my siblings. They applied incredible innovation and effort throughout their first

10 years in the business, before I came on board. They laid the foundation for what we have done together."

℘

Family job descriptions have changed repeatedly as Pete and Wilma, their children, and their children's spouses have overseen the growth of The Tire Rack from a mom-and-pop-sized operation to a large business. Pete says he has found the entire process to be gratifying, for against all odds, the business has retained its family image. From the top down, the distinguishing hallmarks of his brand of leadership are clearly visible.

"Our image in the industry is that of a family business with integrity, where everyone works hard," says Connie. "Though we have over 300 employees at our South Bend headquarters, many people tell me they feel like they work in a small family business. Our employees know they should do the right thing, the honest thing. I think they find that to be a relief."

Pete emphasizes how important honesty and dependability are to him and Wilma, no matter what an employee's last name is. The Tire Rack pays more than many local businesses, he says, and employees are offered good benefits. In return, they are expected to show up every day, be on time, be willing to get along with others, and not let their problems at home keep them from doing their job. The expectations are the same for everyone.

"It all comes down to attitude, which is just so important," he stresses. "It is also important that employees be honest when they have made a mistake. And one last thing: An employee should be willing to learn new things. We have all done that. We are still doing that.

"I must admit: This is the best time in my life because the business is doing well and the children are in it. The children make it so much better. People often ask me how we wound up with our sons and daughters being married to such good businessmen and women. Not just our children, but the men and women they married – they all have good skills and a good work ethic. I just laugh and say it was a requirement for marrying into the family! I'm not sure how it happened, really, but I am proud of them all."

"We don't make a big deal of titles – we wouldn't want to do that – and neither do our children," Wilma adds. "Everyone works hard and does well in his or her area of expertise. The children are all seen as down-to-earth and approachable, I think. No one is pretentious.

"Pete's right: The business does well – now," she continues. "That makes it easier for the children to work together, I think. It might not be as easy if the business was struggling. But that's one reason we have to always keep working at it. We can't just sit back and take it easy. Pete and I can do that now if we want to, but not the children. Business is just so competitive. Someone else will always push ahead. You cannot stand still. You still have to handle your work as a business, even though you are working with family."

Pete grins as he reflects on conversations he has had with his sons and daughters and their spouses over the hows and whys of his life as a Midwestern entrepreneur. What led you to make this decision? Why did you do it that way? Would you have ever given up?

"The children have all asked me, at one time or another, why, of all places, we are located in South Bend," he laughs. "We could be almost anywhere else, preferably someplace sunny and warm. I imagine the grandchildren wonder as well.

"But the Midwest is the only place I felt I knew anything about when I was discharged from the Army, and I never really considered living anywhere else," he continues. "I knew I could always find work here. Besides, you don't really think much about the cold when you are as young as I was back then. As it worked out, a lot of our early success with automobile-related businesses was directly related to the changing of the seasons we experience in the Midwest. The seasons bring a lot of additional automobile expenses with them, especially cold weather. Even the Lawn and Garden Center profited from the change of the seasons.

"We have learned over the years, as The Tire Rack has grown, that South Bend is one of the best locations in the country for shipping. We're close to lots of major roads that dissect the country, and we're close to Chicago. We are pretty much in the center of the country. We didn't plan it that way. It just happened that way, and we have benefited from it."

Pete and Wilma's children may joke – and sometimes moan – about the location of The Tire Rack, but today all of them except one live and work in Indiana. It was the opportunity to work with and live near family that drew Pete's siblings to his side when they first immigrated. Likewise, the success of The Tire Rack, combined with the opportunity to live near their parents and siblings, has kept most of the Veldman offspring in the upper Midwest.

Sons Tom and Mark are principals in the company, as are sons-in-law Mike Joines and Matt Edmonds. Daughter Audrey was a full-time employee when she died, tragically and unexpectedly, in 1996, following a brief illness. Daughters Connie and Sharon, and Tom's wife, Anita, work part-time. Only son Dave and daughter Marcia do not work for the business at all, although Dave, who still lives in Colorado, has helped with commercial real-estate transactions as new warehouse distribution centers have been built around the country. Marcia and her husband, Steve Cotter, live and work in Bloomington, Indiana, where Marcia runs the Bloomington Community Farmers Market.

Back in the summer of 1984, Sharon was working full-time

with Pete and Wilma in their various businesses when Connie and Mike moved with The Tire Rack from Indianapolis to South Bend. About a week later, Sharon married Matt Edmonds, a Notre Dame graduate with a degree in architecture. Matt says that it was obvious from the very beginning that he was getting into a business-oriented family.

"Even when we were dating, if Sharon and I were headed to Indianapolis," Matt explains, "Pete would say something like, 'Hey, Matt, can you drive a load of tires down to Mike for me?' Obviously, there was only one answer.

"I was working for an architectural firm that specialized in church design when Sharon and I got married," he continues. "I helped out some with The Tire Rack, mostly helping Wilma with the small advertisements that they placed in automobile magazines, but my full-time job was as an architect. After Sharon and I had been married for a few years, about the time we were starting a family, I was offered a good position with an architectural firm in Indianapolis. The firm knew we wanted to stay in South Bend because of Sharon's work and family, and they offered me a way to commute back and forth without moving permanently, at least not until I was sure I liked the job. When I told Pete about the offer, he countered it by asking me, 'Why don't you see if you like working full-time for The Tire Rack? Give it a year, and if you don't like it, take the job in Indianapolis.'

"That's how Pete has always been. He always thinks a little differently than anyone else. As an architect, what did I know about tires? To this day, I think Pete wanted me to work for him because I knew how to build an office wall, which is what I found myself doing more than once as The Tire Rack moved from one building to another. But I said yes. I spent the first year working with Pete in the warehouse, learning how the business operates from the ground up. It was his way of bringing me along, and it's still his favorite way to train new employees. Today, some of the grandchildren are coming in as possible long-term employees, and they often start in the warehouse, working with Pete. He likes to see employees grow and improve, no matter who they are or what they do. If you start out sweeping the floors in the warehouse, Pete wants to see you get better at it."

Matt never considered leaving The Tire Rack after his year with Pete, even if his role was at first undefined. He says that with any other father-in-law-as-employer, he may have felt uncomfortable stepping into what has, over a period of years, become his area of expertise: marketing and public relations. But no matter how Matt initially felt about working in the family business, no matter where he thought his rookie year in the warehouse might lead him, Pete never doubted that someone creative and detail-oriented enough to design buildings could benefit The Tire Rack.

Matt was another in a long list of "quality people" that Pete wanted to have on his side. How Matt's skills would best be used remained to be seen; what was immediately important to Pete was his son-in-law's existing talent and his potential. It's a winning formula Pete has used over and over as an employer: First find the person, then find the job.

As Pete says, "Wilma and I always brought in the talent. I have always been on the lookout for people who would benefit the company and who would be good to work with. I've always hired people who knew what I didn't know. Some of them were family and some of them weren't. The difference with good employees is that you only need three or four people instead of eight or 10."

It did not take Matt long to find his niche. "I eventually took over advertising from Mike and Wilma," he says. "From there, my job has evolved as the company has grown. I now oversee sponsorships, the creative aspect of our marketing, and public relations.

"When it comes to promoting Pete and Wilma, you can say that I have the easiest or the hardest job in the world," he continues, "because they don't want the spotlight on them. They are truly two of the most generous and unassuming people you'll ever meet.

"Pete brought himself up in the business world, and he's brought up a whole lot of people with him, including his family. But his is not a story of a gentleman establishing a business and then picking a successor. If a family member is interested in working with him, Pete wants him or her to have the opportunity to do so. He has always made that clear. 'You guys are all equal,' has always been his attitude. Now that he is stepping back from the business a bit, his attitude is: You decide how the business will go from here.

"Not that Pete has bowed out, of course. He is almost 83 years old, and he and Wilma still work. Pete is happiest in the warehouse, just like always. Some of my favorite stories are when a customer has complained to Pete about having to wait too long to have tires put on, or has expressed some other minor irritation, not knowing who Pete is.

"One man said, 'I'd sure like to speak to the president of this company and tell him what I think.' Pete was changing the tires on the man's car and he just very quietly handed him his card, with the words President Emeritus printed on it. He said something like, 'I'm listening. Now, what's the problem?'

"Pete is kind of like that about everything," Matt closes. "If there is any kind of problem in the business, or in his personal life, he doesn't shy away from it. He doesn't stand back when life is hard. I have learned a lot by watching him. And Wilma is just as strong. It was a terrible time for all of us when we lost Audrey. But Pete and Wilma were so strong, so very concerned about how everyone else felt. It wasn't just about them. It has never been just about them."

❧

TO AUDREY, our cherished daughter, dear sister, and loving aunt:

*J*ust *a little more than thirty-four years ago, you were welcomed into this world by the open arms of your mother. Early Tuesday morning, you returned to your mother's arms as your last act of love before returning to God. You filled those thirty-four years with a lifetime of experiences that we all had the joy of sharing with you. We would like to remind you and ourselves of just some of those good times now in order to help us, and all those people who mourn your death, to bear our great loss.*

We must start where you always started – with the children. We truly believe our best gifts to you were our children. You loved them so much and they returned your love so fully. On each of the last two evenings, your nieces and nephews have read to us letters and poems that they, on their own, have written to you since you died. They spoke of special times together – cousin slumber parties at your house, trips with our families, the different ways you spoiled them, and so many other personal moments and remembrances. But most of all they spoke of love – how they loved you and how very much they will miss you. In a very real way, you had more children than any of us. Your gift of love to them will not pass with your leaving.

You will be greatly missed at The Tire Rack. Over the course of many years and many jobs throughout the office, you have known everyone who has ever worked at The Tire Rack. They already miss the trademark shuffle of your shoes as you made your way through the office. We could hear you coming and enjoyed you when you arrived. Your sense of humor and ready smile will leave everyone at The Tire Rack with wonderful memories of you.

Thus begins a letter of farewell that Tom wrote on behalf of his parents and siblings shortly after his sister Audrey died on January 9, 1996. What had been diagnosed as the flu by more than one doctor a few days earlier was something much more serious. It ended with Audrey collapsing in Wilma's arms in the kitchen. She never revived.

Audrey was 34 years old when she died, single, much beloved by her nieces and nephews, a gregarious employee of The Tire Rack with an easy smile. Her death shook Pete and Wilma and their family to the core, and it reminded everyone of what they had always had in each other. With fresh eyes, Pete and Wilma and their children looked at the aunts, uncles, brothers, sisters, nieces, and nephews gathered at their side and reaffirmed just how blessed they had always been.

By bringing all of us together in tragedy you have reminded us of the importance of family. Mom and Dad and your brothers' and sisters' families have come together in these last days and have found the strength and love to carry us through our pain. All of your aunts and uncles joined us for Mass on the day you died or called us from Holland or started driving to join us. Your death kindled in us a need for family that was met with a heartwarming response. . . .

Thirteen years have passed since Mark read Tom's letter at Audrey's funeral Mass. The young nieces and nephews have grown up; several have graduated from college. Pete and Wilma have taken a step toward semiretirement, and the business has expanded beyond what almost anyone – except, perhaps, Pete – could have imagined. But the family's loss has never been completely assuaged. The feeling remains that they are missing someone important to them all.

"Audrey was so much fun, and she loved children. I think about that all the time, how something that I see or hear would have made her laugh," says Wilma. "Everyone loved her and looked forward to her coming in to work every day. Early on, she worked as one of The Tire Rack's receptionists. She was a good person to have out front. Then she worked in accounting.

"We had no idea that she was so sick. She saw three doctors in four days, but they all said it was something she would get over. I think about the fact that she was never afraid of death, and that she never had to suffer through losing any member of our family, none of us. Those are the two good things that I try to think about. But if it wasn't for faith – I don't know how any parent could ever accept losing a loved one so suddenly. It's been said before, but losing your child is very, very hard. It has been the hardest thing Pete and I have ever faced."

✌

Audrey is especially close to her parents' and siblings' thoughts when the family gathers to celebrate occasions such as milestone birthdays, graduations, and weddings. (All total, Pete and Wilma have six married children and 19 grandchildren. It's a big crowd.) The family has shared several of those occasions in recent years. In 1999, Pete and Wilma's children threw a surprise party to celebrate the 50th anniversary of Pete's immigration. A large group of friends and relatives ate together, laughed at funny skits, and bowed their heads in a prayer of thanksgiving offered by Tom. Dave almost stole the show when he walked in the front door, completely unannounced, from Colorado.

In 2002, the family celebrated Pete and Wilma's 50th wedding anniversary by going on a cruise. Everyone knew that Audrey, a self-confessed "sun worshipper," would have loved it. When Pete turned 80 in 2006, the family met for a weekend along the South Carolina coast, where the grandchildren presented their dear Opa with a scrapbook listing 80 reasons why they love him. Another party weekend was held in Wilma's honor when she turned 80 the following year. Again, almost every member of the immediate family spent a few days together, this time in Indianapolis, going from one event to another. Dave and his wife, Linda, were there. Grandchildren flew in from colleges and jobs around the country. The highlight of the weekend was a song written especially for Wilma by daughter Marcia and nationally known folksinger, Carrie Newcomer.

"Love is the Bottom Line" is the title and refrain of the song Newcomer performed at a celebratory dinner held in Wilma's honor on Saturday night. The song tells the story of Wilma's life. The last verse includes these words:

She (Wilma) walks with each joy, and every sorrow,
Feeds the ducks and hopes for a gracious tomorrow,
Loves with a fever because it's all precious time,
And love is the bottom line.

Wilma still beams when she talks about the weekend, and she loves the song. For it is her love for her family, and their love for her, that feeds her hopes for each new day – and helps her remember the past with joy and not only sorrow. She knows the reality of "precious time," and she recognizes the privilege of living a life that has been anchored with love as "the bottom line."

Wilma has worked hard to keep Audrey's memory alive for the family, especially for the younger members whose recollections of their aunt will naturally fade as time goes by. For many years now, she and Pete have hosted their children and grandchildren on Christmas Eve. Since 1996, Audrey's absence has added to, not detracted from, the night's activities. It has given their grandchildren one more unique Christmas memory, much like their parents' memories of Oma and Opa serving everyone breakfast after Christmas Eve midnight Mass, at a long table snaked through the old house next door.

As Wilma explains it, the family attends early church on Christmas Eve. Afterward, everyone gathers in her and Pete's living room to usher in the holiday.

"I will have made a big dinner and set a nice table," Wilma says, her smile returning. "After we eat, we all go downstairs – where there is an organ – to sing Christmas carols. We come back upstairs in a procession. The youngest grandchild carries baby Jesus and places him in the manger. We pray together, and then we open gifts. And now, every year, we light a candle and spend some time talking about Audrey. It's a little different every time, but we want to keep Audrey with us. It has become an important part of the evening for us all."

Another tangible way Pete and Wilma have worked to keep Audrey's memory alive is through a school they established in her memory in rural Tanzania. The Audrey Veldman Agro-Technical Education Center has grown every year since it opened in 2001; about 60 students are currently enrolled, all seventh graders and older. The school is associated with the Saint Brendan Parish in the village of Kitete, and is under the direction of an all-African contingent of Holy Cross priests and teachers. Located in a remote part of the country, near the famous Ngorongoro Crater, solar panels are the building's only source of electricity.

In addition to religion, English, math, and basic computer skills, boys can take classes in carpentry and masonry. Girls can supplement their general education with classes in tailoring and machine knitting. Most of Pete and Wilma's children and several of their grandchildren have traveled to Africa to see the school in action and to go on safari. The simple school structure, the students, the location, the animals – it all thrills Pete as much as he thought it would when he was a boy considering a life in missions as a way to see the world. He has now traveled the globe, but for him, little compares to Africa.

"The school is near the Serengeti National Park, where animals roam by the thousands," he says. "It is really something to see. Wilma and I received the most gracious welcome when we visited the school, from old and young people alike. Women and children danced, and men and boys played the drums all through our visit. Father George, an African Holy Cross priest who brought the need to our attention and helped start the school, is one of the most dynamic people you will ever meet. He is very capable, with an endless supply of energy and enthusiasm. There could be no better tribute to Audrey than to see the students of the school moving ahead."

"There are such great needs in Africa," Wilma adds. "This is something we have been very glad to do, and to do it in Audrey's memory has made it even more special."

❧

Moving ahead has always been Pete's operational mode. Time and again, he and Wilma have chosen forward movement over stagnation, calculated risk over paralyzing fear, hope over despair. Like his father at the close of World War II, when Bernard pointed his family of 12 children in the direction of freedom and opportunity, Pete has relentlessly encouraged others to move with him.

Pete could sit back and take it easy at this point in his life. That he and Wilma still choose to work part-time surprises many of their friends and relatives. No one in Holland can believe that he is still working. But Pete is doing what he wants to do. He would much rather be in the ring than on the sidelines. His stance is that of a young man circling his opponent: He is constantly thinking of ways to expand the business, ways to better serve customers, ways to remain on the cutting edge of sales, ways to encourage his employees.

No matter where Pete is – in the warehouse, on a plane, in his office – he is always thinking. He remains motivated by vision – how to get from here to there, and what "there" may look like. On the desk of his little-used office rests a computer, which is used even less. A substantial stack of automobile magazines rests along a glass wall, deposited by Tire Rack employees who have finished reading them. Pete has the magazines sent to soldiers stationed around the world.

"Soldiers are always looking for something from home," he says, "and lots of soldiers are interested in cars. Do you know a soldier who would like to get a package?"

"Why?" Pete and Wilma's contemporaries ask. "Why are you still working so hard?"

"Since I never had time for any hobbies, this is what I do," Pete answers. "It's not for the money. If you don't have any money, you look to make some. You enjoy making it and having it. Once you have made some, it's not that important."

Pete and Wilma's children know that their parents are doing what they want to do. They have for years been more than spouses; they are business partners with complementary strengths.

"Dad and Mom are a great team," Mark says. "Their combination of skills has served the business well. He has never seen an advertisement idea that he hasn't wanted to try, while she has always looked at every dollar. She wants to know how every dollar will be used, how it will work.

"Dad has endless energy to consider new options," Mark continues. "He truly has as many ideas as the young people in the business. When his ideas are declined, it doesn't slow him down. He will come back again and again to an idea if he thinks it will work. And sometimes, we will come to a decision on something that he has been pushing for a very long time. We'll just have been slower getting to where he is."

Pete still likes risk. To him, risk is another word for opportunity – and opportunity should be seized. He likes to see his sons and daughters think innovatively, outside of the box. Long before it became fashionable to do so, Pete was urging The Tire Rack's human resources department to rethink healthcare. For many years now, Tire Rack employees have been encouraged to advance their physical fitness and health. The flagship building opened in 2001 with a free gym for all employees. Weight Watchers and smoking cessation classes often meet on-site. Walking and exercise groups compete for prizes.

Part-time work. Job-sharing. Telecommuting. Because Pete's route to success was circuitous, he is comfortable with the non-linear path other employees may take. He is always open to considering new possibilities, and he is often the first to promote change. He was pushing for The Tire Rack to develop a reliable mechanism for Internet sales long before other business leaders felt comfortable with online consumerism. Many years later, his foresight has placed the business way ahead of its competitors.

"Dad has always valued education," Mark says, "but he also truly values the education of experience. He is very good at identifying people's strengths and letting them run with them. He doesn't engage in a lot of looking over the shoulder.

"When I was a sophomore at IU, I took over the original Tire Rack business in Indianapolis. Mike and Connie had moved to South Bend a few years before, to get the mail-order business going. The original store had been limping along ever since Mike left. It had gone through several managers and had not made a profit in a long time. Dad asked me to run the Indianapolis store the winter semester of my sophomore year. He made a deal with me: If the business made a profit, I could keep half of it. He had nothing to lose; if I made anything, so would he.

"I was a lot younger than most of the men I worked with, but I did it. We made a profit every month I was there, until Dad closed the store the following summer when the lease expired. I didn't do the bookkeeping, but I handled sales and I worked in the bays mounting tires. The few of us who worked up front always wore jeans to work, and whenever there was a lull in the day we put tires and wheels together. If the bays were full, we helped out there, putting on tires. We stayed busy every minute of the day. When we closed the store, we offered everyone who was interested a job in South Bend. A few employees took us up on the offer.

"It took me five years to graduate because of the time off I took to run the store, but Dad – and Mom – always expected I would finish college, and I did. I just took a different route. That semester and all of my summers working for Dad were an invaluable addition to my degree. Plus, the time I spent running the store helped me pay for college, which I did, though my older siblings like to think Marcia and I got a free ride.

"I graduated from college in 1990, about the time we opened our first remote warehouse, in Reno, Nevada. I was sent there for a year, to get everything up to speed. I thought it would be hard, but it turned out to be one of the easiest jobs I've ever had with the company."

Mark has since worked in many areas of the business. He worked with Mike in purchasing. He worked with Matt in advertising. In 1996, he was closely involved in the creation of The Tire Rack's first website. The company received its first online order in 1998, and Mark hasn't looked back since. He refers to his year in Reno as "the good old days."

"It took a while for the Reno warehouse to begin picking up orders," Wilma explains, "and every morning, Mark and a few other employees enjoyed their coffee and donuts. He no longer has that kind of time."

Mark now oversees a growing number of employees who manage all of The Tire Rack's Internet/e-Commerce resources and national accounts. He commutes regularly from Bloomington, Indiana, where he lives with his wife, Anne, and their two children. It took a while, but Pete, Wilma, and their children eventually came up with a workable solution when Mark announced that he and his family would like to live away from South Bend.

"I've never worked longer days or harder in my life, though I'm no longer in the South Bend building every day." Mark says. "I drive in from Bloomington at least every other week for two days. The only thing that has changed for me is that I now drive a more fuel-efficient car."

ℰℐ

Pete, Wilma, Tom, Mike, Matt, Mark, Connie, and Sharon gather around a table in a large conference room two mornings a week for a family business meeting. The meeting may or may not have an agenda.

"We are all completely engaged in the daily operations of the company," Matt says. "If we need to ask something about another person's work area, we ask. We may have a big-picture item to discuss, something that involves a lot of customers, or we may spend our time talking about one customer. Whatever is on the table for discussion, we don't leave until we are done."

That's the way it should be, according to Pete. It's the way he has insisted that it be, ever since he began working with his brothers and sisters at the service station on the corner of Mayflower and Western.

"In a family business, you should always be able to speak your mind," he says. "When you see something that perhaps needs to change, you should be able to talk about it and get a better understanding of the problem. Sometimes that can be hard to do. I know that. It's not always pleasant, but it's necessary. If we don't agree on something that has to do with the business, we'll work it out one way or the other."

Wilma briefly considers Pete's words. "We always said that if it didn't work out for our family to work together, then the business wouldn't be worth it, no matter how successful it is," she adds.

Dave, who is not at the business meetings because he does not work with his parents and siblings, sums it up from afar:

"Over time, The Tire Rack has become Mom and Dad. They are the heart and soul of it. Their family is there. Their friends are there. They are incredibly respected in the industry. Dad doesn't want to be bored. I see him get along with all of these guys in the warehouse. He treats them no differently than he'd treat the president of Bridgestone. That's just Dad. And that's just Mom."

A framed map of the world hangs in Pete and Wilma's home office. It is not covered with glass. Wilma has carefully marked, with a black marker, every city she and Pete have visited over the years. The map is covered with black dots. Many of the world's major cities are marked, and scores of smaller cities as well.

Pete and Wilma have traveled the globe on behalf of The Tire Rack: Europe, Japan, China, Africa, Australia, New Zealand. They have crisscrossed the United States visiting grandchildren, including three who competed in college athletics at the Universities of Oregon, Pennsylvania, and Georgia. They have vacationed with their family. They have frequently visited the children of Mr. and Mrs. Seesing, the Missouri couple who sponsored Pete as a young immigrant. Family. Friends. Business acquaintances. At least once a year, they return to Holland. It is not an exaggeration to say that Pete and Wilma are always on the move. Their trips are fun, inspiring, and meaningful.

"For me, traveling is a dream come true," says Pete. "I always wanted to see the world. And I have."

Wilma remains an avid University of Notre Dame sports fan. (During football season, she sometimes signs her emails, "Go Irish!") Pete occasionally attends football games and tailgaters with her. They can be found at their favorite pancake house most mornings. After work, they often attend sports and academic events that involve their school-age grandchildren. They regularly attend community dinners and fundraisers. They go to Mass, walk together when the weather is good, and work out. Pete reads. Wilma keeps a beautiful perennial garden.

Theirs is a full life, a fulfilled life.

On days when the roads and sky are clear, Pete drives a pristine, 12-year-old black Jaguar to work. His children complain that it doesn't have enough safety features.

"I don't know what they're talking about," Pete protests. "My car has seat belts – and I wear mine."

"Pete, you know what they mean," Wilma replies.

He nudges her with his elbow, his blue eyes twinkling. "Come on, Wilma. There is nothing to worry about. I know where I'm going.

"I'm headed in the right direction."

ɞ ɞ ɞ

Pete's Business Principles

1. Do not speak badly of your competition, and don't allow an atmosphere to develop that encourages your employees to speak badly of the competition. In time, almost everyone's reputation rightly reflects the kind of work they do. And you never know – today's competitor may be tomorrow's customer or business partner.

2. Expect to work hard. Success at anything requires hard work. If you have employees, they will take their cue from you.

3. Keep your eyes open for new opportunities. Pay attention to what is happening around you. Continually anticipate and evaluate the future. Times will change, and people and businesses will change with them.

4. If you work with your family, you must learn to leave business behind when you go home at the end of the day. There will be disagreements – that is the nature of business. Sometimes you just have to agree to disagree. Let business be business, and family be family.

5. Don't overextend yourself financially, especially when you are starting out. Learn a lesson from the many service station owners who did not understand cash flow. Though they occasionally took in a lot of money, they bought too much

equipment or took out too much cash and could not cover their operating costs.

6. Take a real interest in your employees and create the best possible work environment you can for them. Think of your employees as associates and remember that they are the ones who can make your business successful. It has made such a difference in my life that certain employers took an interest in who I was and what I was doing.

7. When you make business mistakes, correct them as quickly as you can to minimize the losses.

8. If you don't like the kind of work you are doing, find something else, or you will never be successful. When you truly like what you are doing, you will not think of it only as "work." It will be what you want to do.

9. It's fun to work with your children, but don't make it easy for them. They should be more qualified and work harder than any other employee, and they should be genuinely interested in the work.

10. Working with people is so important. If you don't like people, don't go into business.

Afterword

Bernard and Wilhelmina (Opa and Oma)

Pete's parents returned to Holland to visit family and friends before they died, but they never lived there again. Back in South Bend, they were known for attending daily Mass at Holy Family Church; they regularly walked the distance from their house to church smiling, holding hands, speaking to anyone they encountered along the way. They delighted in the circumstances that had led them to immigrate in their mid-60s.

Agreeable as always, Bernard worked with Pete and several of his sons and daughters and grandchildren at Veldman's Service Center on the corner of Mayflower and Western until failing health stopped him. Wilhelmina, meanwhile, reigned as family matriarch in her own inimitable style. She read books and studied English and provided a home for her single children until they married. She welcomed her extended family as often as they could visit, especially on Sunday mornings, when almost everyone gathered at her and Bernard's house after church to eat, drink, laugh, argue, and play cards. For many years, she snaked a long table through the house "with the big rooms and high ceilings" and served everyone breakfast after midnight Mass on Christmas Eve.

Bernard died at home in April 1974 after a brief battle with cancer. He was 75 years old when Wilhelmina summoned Pete and his siblings to the bedside of the fun-loving man with the heart of an adventurer.

"I was holding his hand when he opened his eyes one last time and looked at Oma," says Tom, who was especially close to his grandfather and had been invited to join the adults in the room.

"It was a touching time," recalls Marcia. "Opa died at home, in his bed. Everyone came and said their good-byes to him there. It was really sad, but it was also really special. And it seemed more like a part of life."

Wilhelmina eventually moved into a smaller house on the city's west side where she remained within close reach of her family.

"By the time she moved, the old house had become very old indeed," says Pete.

In later years, Wilhelmina's grandchildren took turns staying overnight with her. Oma was known for inviting her grandchildren in for lunch and letting them enjoy a small glass of wine with her as they discussed various topics of interest.

Tom once interviewed his grandmother for a college course. In her words, she spoke of the joys and trials of immigrating, of the number of American women who were working outside the home, and of the differences between American and Dutch weddings and funerals. She expressed no regrets over leaving her home country as a retiree.

The language was the hardest thing. We went to Central High School once a week. We had a good time there. There were people from all over the world – from Germany, from Italy, from Egypt was one, from Hungary, Austria. Everyone talked English differently, but it was good. We didn't have grammar, but we learned how to speak. I make mistakes, all the time, but I can correct myself. We were happy that we did it.

Most foods that I cook, I changed over to American ways. But the food from Holland that we like, I make that, too.

I would not be an American citizen; it is not necessary, I don't know for what. Voting, that is all, but there are enough people voting. But my home country is America, now. I will not go back, I am glad that we did it. This house is my home. It is much like houses in Holland. It is a place for my children to come home to. Many times talking to Papa we said if someone asked us, "What would you like more to have for yourself?" we would say, "Nothing." We could not ask for anything more.

"Mama was sharp right up into her 90s," Pete says. "But she was smart enough to engage you only in what she understood. She didn't participate if she didn't know what you were talking about – and she didn't let on that she didn't understand. She died at home when she 94 years old."

Wilhelmina traveled to Washington, D.C. to visit and take in the sights when she was 84 years old. Tom was clerking for a federal judge in the capital city at the time. Among other things, Tom arranged for his grandmother and his sister Marcia to go on a special tour of the White House.

It was a thrill Wilhelmina never forgot.

Wilhelmina (Willemien) and Hent Coenen

Pete's oldest sister, Willemien, and her husband, Hent, never immigrated. For many years, they and their five children lived above a garden shop they ran in Didam. From there, Willemien traveled to South Bend many times to visit her parents, siblings, and numerous nieces and nephews.

"Willemien and I were only a year apart in age and grew up to be the best of friends," Pete says. "My immigration was very difficult for the two of us because we had no idea what the future would bring. Willemien would have been here, had it not been for Hent's business, which was passed down in his family. She loved America."

The fact that World War II occurred while Pete and his sister were teenagers left an indelible mark on both of them. Pete says they never openly discussed what happened the day they were almost gunned down by German soldiers as they ran from Didam. They preferred remembering the day after – the day Didam was liberated. But spoken or not, Pete and Willemien never shook the memory of the young woman who fell between them. Pete's children learned the story of his and their aunt's close brush with death only in very recent years. He could not bring himself to talk about it while his sister was alive or for many years afterward.

"Willemien was only 60 years old when she died from cancer. She was the first of my siblings to die. She left behind a grieving family and many grieving friends," Pete concludes.

Theodora (Dolly) and Henk Ensing

Dolly and her husband remained in Canada, where they eventually became farmers some years after Pete traveled from Three Oaks to help them find their first jobs as immigrants. After raising eight children in Ontario, Dolly turned her attention to volunteer work there and in Florida, where she now spends the winter months as a snowbird. No matter where Dolly is living, she is a fixture in local homeless centers and soup kitchens. She also collects clothes, furniture, and anything else she can find to help migrant workers and their families.

"I always compared Canada to the United States after Dolly and Henk immigrated there," says Pete, "but my preference was always for the U.S.A. Dolly is one of the most serious workers in the family, though her education was interrupted by the War. She was more affected by the War in other ways as well. She was a little younger and the air attacks and deaths affected her for a long time afterward.

"Thanks to Dolly, Mama was able to stay in her home until she died," he continues. "Dolly moved in and was a big support to all of us when Mama became ill. That has always been Dolly's nature, to provide support to those in need."

Rieka and Ben Seesing

Pete's sister Rieka and her husband, Ben Seesing, also remained in Holland. It was Ben – or Bennie, as he was called when he and Pete were young farmers facing an uncertain future after liberation – who told Pete about a distant Missouri relative who was willing to sponsor an immigrant. Ben was not interested in the invitation that Pete considered "the chance of a lifetime."

"Rieka was the one in the family who got along with everyone," Pete says. "She never seemed to be in trouble. She must have been Mama and Papa's favorite. The only time I found her to be somewhat unfair was when she stole my best friend and married him! Bennie and I had been sport celebrities in our small town where we ran a footrace for many years. But when we tried it in the big city, we were right back to square one. From then on, we stayed in Didam where we could win."

Rieka and Ben settled in one of Holland's numerous polder districts, where they raised tulips in rich soil reclaimed from the Zuiderzee (southern sea). "Welcome to the bottom of the sea" reads a sign as one enters the area that is famously surrounded by dikes. The tulip farm is now run by a son, one of Rieka and Ben's five children.

Pete's longtime friend and brother-in-law died in 2007.

Allardus (Al) and Elisabeth (Liesbeth) Veldman

In 1974, after working with Pete for 18 years, Al leased an Amoco service station in Roseland and moved his family to South Bend's north side. It is the first station a driver comes upon as he or she exits the Indiana Toll Road. It is also very close to the University of Notre Dame and St. Mary's College. The service station is especially busy during Notre Dame football-game weekends, as parking for the stadium is nearby. Over the several years Al owned the business, he and Liesbeth and their five children got to know many of their repeat Notre Dame customers personally.

"They had a great family business for several years and Al was able to retire early," Pete says. "For a while, he and Liesbeth spent winters in Florida. Today, Al is an active Rotarian, enjoys working in the homeless center, and is a serious postage stamp collector. He and Liesbeth enjoy spending time with their children and grandchildren. Al has always looked on the bright side of things. He was never down all the years we worked together. He was not even depressed when he was living in Canada and seemed doomed to low-paying, labor-intensive jobs.

"I was Al's best man when he and Liesbeth got married in Canada," Pete remembers with a laugh, "and I barely made it on time. Wilma and I traveled north all night with my old Army friend, John Kruis, and his wife, Ida. We stopped to eat, play pool, and for John to listen to some of his favorite music, and we were nearly late for the wedding."

Bernardus (Ben) and Florence Veldman

Ben had been seasick for 11 days when his ship finally reached America. Tenderhearted and hardworking, he moved in with Pete

288

and Wilma and their two little boys in Three Oaks and immediately got behind the wheel of a tractor. After he graduated from the University of Michigan with a degree in mechanical engineering, Ben quit working at the service station with Pete and Al and moved to Wisconsin. He eventually relocated to South Bend to work for the Bendix Corporation.

Ben married Florence Jaworski in 1961. They met while he was working at one of the service stations during a college break. Together the couple raised six birth children, eight adopted children, and over the years, 54 foster children. Many of the children who found a loving home with Ben and Florence were from other countries.

"Going to their house was like going to the United Nations!" Pete always says. "But Ben was the best one of us all," he adds, tears in his eyes. "All those children. . . ."

After his retirement from Bendix and until his death in 2006, Ben could occasionally be found at The Tire Rack, putting his engineering skills to good use, working with Pete in one way or another. Ben's widow, Florence, still comes in on "statement day" to stuff envelopes for the company. She is often accompanied by one of the many now-grown children she and Ben provided a safe haven for.

Theodorus (Ted) and Theresa Veldman

"Ted decided to take over the beautiful farm in Holland with the great orchards, the house with the high ceilings and huge rooms, the barn we all played in as children, and the lake we enjoyed for swimming in the summers and ice-skating in the winters," Pete says. "He was only 16 years old when I left for America. We hadn't yet talked about who would stay on the farm when we all got older and someone needed to look after Mama and Papa. Ted just did it, willingly. He and Theresa lived in the old house with our parents."

After Pete's parents immigrated to South Bend, Ted and Theresa felt free to follow suit. Ted joined his brothers at the Mayflower Road and Western Avenue service station in 1964. He and Theresa rented a small house of their own and quickly acclimated themselves to life in America. Eventually, they adopted two boys and two girls. In 1977, Ted leased his own service station on the corner of Ironwood and Edison; after some time, he moved to a service station south of town, on the corner of Ireland and Michigan. In 1981, Ted opened Veldman Auto Parts on Western Avenue, west of Veldman's Service Center. The business specializes in selling used auto parts.

Ted and his sons still operate Veldman Auto Parts today.

Maria (Mary) and Hank Goris

Pete's sister Mary first immigrated to Canada to marry another Dutch immigrant, Hank Gorris, and become a farmer's wife. But Hank had been a pilot with the Dutch Air Force and flying was his first love. Having trained as a pilot in Texas, he had his heart set on flying professionally in the United States.

By the time Pete's parents decided to join their children in South Bend, Mary and Hank were living in the old garage apartment next door to Pete and Wilma. Mary had a part-time job as a waitress and Hank worked full-time for a Volkswagen dealer. Flying, however, remained Hank's goal, and he spent every free moment working as a flight instructor at a local airport.

Hank's persistence finally paid off, and he and Mary eventually settled in Wisconsin, where he flew for Kimberly-Clark, a mass producer of paper-based consumer goods. After an automobile accident ended his flying career, he and Mary moved back to South Bend to be closer to family. Hank returned to farming and Mary worked with the elderly, developing programs for senior citizens. But because most of Mary and Hank's six children live in Wisconsin, the couple returned there some years ago to be near them and their grandchildren.

"Because of our age difference, I remember very little of Mary's early years, other than that she was and remains an extremely nice person who always has a smile," Pete says. "I also recall that Mama was once very worried about Mary's health, when she was not well for several months. That passed, however, and Mary once again became a ray of sunshine.

"Mary and Hank enjoy their children and grandchildren and are great fans of the Green Bay Packers. Mary has returned to her work with the elderly. I think it must be her calling. We enjoy them and often play cards late into the night when they come to visit."

Johanna (June) and John Wynen

"John went to work at the service station and the Lawn and Garden Center and June went to work in a restaurant right after they immigrated," Pete says. "The management knew June was only going to be at the restaurant temporarily, but she loved the work and was very good with her customers. However, June knew she needed more education and she eventually went back to school at IUSB (Indiana University South Bend), where she got a degree in accounting. After she finished there, she spent many years working for a group of doctors, managing their offices and finances. She did a great job and was very well thought of."

There is a funny family story about June's first job as a

waitress. She was working hard to improve her English when a customer ordered a hot dog. June knew the word for "hot" and the word for "dog." She wrote down the order but she was more than a little confused – she was horrified – to consider the kinds of foods Americans must eat that she knew nothing about.

In between work and school, June and John raised four children of their own as well as a boy who moved in with them after his parents died. As the years passed, John grew more and more involved in running the irrigation business that, at first, had seemed such a natural spin-off to the Lawn and Garden Center. However, it eventually became clear that the fledging business was sporadically too labor-intensive, especially in the spring.

With Pete's blessings, John pulled away from the Lawn and Garden Center in 1969 to form his own irrigation company, Wissco. Both of John and June's sons were initially involved in Wissco. Today, the company that the Wynen family built – and where John worked until his death in 2003 – is ranked as the Midwest's largest irrigation-system contractor for homes, businesses, and golf courses.

"The irrigation business was not always such a good match with the service station," says Pete. "But John and his family made it work."

"June died of cancer several years ago, but she continued her interests in family and business matters until the very end," Pete says. "Like Willemien, she was only 60 when she died. We all miss her very much."

Francisca (Fran) and Frank Beidinger

Fran, who had "no idea" what she would do when she first immigrated with her brother Henry in 1961, worked in the audit department at 1st Source Bank in South Bend for the first three years she was in the United States. She also helped Wilma keep the books for

Veldman's Service Center, and once a month she worked with Pete for three or four hours on the accounts receivable.

"I enjoyed it," says the youngest of Pete's sisters, "because I got to talk with Pete. We chatted a lot.

"I was not terribly focused when I decided to come to America with Henry," she continues. "Henry said he was coming, probably only for a visit, and I said, 'Get me a visa, too.' Then we found out that the Dutch government would pay for us to get a permanent visa instead of a vacation one. So that's what we got. When we first came, I had so much fun working with my brothers. The down times were when you couldn't express yourself adequately because of the language barrier.

"I remember an incident in the war. The soldiers were trying to take a horse, and they were holding a gun to Pete. We were begging him to just let the horse go. We went in to tell Mama, and she said, 'Your Papa and Pete know what they are doing. Don't go back there.' I was around six years old, and I was terrified.

"I also remember the first time Pete came home. He told us he would be hitchhiking on a plane, which we could not begin to imagine. Then he called to tell us he was arriving on the train in just a few minutes. Everybody just happened to be home that day. We were all making our way to the station. It was one of the highlights of my life, I think, the night Pete came home. We stayed up all night, which was absolutely unheard of. I was around 15 years old or so.

"From that day on, I was not so worried that whoever left home was not going to come back anymore. If nothing else, you could hitchhike."

Fran married Frank Beidinger in 1965 and they had four children. "Frank was the car salesman of the family," says Pete. "He sold new and used vehicles in South Bend for several years. Fran returned to school, eventually graduating with a Master's Degree in Social Work from Western Michigan University. She continues working in her field today."

Willibrordus (Willy) and Joyce Veldman

"I was 12 years old when I knew I had to come here, to America. I was 19 when I left Holland," says Willy. "I went to Canada first. A year later I moved in with Pete and Wilma. I can't believe my mother ever let me go. When Pete left, we had never seen a ship, had never traveled to Rotterdam, had never had a death in our family or had anyone leave. It was a big event in our lives."

Willy and his wife, Joyce, and three of their four children still run Veldman's Service Center on the corner of Mayflower and Western. (One son has special needs and lives in a group home in Chicago.) After working with Pete for 20 years, Willy bought the station and the automotive center next door to it when Pete decided to concentrate solely on expanding The Tire Rack.

"After all those years, I thought I could run the station," deadpans Pete's next-to-youngest brother.

Veldman's Service Center recently celebrated 50 years of being in business, reaching back to the days when brothers Pete, Al, Ben, Ted, Willy, and Henry, and brother-in-law John Wynen, were working to establish its presence on the west side of town. Many things have changed for the service station. It now serves multiple purposes as a carwash, convenience store, sandwich counter, and repair shop. But many things remain the same: Willy knows his regular customers. His wife and children work with him. His family prides itself on doing good, honest work. Additionally, Willy is known in the community for his generous support of exceptional children.

"I learned from Pete his charitable way of thinking," is how he explains it.

Henricus (Henry) and Mary Veldman

The youngest of Bernard and Wilhelmina's 12 children, Henry is 15 years younger than Pete. To him, the most pleasant aspect of growing up on a farm in Holland was that there were always people around.

"Even if we were picking fruit in the orchard and lunch was brought out to us, there was a big group," Henry says. "There were always extra people living with us in the house and working with us in the fields."

Henry had not finished high school – and had no prospects of doing so – when he immigrated to South Bend and began working with Pete. Between Pete's encouragement and his own ingenuity, Henry eventually graduated from Purdue University with a bachelor's and a master's degree in mechanical engineering.

"I just told the admissions people that my high school transcripts had been lost!" Henry says. "Pete had also encouraged my brother Willy to go to college, after making him finish high school, so we applied together. When we turned in our applications, Willy got in, but they told me I should wait for a year, probably so I could get a better grasp on the language. About a week later, Willy said to me, 'I'm not going.' So I took his application, switched them around, and went in his place. I started that year."

Henry paid for school by working with Pete and his other brothers at Veldman's Service Center during the summers and over breaks. After he graduated from Purdue, he worked for Boeing Aircraft in Wichita, Kansas. From there, he gradually made his way back to the upper Midwest. Always a huge soccer fan and participant, Henry helped establish youth soccer leagues wherever he lived; most of those leagues are thriving today. Henry and his wife, Mary, raised two children. The couple now lives in Bloomfield, Michigan.

"Pete has had an incredible impact on my life," Henry says. "Really. His house on State Road 2 and the house next door were a typical immigrant settlement. And Pete and Wilma's swimming pool became the family swimming pool. I often think of that when families have something they could share and they don't – I think of what Pete and Wilma did. It was a wonderful gift to the whole family.

"And for my parents to come here when they were 65, to a new country, a new language" he continues. "My father had never driven a car. I think of that when people speak of their lives as being almost over, or when they are not open to change, after they retire. I was glad, though, that my dad never drove on the freeway.

"Pete has really been a big brother to us all. Totally. By starting the business, though he knew very little mechanically, with Pete managing the business side and Al the mechanical side, there were jobs for all of us when we came over. Pete was always amazingly supportive of ideas people had. I was sometimes uncomfortable with how much freedom he gave me at the service station to do things I thought would help. Even though he had more experience, he did not view himself as the one with all the answers.

"In later years, I've been impressed with how Pete has stayed on the cutting edge of technology. Even though I was totally into computers for my job, he would ask me questions early on about using the Internet for The Tire Rack that I had no idea how to answer. He looks for ways to introduce new technology and new methods that can help the business. His brain never stops.

"Pete is very respected. He really is viewed as the elder statesman of our family. We don't all agree on everything. We certainly disagree politically. But when we get together we put that aside and have a good time. It's deceiving to the outsider who may think that we are unified in thought. We are not. Nor do we need to be.

"When I think of the number of people whom Pete helped get started, even when the business split up and maybe did not go at first as everyone thought it should – and it never can, never will – today everyone is on their own, everyone has been successful.

"It is an amazing story."

❈ ❈ ❈

Family Records

CHILDREN OF TOM VELDMAN AND ANITA JACOBS (VELDMAN)
Peter · *May 20, 1981*
Carly · *August 2, 1982*
Julie · *September 14, 1985*

CHILDREN OF DAVE VELDMAN AND LINDA RASMUSSEN (VELDMAN)
Dustin Trauernicht · *February 10, 1982*
Taylor Trauernicht · *November 9, 1983*
Colin · *March 19, 1984*
Caroline · *August 14, 1987*

CHILDREN OF CONNIE VELDMAN (JOINES) AND MIKE JOINES
Brian · *June 29, 1983*
Jeff · *October 14, 1985*
Kelly · *December 26, 1989*
Grace · *October 1, 2001*

CHILDREN OF SHARON VELDMAN (EDMONDS) AND MATT EDMONDS
† Allison · *December 28, 1986*
Caitlyn · *February 1, 1988*
Corey · *November 20, 1989*
Christina · *October 13, 1991*
Connor · *May 21, 1994*
Catherine · *February 10, 1998*
Caroline · *August 22, 2001*

CHILDREN OF MARK VELDMAN AND ANNE COVER (VELDMAN)
Aleida · *November 20, 1999*
Zachary · *August 22, 1997*

Love is the Bottom Line
By Carrie Newcomer and Marcia Veldman

Wilhelmina Aleida was born in Vorden to Bart and Maria Zents,
With eight brothers and sisters on a lovely farm,
Next door to a castle of beauty and charm.
Shoes for Saint Nicholas, oliebollen at New Year's,
Going neighbor to neighbor, singing together,
Rode her bike and yes her blue eyes would shine,
And love was the bottom line.

Then came hard days when war crossed the borders.
In the heart of their home they carved a safe place.
In defiance she flashed a "V" at them all,
Because she knew that love was the greater law.
In 1944, at a clandestine dance,
Handsome Petrus Veldman she met by chance.
He wore a pink shirt and brown shoes, a good man and fine,
And love was the bottom line.

Chorus:
It's good to work hard and tend a garden,
Loving God means loving all.
We are gathered one and all the same,
And it's good to cheer for Notre Dame.
Hope guides us through our lives and time,
Because love is the bottom line.

Peter went first to make room in the New World.
It was three long years they'd have to wait,
And ten long days on a boat to cross over,
With a sewing machine and all the hope she could take.
But there on the dock with a smile and car,
Her new life awaited in this country so far.

Courage doesn't mean you're never afraid at the time,
Just that love is the bottom line.

Chorus

First convent caretakers, then Three Oaks farm,
Little Tom in a basket, safely out of harm.
Then a service station on the west side of South Bend,
Working together as a new dream began,
Then David and Connie, Sharon and Audrey,
Marcia and Mark, all in good time.
Like the rosary, our lives and our prayers are entwined,
And love is the bottom line.

Oma and Opa Veldman moved in next door,
Uncles and aunties, cousins galore.
There was soccer and swimming, she welcomed them all,
Playing cards in the summer, apple crisp in the fall,
Holy Family games with her sons and her daughters,
For the one sick in Europe she would have stole water,
Mary on the mantle looked down so kind,
And love was the bottom line.

Chorus

Eighty years of blessings beyond expectation,
Fifty-four years of true love, travel and celebration,
Seventeen grandbabies have slept in her arms,
And she's cherished her visits back to family and farm.
She walks with each joy, and every sorrow,
Feeds the ducks and hopes for a gracious tomorrow,
Loves with a fever because it's all precious time,
And love is the bottom line.

Words and Music by Carrie Newcomer
With Permission © Carrie Newcomer

Chorus

Our Family's Letter of Farewell

To Audrey, our cherished daughter, dear sister,
and loving aunt:

Just a little more than thirty-four years ago, you were welcomed into this world by the open arms of your mother.
Early Tuesday morning, you returned to your mother's
arms as your last act of love before returning to God. You
filled those thirty-four years with a lifetime of experiences
that we all had the joy of sharing with you. We would like
 to remind you and ourselves of just some of those good
times now in order to help us, and all those people who
mourn your death, to bear our great loss.

We must start where you always started – with the children. We truly believe that our best gifts to you were our
children. You loved them so much and they returned your
love fully. On each of the last two evenings, your nieces
and nephews have read to us letters and poems that they,
on their own, have written to you since you died. They
spoke of special times together – cousin slumber parties
at your house, trips with our families, the different ways
that you spoiled them, and so many other personal moments and remembrances. But most of all, they spoke of

love – how they loved you and how very much they will miss you. In a very real way, you had more children than any of us. Your gift of love to them will not pass with your leaving.

You will be greatly missed at The Tire Rack. Over the course of many years and many jobs throughout the office, you have known everyone who has ever worked at The Tire Rack. They already miss the trademark shuffle of your shoes as you made your way through the office. We could hear you coming and enjoyed you when you arrived. Your sense of humor and ready smile will leave everyone at The Tire Rack with wonderful memories of you.

Your smile is a cherished memory for all of us. Many things particularly illuminated that smile. Vacations would do that – particularly vacations that provided opportunities to relax and sunburn. NASCAR was big – especially if Jeff Gordon won. Professional football was another – especially since your team always won. It's a shame that you won't have the chance to extend your record for supporting the most consecutive Super Bowl winners – always selected by the end of the fourth quarter.

But your football record wasn't perfect – you stuck with Notre Dame through thick and thin. Your aerobics class, with Peggy, will lose its most consistent participant and biggest smile.

These are just a few of the gifts of remembrance that you left with us from your lifetime. But even after your death, you have continued to bless us. By bringing all of us together in tragedy you have reminded us of the importance of a strong family. Mom and Dad and your brothers' and sisters' families have come together in these last days and have found the strength and love to carry us through our pain. All of your aunts and uncles joined us for Mass on the day you died or called us from Holland or started driving to join us. Your death kindled in all of us a need for family that was met with a heartwarming response. You also gave us a true appreciation for how many lives you have touched. Hundreds and hundreds of people passed through the funeral home yesterday. They all came with the same message – Audrey was so kind and happy and brightened their lives with her smile and good humor. We were so touched by that expression of love for you.

We would all love to bring you back. You left too quickly.

You didn't give us a chance to say good-bye or to say the special things that we only seem to share when faced with life-threatening illness or old age. Now we are telling you all those things in the hope and with the faith that you can still hear us even though we can't see you. Even if we could ask you to return, we have the feeling that you would give us the answer you liked to give when you really meant "No" but didn't want to say it – yes, the famous "Yeah, but." We would ask you if you would be willing to come back to us for a time and you would probably say, "Yeah, but it is so peaceful and beautiful here. And I've just started to catch up with my Omas, Opas, uncles, Aunt Willemien, Allison, Cass, and the rest of the family." Then we would tell you how much we miss you and don't want to be without you and you would respond, "Yeah, but heaven is a place of happiness of a kind that you can never know on earth." And you would be right. We must accept that we can no longer experience your physical presence and must have the faith to know that we will see you next in heaven when God decides that we should.

The morning that you died, we sent an e-mail message to Fatima, Portugal. Our friends there took our petition to the famous shrine dedicated to Our Lady where it was placed at the foot of Mary's statue in the Chapel of the Apparitions. There, thousands of pilgrims raised their voices in prayer for you, just as we have here. We are sure that the message has gotten to you by now, but for those of us who haven't heard it, here is our petition and our first prayer to you in heaven:

"Dear Mary, Queen of the Holy Rosary and our Mother, please remember Audrey to Jesus. We will miss her very much, but we trust that she has found a place of happiness with you, and all the saints and angels. Ask Audrey to pray for us as we go forward without her. We will keep the promises to you that we offered for Audrey's recovery in the sure and certain hope that she will find her ultimate recovery with Jesus."

Dearest Audrey, we will miss you terribly, we will never forget you, and we will always love you.

Please pray for us.

Our Prayer

50th Anniversary of Peter Veldman's Immigration
April 25, 1999

Dear God:

We begin this prayer in the name of the Father, and of the Son, and of the Holy Spirit.

Please bless all of us who are sharing in this celebration. We pray for all the needs of all persons, living and dead.

We pray for Alvin Joines. Please grant that he may be blessed with a rapid and complete recovery. Both Alvin and Glenna are missed at this gathering and we hope to share their company again soon.

As we celebrate with Pete today, we thank you for the gifts of friends and family, many of whom are here today. We remember with great love those friends and family who have died. This party would be so much more complete with good friends like John Kruis, Hank Wienhols, and Ted Bergeron. And wouldn't we give anything to share this evening with Audrey, Opa, Oma, Aunt Willemien, Aunt June, Uncle Henry, and all of our cherished family members whose loss is still felt so deeply. We continue to be blessed by their lives and our fond memories.

Thank you for Mom and Dad's decision to move to America. So

many of us have benefited from the consequences of that decision. Our education, livelihoods, and every aspect of our personal lives have been affected by that good decision made 50 years ago.

Thank you for bringing our Aunts and Uncles to America and Canada. We have benefited from and enjoyed our time spent with them: working in the business with our Uncles and, sometimes, our Aunts, playing soccer with Henry and Ted, walking to school with Willy and listening to him talk in his sleep, sharing time with Aunt Dolly as she cared so ably for Oma, spending Sunday afternoons with the extended family, singing as best we can at the caroling parties, and so much more.

Most of all we are thankful that so many Aunts and Uncles came to America and that Opa and Oma were able to join us in South Bend. Having Opa and Oma as next-door neighbors was the greatest gift of all. It was our last stop when we left and the first visit when we returned because they made each visit so special. Opa died 25 years ago today. Many of us were with him on that day and most of the days of his illness and there are many lasting memories from that time. But probably, most of us prefer the memories of Opa playing cards, working in his garden, doing the credit cards at work, selling the Bingo cards at Holy Family, attending 8 a.m. Mass every day, telling a good joke and laughing at it, and, most of all, loving Oma and all of us. Twenty-five years is a long time, but those memories are fresh and lasting.

For all these blessings and so many more, we thank you. Please grant us the blessing of celebrating many more anniversaries with our family. Hold us all in the palm of your hand. Amen.

✳✳✳✳✳✳✳✳✳✳✳✳✳✳✳✳✳✳✳✳✳✳✳✳✳✳✳✳

ACKNOWLEDGMENTS

I was discussing freelance work with a friend one day when she asked me, "Have you ever written a biography?" Her comment led to my meeting Pete and Wilma Veldman. I am grateful for the opportunity they gave me to tell Pete's story. It has been a humbling experience. How can anyone do justice to the life of another person? Pete has graciously treated me like anyone else he has ever worked with: He set a goal before me, gave me wide parameters, and let me figure out how to accomplish what he had in mind. Wilma has been beside him every step of the way, keeping an eye on the clock, correcting details, making sure the writing is moving ahead. They are a delightful team. I have listened and learned a lot about both of them over countless cups of coffee shared early in the mornings, before they head off to The Tire Rack. I hope our conversations will not end.

I would not have finished this without the support of my family, friends, and colleagues, who did everything from helping me set up a new computer to reading early versions of the manuscript to cheering me on when the end was not yet in sight. At least some names should be mentioned: Erik Peterson, Peggy Jones, Don Nelson, Nancy Ickler, Ann Power, Laura Shrader, Rebecca Waring-Crane, the staff at the South Bend Public Library, a docent at the Studebaker National Museum, Andrew White, Angie Rogers and Kelly Wiard at The Tire Rack, Pete and Wilma's children and their spouses: Tom, especially, spent hours ironing out conflicting family dates; Anita, Dave, Connie, Mike, Sharon, Matt, Marcia, and Mark. Ruth Harmelink previously recorded conversations with Pete and the rest of the Veldman family; her tapes have been invaluable. I have for many years been part of a women's study group; those women have sustained me. I am grateful for each one of them.

My parents, Andrew (Buddy) and Norma Midgett, my siblings, and their children – all have asked me questions and shown such genuine interest in this project. To my children, Lillie, Virginia, and Evans: Thank you. You picked up the slack at home and made me laugh. Your willingness to try new things has encouraged me more than you can know. And then there is David – husband, critic, mentor, friend. You always said I could do it.

ABOUT THE AUTHOR

Andrea Midgett lives in South Bend, Indiana,
with her husband, David Lodge, and their three children.
She grew up along the Outer Banks
of North Carolina listening to family stories.

Cover and Book Design by Don Nelson